Character
Matters

A Daily Step-by-Step Guide
to Developing Courageous Character

Dr. Stephen
& Megan Scheibner

Character Health Corporation
CARY, NORTH CAROLINA

Character Matters:
A Daily Step-by-Step Guide to Developing Courageous Character

By Dr. Stephen and Megan Scheibner
Copyright © 2013. All rights reserved.

Produced and Distributed by:

> Character Health Corporation
> 101 Casablanca Ct.
> Cary, NC 27519

> CharacterHealth.com

ISBN: 978-0-9849714-2-8

Printed in the United States

Dedication

To all our faithful supporters who read our
character quality emails each week...

This book is our gift to you.

Don't grow weary of doing well!

How To Use This Book

A s you'll notice, this book doesn't contain a traditional table of contents. Unlike a traditional book which would be read chapter-by chapter, this book is designed to be used in two ways.

First, this is an excellent resource for family devotions on a daily basis. Simply begin on a Monday and work through the book one day at a time. Slip in a bookmark to hold your place and each day you're ready to go.

Secondly, the book is intended to be a much-used resource. When you are dealing with a specific character quality, such as: integrity or honesty or faithfulness or compassion, turn to the index in the back of the book. All of the Character Quality pages dealing with that issue are listed by page number. Look through the listed pages and choose the one that best fits your needs. As a bonus, looking through the index will often prompt other areas of discussion or encouragement.

For areas that you come back to over and over again, I would suggest marking your book. Make it personal and make it work for you and your unique family!

God Bless,
Steve and Megan

Foreword

Our hope is that the book you hold in your hands will be a helpful resource for years to come. Whether you use it as a daily family devotion, or turn to it for help with a particular character issue, the scriptures and accompanying character and parenting points will provide countless opportunities for training and discussion.

In order to raise Christ-like and character healthy children, it's imperative that we understand what biblical character entails. With that in mind, the material contained in these pages is meant to challenge parents and children alike. Our children will more easily learn those qualities that we are modeling, rather than those that we simply tell them to perform. Christ-like character isn't just for our children!

To use this book as a family devotional guide, simply begin on any Monday. Each week's reading will cover six different character qualities. Sunday is set-aside for review and family prayer. Please don't skip the Sunday activities! As we pray for tender and teachable hearts, God will find fertile soil to bring about His change and growth. As well, make sure that you look up the accompanying scripture each day. God's Word will bring about change in our hearts and in our children's hearts that no other writing can accomplish.

To use the book as a stand-alone resource, simply turn to the index provided in the back of the book. There you'll find the character qualities conveniently listed in alphabetical order. If, for example, you are dealing with the negative action of lying, look for the contrasting positive character quality of honesty in the index. Most character qualities will have several pages listed as resources. Use any, or all, of those suggested pages to prompt discussion and bring about character training in your home.

We're excited to see what God is doing in so many dedicated families. As we intentionally train our children to glorify God through character-healthy decision-making, our homes and communities will be transformed and our God will be magnified. May God greatly bless your faithfulness!

In Christ,
Steve and Megan

"And let us not lose heart in doing good, for in due time
we shall reap if we do not grow weary."
—*Galatians 6:9*

I'll Get Even with You for That!

Have you ever had a friend that was known for having a spirit of retaliation? It is easy to want to "get back" at someone when we have been wounded or wronged, but the Word of God instructs us to behave differently. Choosing the road of retaliation builds a harsh and unapproachable testimony. God wants his children to bring forgiveness and healing to hurting situations not a tit-for-tat attitude. Entrust your grievances to God; He will take care of you!

Proverbs 24:29

Parenting Point

Do you find yourself refereeing children who got caught in the "get even" trap? So many times, as I was trying to fact find in order to discern what had occurred in a given situation, I realized that what had begun as one child's wrongdoing had escalated because of another child's retaliatory spirit. We walk a fine line as parents. We don't want our children to return evil for evil. We encourage our children not to tattle on the bad behavior of others. Yet, there are times that our children are mistreated or wounded by one another. It is important to give them an outlet and a refuge for help in those times of need. We taught our children a simple "Go to...Go with...Go for" formula. When another child had offended them by words or actions, we instructed our child to first go to the offending party and share how they were feeling. If the offending child sought their forgiveness, the issue was done and we never had to be involved. If, however, the offending child refused to repent, we instructed the injured child to offer to go with them to tell us what was happening. This important step kept our children from simply gossiping and tattling about one another. If the offender still wouldn't respond properly, the injured child was then free to come tell us. Having to deal with their sibling in an appropriate manner before coming to us, took all the joy out of being a talebearer. It also kept ugly situations from escalating while still offering a place of refuge for the offended child. Obviously, the end goal is to help our children learn how to biblically deal with conflict. Yes, we must help them and intervene when necessary, but it is important for our children to learn to resolve difficulties independently of our intervention.

9

Speech That is Pure

Read today's verse. What does it mean to have perversion in our tongues? The dictionary defines perversion this way: the alteration of something from its original course, meaning, or state to a distortion or corruption of what was first intended. The original perversion took place in the Garden of Eden when Adam and Eve's sin perverted their relationship with God. In regards to speech, God lays out His definition of undistorted speech in Philippians 4:8. Does your speech match God's definition or does it pervert and distort what God calls good?

Proverbs 15:4

Parenting Point

Is your home the place that family members just "let down" and loosen their standard of speech? Although that is a normal occurrence in many homes, today's verse reminds us that the perverse speech we allow is actually instrumental in crushing the spirits of those who dwell in our homes. In actuality, our homes should be a sanctuary where our speech is seasoned with grace toward one another. Using Philippians 4:8 as the standard for speech in our homes will not only train our children how to communicate biblically, but it will be a protection from crushing their sensitive spirits. Instead of telling others to "toughen up" or "get over it," we need to pray for mouths that are careful not to hurt or wound. Bathroom humor, coarse jokes, and bad language all place heavy burdens on the shoulders of our children. They do not know how to process and discard the filth that they hear through their ears, and our homes should never be the place that they are handed such burdens. Rather than edifying, harsh words, yelling, and name-calling can be another means of crushing and frightening our children. As adults, sadly we've become somewhat hardened and desensitized to perverse communication. Pray for a heart that is sensitive to unbiblical speech and for lips that bring soothing and peace.

Obedience Shows What You Believe

How committed are you to personal obedience to the Lord and His commands? As today's verse makes so clear, our obedience is the mark of our love relationship with God. Too often we foolishly slip into an attitude of "You're Not the Boss of Me!" Whenever we find ourselves demanding our own rights or stridently announcing our independence, we must examine our relationship with Christ. Often, the instruction or correction that another person brings into my life is simply God trying to get my attention. Yes, we have freedom in Christ, but as I Peter 2:16 reminds us, that freedom does not mean freedom to sin, or to forgot that we are bond slaves of God.

John 14:15

Parenting Point

Although most of our children would probably not boldly announce that we can't tell them what to do, often their expression or body language clearly shows that such an attitude is dwelling in their hearts. It is important to teach our children to obey us completely, quickly, and without questioning our authority. The day will come when they can ask us to explain or help them to understand an instruction, but until they are characterized by obedience, that day is not here. The goal of obedience is not simply well-behaved children that bring honor to their parents. Of much more importance is the goal of obedience to the Lord. I want my children to understand that as they are obeying me completely, they are building habits of obedience that will make it much easier to obey God. Allowing disobedience will have the exact opposite result; our children will struggle to submit to Jesus as their Lord. Practice today builds strong character for tomorrow!

The Heart That Mourns

There are times when we need to be characterized by a heart that mourns. I think everyone recognizes the need to mourn over a death or a loss but mourning over our sin is just as necessary. Until we recognize the destruction that our sin causes in our earthly and spiritual relationships, we will lack the commitment necessary to abandon that sin. Don't limit your mourning to earthly sorrows; mourn for and repent of your sin appetites and watch the Lord turn your mourning into dancing!

Ecclesiastes 3:4

Parenting Point

Have you taught your children the importance of mourning over their sins? While it is easy to teach our children the necessary steps of asking forgiveness and seeking restoration, without a heart that mourns over the damage caused by sin, those actions can become simply formulaic; easily said and just as easily forgotten. The first step in teaching our children to mourn for their sin is to allow them to see the grief that our own sin causes. It takes transparency to share how our failures have caused us to mourn, but that vulnerability will make it possible for your children to share their mourning over sin with you as well. The second step in teaching our children to mourn over sin is to take them to the Scriptures. When they learn how God's heart is wounded and grieved by our sin, they will begin to understand how David could cry out, "Against You, alone have I sinned." It is important that our children realize that they do not sin in a vacuum. Their wrong choices affect everyone in their family and often their friends and acquaintances also. As a family, when someone is sorrowing over their sin, join in their sorrow by praying for and with them. When we learn to truly mourn over our sin, we will hesitate to sin again. The discipline of mourning will yield the peaceable fruit of righteousness in our lives and in the lives of our children.

Honesty in Action

Have you ever wondered what specific actions you could take to promote peace in your home? Read today's verse. According to this verse if we are careful to speak truth to one another and to judge with truth, we will experience peace. And, as we set that standard of carefully spoken truth and judgment, others will be encouraged to follow our example and further build an environment of peace.

Zechariah 8:16

Parenting Point

I believe that most of us are careful to weed out and discourage dishonesty. I know that I teach into honest speech and mete out with discipline purposeful lying; however, am I as diligent when it comes to rewarding and praising our children for choosing to tell the truth? Sometimes, it is normal to simply expect our children to do what is right without any undue notice being taken of their good behavior. When it comes to being honest, though, I think it is important to build the courage necessary for our children to continue to maintain a high standard of honesty. It takes courage to tell the truth! There are times that my children know that I would most likely never unearth the truth or even know that I had been deceived. When they come to me, in those times, and courageously tell me the truth, regardless of the consequences, it is my privilege and responsibility to recognize their bravery. As I praise my children for telling the truth in those situations, I am infusing them with courage. Of equal importance, when I recognize their faithful and consistent character of truthfulness, I am reaffirming the importance that we place on being honest. In our home, we have a "You Did Great!" plate. Sometimes that plate is awarded for academic or sports achievement, but the most important time that I award the plate is for the display of positive character. When I place the "You Did Great!" plate in front of a child and announce that they are receiving the honor of the plate because they are characterized by telling the truth, I am building a positive peer dynamic. My other children will see that truthfulness is recognized and rewarded in our home. Sometimes, we are so busy dealing with negative character qualities, that our children's God-honoring behavior goes unnoticed. Pray and ask the Lord to prick your heart and help you to recognize and reward those faithful children and their faithful character.

Joy

A Heart That is Free to Laugh

Today's Scripture assures us that there is a time to laugh. Do you feel free to laugh when the laughter is appropriate? As Christians, we ought to be the most joyful and lighthearted people on Earth. Our sins are forgiven, and we know that we will live with God eternally. Sadly, too often the common characteristic of Christians is a glum face and dutiful attitude. It's time to put-off gloominess and put-on laughter; the joy of the Lord is your strength!

Ecclesiastes 3:4

Parenting Point

Can we teach our children to be happy? I believe the answer is yes! For some of our children, their natural disposition and personality is one of cheerfulness and an upbeat disposition. Those children will need few reminders to be happy; however, we also have children living in our homes who tend toward being melancholy. They seem to see the cup as half empty rather than half full. We can, and should, help these children learn to put-off their misplaced unhappiness and replace it with contentment and joy. When my children were small, I often reminded them to obey, do their chores, take their naps, etc., with a "Happy Heart." We practiced what a happy heart looked like by posing in the mirror. I would demonstrate a smile and bright eyes and then have the children mimic me. Encouraging them to have a happy heart helped them remember to be cheerful the majority of the time. Then, when they truly were having a bad day, I was always available to sympathize and comfort them. Because they had worked to build the habit of happiness, I could trust that their downcast countenance had an appropriate cause. I'm naturally more serious and melancholy by nature and reminding myself to have a happy heart can change my day from glum to fun! When it comes to a happy heart, sometimes actions must precede belief.

The Week in Review

Take some time to gather as a family and discuss the character qualities that you learned this week. Here are some questions to get the conversation started.

- List the character qualities we studied this week.
- Which character quality was the hardest for you to practice this week?
- Did you see a family member consistently practicing one of this week's character qualities? Which family member?

Use your imagination and add questions of your own. After your time of discussion, spend some time praying together, thanking the Lord and sharing one another's burdens. Pray ahead of time for teachable hearts to incorporate and put into practice the character qualities your family will learn in the upcoming week.

Easily Influenced Eve

How firm are you in your beliefs and commitments? In order to be a faithful follower of Jesus Christ, we must develop a character that is steadfast and immovable. As today's Scripture emphasizes, Eve lacked that type of strength in her character, and the consequences of her subsequent bad decisions remain with us today. Search the Word, pray, and form firm convictions, then commit to the Lord that only He — not your circumstances or relationships — will guide your choices and decisions.

Genesis 3:1-6

Parenting Point

Do your children know that your yes means yes and your no means no? Too often we allow ourselves to be moved by their manipulation, tears, or whining. Our children need the security of a mom and dad who say what they mean and mean what they say. Before you ever make a decision, think through the ramifications of that decision. If, after consideration, your decision must be no, confidently stand by your carefully considered decision. We get ourselves into trouble when we are quick to make decisions and then we lack the conviction to carry out the decision that we just made. Our children will push against us and our boundaries to try to get their own way; that is natural. However, the wise parent will avoid giving in to that type of manipulation. When we stand firm in a previously decided action, our children will grow in security, and they will know that they can trust our word. Then, on the infrequent occasions that we are forced to change our mind, or if we decide that what once was off-limits isn't so important after all, our children will be able to rest securely in our new decision. Parents who are easily influenced by the latest parenting craze will raise children who are just as easily influenced by their peers. As a family, take time to develop your family's convictions and beliefs. Then, use your family dynamic to hold one another accountable to living out those decisions.

Humility Defined

What does it mean to put on a heart of humility? Humility comes from the word humble and means a modest or low view of one's own importance. The most important of men could have an attitude of humility. In fact, humility is exactly what the most influential man who ever lived exhibited. Jesus Christ is our model and example of humility. Regardless of your titles or accomplishments, "putting-on" a heart of humility will make you a mirror, reflecting the humility of your Lord.

Colossians 3:12-14

Parenting Point

How do we teach our children the essential quality of humility? From the time they are babies, it is so easy to share all of their extraordinary feats with everyone we meet because, obviously, there has never been another baby like our baby!! Unfortunately, that attitude on our part doesn't do anything good to help develop humility in our children. (Or ourselves, for that matter.) The best way to teach humility is by utilizing the wonderful tool of humbling work. Daily chores and assigned work within the home are one of our greatest teaching resources. Our homes offer a myriad of humbling jobs just waiting to be completed. Remember, this isn't about punishment or slave labor. This is about teaching our children to be humble and available servants! I always made sure that the dirty jobs I assigned were of importance for the smooth operation of our home. Just making up dirty jobs that are of no help to our homes is busy work and our children will feel exploited, not useful. As our children clean garbage cans, scrub toilets, wash floors, and take out the trash, they will be learning important lessons about family life. No one in our home is above doing the dirty work! As they see us willing to do anything and everything that needs to be done, they will become willing servants as well. If our children only do the "fun" or easy jobs while we do the dirty work and heavy lifting, they will begin to see themselves as worthy to be served rather than becoming eager to be servants. Serving others is humbling, but it gives us wonderful opportunities to put into practice love, compassion, and generosity. Eager service paints a picture of humility to a watching world.

Consistency

Although it is important to be always growing and always learning, often the problem isn't is what we don't know yet; rather, the problem is found is living up to what we already know to be true. Consistency is a character quality that can only be developed through hard work and habit-forming choices. Ask yourself this hard question: What has God already shown me that needs to be changed in my life, that I have not obediently changed? Consistent obedience will lead to a deliberate and fruitful walk with the Lord.

James 1:23-25

Parenting Point

Sometimes, we can inadvertently teach our children to live lives of inconsistency. When you ask your children why they are continuing in an unfruitful activity or why they haven't stopped a forbidden activity, what is their response? Too often, my own children would respond, "I forgot." While forgetfulness may occasionally be a truthful answer, too often the truthful answer is, "I didn't feel like it." When we allow our children to claim forgetfulness, when the actual truth of the matter is a lack of concern for clear parental instruction, we are teaching them to lie. Allowing them to persist with an untruthful, "I forgot" answer will build habits, but they won't be the positive habits you want to see. Pay careful attention to their actions and responses, this is no time to cut them or yourself a break. As you help them live up to what they already know is the right thing to do, not only will you be teaching them how to be consistent, you will be developing more consistency in your own life, as well.

Real Deal Zeal

What comes to mind when you hear the word "zealous?" Does this word have a negative or a positive connotation? The dictionary defines zealous this way: marked by fervent partisanship for a person, a cause, or an ideal. There are so many areas in which it's easy to show our zeal. Whether we are zealous for a political candidate, a sports team, movie stars, or dietary choices, our zeal spills over easily into our conversations and choices. Sometimes, however, I wonder about our spiritual zeal. When it comes to the Lord Jesus Christ, do we have the same attitude of zeal? Is our zeal the "real deal," or is spiritual zeal something we save for Sunday at church? Eternity focused zeal, with Jesus as its core, will be a winsome testimony that draws others to Him!

Titus 2:11-14

Parenting Point

I love being my children's greatest cheerleader! Whether it's cheering for them at a baseball game or swim meet or extolling their latest academic feat, I'm quick to pull out my parental pom-poms and do the "You were great!" cheer; however, I wonder if I'm as zealous to cheer on their positive character choices. As our children's parents, we have the greatest opportunity to encourage and cheer for the good choices they make. When we see our children exhibiting good character by sharing, or telling the truth, or working diligently, etc., we should be at least as excited about their character victories as we are about their worldly victories. When we recognize and applaud their good character, we are paving the way for them to make even more character healthy choices. Whether it's receiving the "You Did Great" plate or simply hearing, "Well done." we owe it to our children to notice their purposeful acts of good character. Make a point to tell your children how pleased you are by the character they exhibit. At the same time, let them know that their good character presents a wonderful picture to others of their Savior. Don't stop cheering on their worldly accomplishments, but remind them that the testimony of godly character that they are building will last for an eternity...long after the base-clearing homerun or impressive report card!

Contentment • Faith • Trust

A Faulty Focus

As we've discussed this week, it is important to develop the character quality of focus; however, what do we do about a faulty focus? Years ago, a dear pastor used to remind us to "gaze at the Lord and glance at our circumstances." Good advice! When our troubling or difficult circumstances become the continual focus of our life, we will become unproductive and unsettled Christians. Instead, we must discipline ourselves to keep our focus on the Lord and then to deal with our circumstances through His direction and leading. This "gazing" doesn't come naturally, but the more diligent we are to pull our focus back to Christ, the easier the gaze will become for us.

Philippians 4:8

Parenting Point

Is it easy for your children to become bogged down and ensnared by the circumstances of life? I know it's easy for my own children! Simply waking up to rain on a day that something outdoors was planned can be enough to ruin their day. As their parents, we must teach our children to look for the lessons that God has for us in the disappointing circumstances. With your children, memorize the verse listed above. When difficult or disappointing circumstances come their way, help your children to look for what is good, true, lovely, etc. in their present situation. Teaching them to gaze at the Lord and to treat their circumstances as "momentary light affliction" will be a tool that will strengthen their character both today and far into their future.

A Character of Nobility

Do you have a noble character? In today's culture nobility would seem to belong to rulers or those with royal blood; however, as today's verse reminds us, in God's plan we are a chosen people-indeed, a royal priesthood. The dictionary defines noble this way: having or showing high moral character such as courage, generosity, or honor; showing magnanimity. So consider the question again. As a royal priest and one chosen by God, is nobility the mark of your character? I Peter goes on to tell us why it is so important that we exhibit such character: it is to proclaim the excellencies of our God. What an honor to be chosen as nobles that can point others to our magnificent King!

I Peter 2:9

Parenting Point

How high is the moral character of your family? Are your children courageous? Generous? Honorable? It is important that we periodically take the time to evaluate the moral character exhibited by our family. Simply instructing children to show good character is not enough. They need to know the "why?" behind the instruction. For this reason, it is imperative to build a family identity. Young children will work hard to show good character because they want to accurately represent your family, and it is important to then help them understand that your entire family is a representative for the Lord. A family identity can lay the groundwork for the importance of good character, but if our children only obey because they are the Smiths, or the Bakers, or the McGillicuddys, etc., their good character is of limited value. It is only as they recognize and begin to internalize the purpose of their obedience - to glorify God - that our family testimonies can gain impact and draw others to the Lord. When your children exhibit good character, praise them! Tell them what a great representative they are for your family, and more importantly, for their God.

The Week in Review

Take some time to gather as a family and discuss the character qualities that you learned this week. Here are some questions to get the conversation started.

- List the character qualities we studied this week.
- Which character quality was the hardest for you to practice this week?
- Did you see a family member consistently practicing one of this week's character qualities? Which family member?

Use your imagination and add questions of your own. After your time of discussion, spend some time praying together, thanking the Lord and sharing one another's burdens. Pray ahead of time for teachable hearts to incorporate and put into practice the character qualities your family will learn in the upcoming week.

Trust

When I teach my Core Values classes to the Navy, I always ask the class, "How long does it take to earn back a bond of trust once it has been broken?" You can imagine the answer to that question. Almost everyone agrees that trust is extremely hard to regain. Not impossible, but hard. Trust is the core of commitment and integrity. Trust is defined as confidence in and reliance upon good qualities, especially fairness, truth, and honor. It is the position of somebody who is expected by others to behave responsibly or honorably. Perhaps that is why broken trust hurts so much when we are let down by those we counted on to behave responsibly and honorably. Even though we let each other down far too often, we can rest assured that God will never let us down. He is always trustworthy, fair, and honorable. Spend a few moments this morning lingering with the following verses and remember to thank God for his trustworthiness.

Proverbs 3:5-6

Parenting Point

Be careful Mom and Dad! It is so easy to become untrustworthy. How often do we make promises to do something with the children, only to turn around and cancel or "forget?" They never forget our promises to them, and a simple oversight on our part can teach them that our word is not worth much, if anything. It may seem ridiculous to you, but I now put "game time" and "activities" with my kids and wife on my calendar and treat those appointment with the same importance that I treat clients or prospects. I want my kids and my wife to know that I am trustworthy. By the way, if you've blown your family's trust in the past, seek their forgiveness and start over. Pretending like it never happened does no one any good. We all blow it from time to time, so handle it biblically, seek forgiveness, and get right with your family. You'll be glad you did, and the example you set for your family as you humbly seek their forgiveness will produce great fruit for the future.

Joy

Love Finds No Joy in Unrighteousness

What things bring joy to your heart? Are you made joyful by the same things that would make the Lord Jesus Christ joyful? Even though we would make the choice not to involve ourselves in certain unrighteous acts, we often spend time and money to observe unrighteousness. We encourage more unrighteousness by laughing at those things that bring sorrow to the heart of God or glorify our past unrighteous acts. When this is our path, we are exhibiting a lack of love for God. Godly character requires that we don't rejoice in what is unrighteous. What brings you joy today?

I Corinthians 13:6

Parenting Point

What things cause your children to laugh out loud? Are they situations and people who are glorifying God through their choices? Or are your children captivated by the latest bathroom humor or off-color joke? Be an observer of your children. Proverbs 29:15, in particular, addresses the shame brought into a mother's life by a child left to their own way. Moms, take this admonition to heart! We must be acutely aware of the heart delights of our children. If the things that bring them joy are the same things that would bring joy to the heart of Jesus, great! However, if the things that bring them joy would bring sorrow to the Lord and shame to us, then we must act decisively. Certain children will be more drawn to unrighteous jokes, books, and movies than others. Your children that seem to love acts of unrighteousness the most will require more diligent oversight and training in this area. Talk to them in private about the rejoicing in unrighteousness that you have observed. Take them to scripture and help them develop a set of memory verses that deals directly with the lusts of the flesh and worldly appetites. Scripture hidden within their hearts will be a safety net when you are not in their immediate vicinity. Pray with and for these children that they would learn to love righteousness and hate unrighteousness. Encourage them when you see them walk away from opportunities to exalt unrighteousness. Building a love for righteousness while they are young will be a powerful protection when they are grown.

A Blessed Peacemaker

Everyone enjoys being around a peacemaker. Peacemakers are the type of Christians that can take a stressful situation and act as a calming agent. It is not easy to be a peacemaker. It is much more in our nature to stir the pot through criticism or contention. Although being a peacemaker may come more easily to some than others, it is a character quality necessary to the integrity of every believer. Not only are peacemakers a blessing to others, but God is delighted to call them His sons and daughters.

Matthew 5:9

Parenting Point

Our children will not naturally embrace peacemaking. It is much easier for them to join the fray rather than to be instruments of peace and healing. Although it isn't easy for them, as you consistently train them in peacemaking and model peacemaking for them, they will begin to be known as problem-solving peacemakers rather than pot-stirring troublemakers. What a great reputation to gain!

Decisiveness • Leadership

Decision Time

As we learned yesterday, decisive Christians are pro-active, problem solving Christians. This distinction isn't just for a select few. As believers, we all have the responsibility to grow in our character health, and decisiveness is a necessary part of that character growth. As we grow in decisiveness, we become better servants for the Lord. The church is suffering from a lack of problem solving decisive servants. Too many Christians fail to step up to the plate because they assume someone else can fill the need. There are plenty of needs to go around! Won't you make the decision today to become a character-healthy leader?

Ecclesiastes 3:1

Parenting Point

It is so important for our children to learn to be decisive in a Christ-like and character-healthy way; however, it is equally important to teach them that they must earn the right to be leaders and decision makers. All of our children, but especially our boys, became frustrated when they had ideas and plans yet no one seemed to want to follow their directions. Although 10-year olds have some great ideas, they haven't yet earned a position of leadership. Learning to patiently wait and do the hard work necessary to gain the respect of others is an absolutely essential life skill. Help your children to confidently make decisions, but don't allow them to inhabit positions of leadership that they haven't yet earned.

Giving Without Partiality

O ne way of showing the character quality of love is through giving. The scriptures clearly testify that God provided the ultimate service to mankind through the sacrifice of His Son. In a like manner, Jesus showed love to undeserving men and women through the gift of His death, burial, and resurrection. We can never match Jesus' gift of unconditional love, but we can certainly follow His example by giving to both the lovely and unlovely, the deserving and undeserving.

I Timothy 2:5-6

Parenting Point

Gift giving would seem to be the easiest way of showing love for others. Let me encourage you to take a moment to examine the how and why of the gifts you give; then, you will be able to teach your children how to be sacrificial and unconditional gift givers. Think about the gifts that you like to give. Are they always the gifts that you would want to receive yourself? That is overly simplistic gift giving. Take the time to really consider the value of the gifts you are preparing for others. If you have a quiet friend who loves to read and longs for time alone, a gift of lunch out to spend time chatting might not be the most appropriate gift. Instead, a gift card to a local bookstore and the offer of an afternoon of free babysitting might be a more caring gift. Encourage your children to think of others as they choose gifts. If they would be thrilled with the gift of Legos, but their friend is an outdoor explorer, challenge them to think outside of their own box to choose a gift that will truly be a blessing. Yes, folks should simply be thankful for whatever they receive, but that is not our lesson to teach them. Instead, the lesson we must learn is how to give with no mind to our own desires and every thought on someone else's. Teaching your children to consider others in this way while they are young will be great training for their future marriages and homes.

Spiritual Hunger • Faithfulness

The Heart of a Builder

What an opportunity we have as followers of Christ to build into the lives of our family and friends! In the book of Titus, older men and women are exhorted to teach the younger men and women. Spiritually speaking, we all have folks younger than us. Are you taking opportunities to build into the spiritual life of a younger believer? Don't miss a single opportunity to take advantage of this awesome privilege and responsibility!

Ecclesiastes 3:3

Parenting Point

There is no neutral ground as a parent. If we aren't actively building into the lives of our children, we will be tearing down what has already been built. Our children are keenly aware of hypocrisy, and they will recognize if you are holding them to a standard that you do not adhere to yourself. Spend some time with your spouse, or with the Lord for a single parent, and make a list of the character qualities that are especially needful in your children's lives right now. Come up with a methodical and comprehensive way to build into those character qualities. Some ideas would include: Bible study, role-playing, helpful read aloud books, etc. Once you have decided on a strategy, spend time in prayer committing your plans and work of building to the Lord. In love, hold one another accountable to the decisions that you have made. Don't look back ten years from now and wish that you had spent more time building into your children's character. Make the most of every day, because the window of opportunity to influence their hearts is shorter than we think. The world and all that it holds is actively pursuing their hearts, but the world doesn't have to win the war. Your consistent and loving training can guard your children's hearts from the deceptive and destructive philosophies of this world. Arm yourself for battle today!

The Week in Review

Take some time to gather as a family and discuss the character qualities that you learned this week. Here are some questions to get the conversation started.

- List the character qualities we studied this week.
- Which character quality was the hardest for you to practice this week?
- Did you see a family member consistently practicing one of this week's character qualities? Which family member?

Use your imagination and add questions of your own. After your time of discussion, spend some time praying together, thanking the Lord and sharing one another's burdens. Pray ahead of time for teachable hearts to incorporate and put into practice the character qualities your family will learn in the upcoming week.

Obedience:
Show What You Believe

Almost every new endeavor in life starts with obedience. The first days on your first job you were told where, when, and what to do. You were required to be obedient and not much more. In fact, your first few years of life were much the same. Mom and Dad told you when, what, and how to eat, walk, talk, and so on. Obedience is a budding responsibility that is truly entry-level Christianity. The requirement to be obedient never really goes away, and a lack of obedience can become serious business. James 4:17 reminds us that a lack of obedience at any age, position in life, or maturity in Christ, can become offensive to God. If we do not follow God in faithful obedience, it makes our God look small, and that is a sin,

James 4:17

Parenting Point

What areas of disobedience do you allow your children to overlook? Take a minute and write down the areas of disobedience you are allowing them to excuse, such as: hygiene, chores, or a generally poor attitude. Also, how do your children speak to you? Do they respect you with their tone and words? Do they obey you Right away, All the way, the Happy way? If not, write it down and get to work on obedience. Remember, obedience leads to responsibility, which leads to ownership. If you allow disobedience and reward irresponsibility, it will lead to entitlement, and trust me, you don't want that. Next, do the same exercise for yourself. It is difficult to ask your children to be more obedient to God than you are willing to be yourself!

Rich or Poor?

Take some time to read today's verse. What does it mean to be poor? Does a diligent work ethic mean that you will be financially rich? This verse is talking about so much more than money. Learning to be a diligent worker in whatever you put your hand to will reap rich character. Diligence produces self-control, patience, long suffering, priority-living, and so much more. God wants us to be rich in character, and He has provided the way for us through diligent living.

Proverbs 10:4

Parenting Point

More and more I see books, articles, and blogs encouraging young mothers to "forget about the dishes and unmade beds; it's much more important to play with your children." While I would agree that we need to invest time in playing with, reading to, and snuggling with our children, I don't believe that ignoring our responsibilities in order to do those things is a right priority. If our children grow up seeing us shirk responsibility in order to play with them, they will learn to follow our example. We will soon see a new generation of "grown-up" children, struggling to learn how to work when all they want to do is play. Teaching our children to complete the work necessary to run a well-ordered home is just as important as playing board games or reading aloud. Chores, carefully completed before play, provide the opportunity to teach diligence and carefulness. Help your children see the freedom that comes with completed chores. Moms, don't wait until the children are napping or in bed to do the work yourself!! Help them learn to appreciate an orderly and peaceful home by having them assist in keeping it that way.

Integrity of Heart

Integrity is a character quality that shows itself in many different forms and manifestations. Any discussion of integrity must begin with the most important integrity of all: integrity of heart. It is wonderful when other people see us as people of integrity and character, but the most important judge of our integrity is the Lord God, Himself. In today's Scripture, God extols the integrity of heart shown by David and holds it up as an example to David's son, Solomon. Would God be able to use your integrity of heart as a standard and example for your children?

I Kings 9:3-5

Parenting Point

Integrity can be a nebulous term, difficult for our children to understand. Help them to understand this character quality by challenging them to be exactly the same person, regardless of their location, circumstances, or parental input. As parents, we must take seriously our own responsibility to exhibit integrity of heart. Others may be fooled by our outward appearances, but our children will know immediately if we are living the life of a hypocrite. Pray, as David prayed in Psalm 139:23-24, and ask the Lord to search your heart to unearth any wicked ways within you. We all fail. Turn your failure into an opportunity for growth by seeking forgiveness (of your children, if appropriate) and pressing on to serve God with a heart characterized by integrity. Building a testimony of integrity is an ongoing process. Don't allow failures to slow your progress. Instead, use those times to strengthen your resolve and to build a strong desire to honor the Lord through integrity. When your children fail, encourage them to press on and to redouble their efforts to live lives that are led by the Spirit of God and characterized by a testimony of integrity.

Peacefulness

Peace Out!

I s your life characterized by peace? On a daily basis are you more often peaceful or filled with doubt, worry, or strife? Read today's verse. Interestingly, the attainment of peace is equated with acquiring wisdom from above. In other words, the more we know of God and His wisdom, the more peace will be evidenced in our lives. Spend some time with God today and reap the benefits of His spiritual peace.

James 3:17

Parenting Point

Isn't it discouraging to watch how families, especially large families, are portrayed on television and in the movies? There seems to be an assumption that all families are filled with strife, clutter, and out of control children. Hollywood is wrong! There is no need for our families to become hotbeds of turmoil; indeed, the Christian home should be a sanctuary of peace, not only to our own families, but also to those who visit our homes. Is your family lacking peace? Discuss as parents how much time your family is spending immersed in the Word of God and developing that important "wisdom from above." If the majority of our time is spent watching television, using the Internet, or simply filling our time with busyness while evidencing no regard for godly wisdom, the inevitable result will be a lack of peace. Every family has difficult times and situations that cause stress or strife; however, the overall characterization of our homes should be one of peace, contentment, and harmony. If your home doesn't pass the "peace test," determine today what changes you will make to increase your wisdom input in order to strengthen the output of peace in your home.

A Reliable Yes

I s your "yes" a reliable yes? Is your "no" just as reliable? As followers of Christ, we can have the confidence to make decisions and stick with them. How do we gain that confidence? By spending time immersed in the Word of God and seeking the Lord through prayer, we will gain the knowledge and insight necessary to make wise decisions and the courage to follow through on those same decisions, as well.

James 5:12

Parenting Point

Parents who are consistent in following through on what they have said build security into the lives of their children. As the scripture above says, let your yes be yes and your no be no. When we give in easily to our children's demands, we are doing them no long term good. Yes, our children will beg, coax, and wheedle, but once you have made a parenting decision, have the strength to stand by that choice. Be careful not to say "no" immediately. Take the time to contemplate your parenting decisions, but once a commitment has been made, stick to it! Your "yes" and "no" decisions will form walls of protection that your children can count on.

Trust • Wisdom

Trust, But Verify

Is there a difference between being trusting and being naive? I believe there is, and today's verse highlights that difference. The dictionary defines naive this way: showing a lack of experience, wisdom, or judgment. In other words, although we are to be trusting, we are to infuse that trust with wisdom and good judgment. Such wisdom is found in the Word of God. It is easy to speak the language of trust, but truly developing godly trust will hinge upon maturity, which can only be built through diligent study and application of scripture. Are you trusting or naive? Ask God to help you ascertain the core of your character.

Matthew 10:16

Parenting Point

After we do the hard work of parenting faithfully and teaching our children how to trust us and, in turn, trust God, what is our next assignment? Honestly, as a parent of young adults, what comes next is even more difficult for me to faithfully complete. Once our children have grown in wisdom, proven themselves trustworthy, and developed their own trusting relationship with the Lord, we must step back and allow them the freedom to pursue that trust relationship in their own individual manner. There are times that my children have confidently trusted the Lord for provision or direction when I was absolutely terrified of what might be the result. Hmmm... Sounds like I need to work on my own trust relationship! Learning to trust God with my children as they trust God for their daily decisions, is an important and essential next step in parenting. When our children have proven themselves trustworthy, it is our responsibility to trust them! Yes, they will undoubtedly make mistakes and be forced to face the consequences of failures, but it is in these times that they will learn to trust God even more wholly. Step back, Mom and Dad! Be available to offer wise counsel, *when they ask,* pray diligently, and remember...God is trustworthy!!

The Week in Review

Take some time to gather as a family and discuss the character qualities that you learned this week. Here are some questions to get the conversation started.

- List the character qualities we studied this week.
- Which character quality was the hardest for you to practice this week?
- Did you see a family member consistently practicing one of this week's character qualities? Which family member?

Use your imagination and add questions of your own. After your time of discussion, spend some time praying together, thanking the Lord and sharing one another's burdens. Pray ahead of time for teachable hearts to incorporate and put into practice the character qualities your family will learn in the upcoming week.

A Clean Character

Consider this dictionary definition of clean: morally pure, virtuous, having no marks of discredit or offense. Just reading that definition makes a clean character seem almost unattainable, doesn't it? However, as today's Scripture reminds us, it is God who creates a clean spirit in us. He renews the ability to be steadfast in seeking to keep our hearts clean and pure in His sight. In Matthew 7:7 our Lord Jesus reminds us to ask and it will be given to us. Asking God to create a clean heart in you is the type of prayer God delights to answer! So, seek God today. Ask for a clean heart and then use the steadfast spirit He provides to continue to develop a clean character.

Psalm 51:10

Parenting Point

How's the character of heart cleanliness in your home? Clean and steadfast? Or dusty and disheveled? Discerning the true heart-character of a family will require a deep and discerning look at not only what is *done* in a home but in the *attitudes* and *behaviors* surrounding the actions. Sadly, it is possible for our families to "look" clean on the outside while ungodly and unkind hearts are festering underneath. Pray for God to give you clear eyes and sensitive ears to accurately assess your family. If you notice children who obey or serve accompanied by eye-rolling or an unpleasant attitude, address the inward heart problem. Whether it is our children or ourselves, outward compliance without inward submission is the product of a Pharisaical heart. Don't be satisfied with looking clean; take the necessary steps to cleanse and purge the heart character of your family. A family conference, dedicated to eradicating unclean attitudes and affirming the need to desire cleanliness of heart first and foremost, will go far in readjusting the character of a family. Our children need to know, without a doubt, that we care more about who they are on the inside than how they appear on the outside. Spend time seeking and extending forgiveness for hidden heart attitudes. Commit as a family to seek God's help in cleansing your hearts and then steadfastly seek His help to keep them that way.

Are You Willing to Be Scrutinized?

One of the hallmarks of a true follower of Christ is the desire to have a scrutinized heart. Unlike an "old dog that can't be taught new tricks," the disciple of Christ desires to have his/her heart searched, cleansed, and changed by the Savior. As today's Scripture reminds us, it is God alone who truly sees and knows the condition of our heart. Scrutiny takes vulnerability; change takes humility. Are you prepared to ask the Lord to scrutinize your heart today?

Psalm 139:23-24

Parenting Point

When it comes to teaching vulnerability and the willingness to be teachable, our example will always speak more loudly than our words. Our children are watching to see how we handle instruction and constructive criticism. What do they hear in the car on the way home from church on Sunday? Often when we feel challenged or scrutinized by the Word of God, we respond by complaining about the messenger. When this happens our children are learning that the appropriate response to conviction is an argumentative and defensive spirit. Don't be surprised when they respond to your instruction or conviction in the same manner. Learning to be teachable and humble is essential to the Christian life. Your humble and transparent example of teach-ability will speak volumes to assist you in encouraging this important attitude in your home.

Are You a Magnifying Glass?

According to the dictionary "to magnify" means to make greater in size, to enlarge, to glorify, or to praise. Do you have a character of magnification? Does your life make God look great, and does it cause others to glorify and praise Him? Certainly, God looks great all on His own. We can't make Him any greater; however, through our actions, attitudes, and choices we can regretfully make a great God look smaller. Work hard to build a character of magnification, so that your great God is enlarged to a lost world. Magnification is contagious, and soon others will, as today's verse says, "magnify the Lord" with you!

Psalm 34:3

Parenting Point

When we can "show" our children what a biblical concept looks like, it is much easier for them to internalize that teaching. Take some time to show your children how a magnifying glass works. Have them examine a number of items through the magnifying glass, and then ask them to describe what they are seeing. After you have talked about magnification, read today's verse together. Ask them what they can do that would magnify God to their friends. Some examples would be responding respectfully to teachers, having a cheerful disposition, telling the truth even when it's hard, etc. Remind them that God really needs no magnification from us, but that He graciously allows us to enlarge Him to others. Secondly, ask them what attitudes or actions would accomplish the opposite of magnifying God. Help them to understand that they have a choice each day to make their God look great or to diminish His glory through their poor behavior. Spend time as a family praying about ways to better magnify God together. After praying, put those ideas into action!

Bitter, Bitter

If being tenderhearted is the positive character quality a Christian can exhibit, being bitter is the negative heart attitude. Bitterness can destroy the life, health, and testimony of a follower of Christ. Although bitterness has several definitions, two are of particular importance to consider. Bitterness: marked by resentment or cynicism or, causing a sharply unpleasant, painful or stinging sensation. While the first definition speaks to what bitterness causes in our own lives, the second clearly underscores the effect of a person's bitterness in the lives of others. We must "put-off" bitterness and replace it with tenderheartedness and a forgiving spirit.

Hebrews 12:15

Parenting Point

Read today's Scripture aloud as a family. Notice that one of the consequences of bitterness is trouble and defilement. Ask your children what bitterness looks like. Then ask them how they think bitterness could cause trouble in a family. Sadly, even Christian families can be wounded and divided by a bitter and unforgiving spirit. Children who grow up in a home with bitter parents will deal with insecurities brought about by the unrest of bitterness in their home. Mom and Dad, if you have allowed a root of bitterness toward anyone to spring up in your life, do whatever it takes to uproot that nasty weed. Seek the Lord's forgiveness regarding your own bitterness, and ask Him for the strength to take the steps necessary to replace bitterness with tenderheartedness.

Concerned Christians

A re you a concerned Christian? I'm not referring to a busybody or someone who entangles themselves in the affairs of others, but a Christian who is concerned for the *welfare* of others. We live in a world that promotes the attitude of "whatever." This attitude stands in stark juxtaposition to the care and concern that Christians should show for other people's needs, possessions, problems, and most importantly, salvation. A "whatever" attitude may be "cool," but it is aloof. Our Lord was winsome and cared deeply for each and every person He met. True concern for the needs of others will often earn us the right to share the good news about our Lord.

Luke 10:25-37

Parenting Point

Teaching our children to be concerned for others is really just teaching them to be others-oriented. Take some time today to read the story of the Good Samaritan. Ask your children to describe the Samaritan's actions and attitudes as he ministered to the injured man. Now, ask them how they can show concern for others with the same actions and attitudes. Help them to develop practical ways to show their concern for others. Don't allow them to simply settle for the correct "Sunday School answer." Encourage them to learn to show concern at home by caring for their brothers and sisters. As you see them exhibit good actions and attitudes of concern, take the time to praise and encourage your children. When your children are characterized by showing concern for the other members of their family, begin to reach out to those outside of the family. Ministering together will provide your children with opportunities to grow and mature while still working within the security of their family unit.

Humility

Be Humble...or Be Humbled

Consider these synonyms for the word humble: modest, low-ly, meek, submissive, unassuming, low. Aren't those the same words that would be used to describe the Lord Jesus Christ? While the world defines success as powerful, rich, or important, our Lord modeled the ultimately successful life as a humble life. How can we become humble? The more time we spend in the Word of God learning about our marvelous and majestic Lord, the more easily we will bow in an attitude of humility. As we recognize His greatness, any self-importance we cling to will be erased in the light of His glory.

James 4:6

Parenting Point

It is so easy to inadvertently encourage an attitude of pride and self-exultation in our children. When we consistently boast of their great achievements in their earshot, we can cause them to consider themselves more highly than they ought. Yes, our children should absolutely hear our heartfelt words of encouragement and our excitement about their accomplishments; however, we must be careful to praise them for the things that really matter. Godly character really matters! While being extolled as the best batter on the baseball team can bring momentary glory to our child, character that is shown through kindness, honesty, integrity, and humility will bring glory to God. Who do your children look up to? Do they idolize sports heroes with questionable character, or do they desire to have the testimony and character of an athlete like Tim Tebow? Have them memorize today's verse and allow God's Word to transform them from proud to humble.

The Week in Review

Take some time to gather as a family and discuss the character qualities that you learned this week. Here are some questions to get the conversation started.

- List the character qualities we studied this week.

- Which character quality was the hardest for you to practice this week?

- Did you see a family member consistently practicing one of this week's character qualities? Which family member?

Use your imagination and add questions of your own. After your time of discussion, spend some time praying together, thanking the Lord and sharing one another's burdens. Pray ahead of time for teachable hearts to incorporate and put into practice the character qualities your family will learn in the upcoming week.

Planning to Be Proactive

Today's verse shows a clear contrast between a wise, proactive man and a foolish, shortsighted man. Wise men see the danger ahead, and they purposefully avoid that danger. If we want to live wisely as Christians, we must build a purposeful, proactive character that examines every situation and evaluates the danger, spiritual and otherwise, which that situation brings into our lives. The best way to learn what is spiritually dangerous is by evaluating each situation in light of Scripture and what the Word of God has to say about it. In order to do this accurately, we need to know the Bible. Are you prepared to be proactive and purposeful in order to avoid danger? If not, what steps do you need to take to be Scripturally armed to avoid proceeding into danger and then paying the penalty?

Proverbs 27:12

Parenting Point

Do you have children in your home that seem to continually "stray" into trouble or potentially dangerous situations? Some children just seem more prone to end up in the wrong place at the wrong time. In our home, we often joked about the "child who will go unnamed." That child could be counted on to be involved in any troublesome situation or conflict in the home. Although some children may seem more naturally prone to trouble, do not allow them to continue down this dangerous path. Take the time to teach your children to slow down and evaluate situations, circumstances, and relationships. Teach them to ask themselves the important question: "What virtue or value is at stake in the decision I am about to make?" Often, simply thinking through that question will enable our children to stop a course of action before it is too late. Be diligent to consistently teach them what godly character looks like. Daily training to be circumspect, careful, faithful, trustworthy, honest, respectful, etc. will be a safeguard from the path that leads to danger and too often into painful consequences. Even the most impetuous child, as they are consistently taught to practice self-control, can learn to slow down, evaluate, and choose wise life lessons that will serve them well for their entire lives.

Contagious Joy

Joy is one of the most contagious character qualities a Christian can possess. When we routinely praise God and allow Him to lift our countenance, others take notice. Positive words of encouragement, selfless acts of generosity, or a simple bright smile, are all displays of joy that can cause a domino effect in others. Joy is contagious... Look at the domino effect of contagious joy in Acts 3:8-10. Who have you infected with joy recently?

Acts 3:8-10

Parenting Point

How is the joy barometer in your home? We've all heard the saying, "When mama ain't happy, nobody's happy." and in many ways, this saying is true. Parental joy, or the lack thereof, will directly influence the atmosphere in your home. If you are a born-again believer, exhibiting joy is one of your parental responsibilities. Every day we are modeling what it means to have joy regardless of our circumstances and simply because of our salvation. Your attitude is contagious... What are your children catching from you?

Putting on Gentleness

I n some ways gentleness seems like one of the qualities that you are either born with or you're not; however, according to today's verse, gentleness is a hallmark of one who has been chosen by God. It is easy to make excuses for a lack of gentleness: I'm just tired. My whole family is a little rough. I've had a bad day... But, our excuses must be abandoned as we obediently "put-on" the character of a gentle heart.

Colossians 3:12-14

Parenting Point

Is it really possible to teach our children to be gentle? What about our rowdy little boys who are constantly loud and rambunctious? God's Word never instructs us to do anything that He won't empower us to accomplish. Even the busiest and most rowdy children can learn to curb their energy and exhibit gentleness. We begin teaching gentleness as we are teaching our children about being appropriately behaved in different circumstances. Although we should never be rough or inconsiderate, there are certain times and situations that require an extra level of gentleness. Role-play some of these situations with your children. Teach them how to gently hold a baby. Teach your boys how to gently shake a woman's hand. All of my boys learned from their father's example that they needed to treat their mother with gentleness, and we encouraged them to practice that same gentleness with their sisters. Young men who have learned to be gentle and considerate to those at home will become adults who treat their wives with gentle consideration! Girls need to learn gentleness as well. Baby dolls, as opposed to fashion model dolls, teach our children how to be motherly and gentle. Gentleness isn't simply limited to our actions. Spend time teaching your children to use gentle voices and gentle words. Gentleness is the opposite of harshness. Be an example of gentleness, even when your circumstances would seem to provide an opening for harsh words. Gently correct and train your children and make sure that you praise their acts of gentleness.

Soothing or Irritating?

How would your friends define your character? Are you seen as one who brings soothing and calmness to a group, or are you an irritant and one who stirs up trouble? Read today's verse. Boasting, challenging, and envying are all behaviors that act as an irritant to others. While it is good to spur one another on to good deeds, simply irritating and bothering others will only serve to detract from our testimony for Christ. Ask a trusted friend to help you recognize the characterization of your behavior.

Galatians 5:26

Parenting Point

In any family there is generally one member who is characterized by being irritating or annoying. Honestly, I think each of my children went through an annoying phase, but when a child begins to be known for their irritating and annoying behavior, it's time to step in and coach them to a higher standard. Some of the loneliest children I've met are the children who find themselves avoided or ostracized because of their awkward or unacceptable behavior. Take the time to role-play various social situations with these children. Ask them good questions to help them discern for themselves what behavior is proper and becoming for Christian children. When you see them practicing those good behaviors in real-life situations, praise them and encourage them that not only are you pleased, but also that God is pleased with their kind and considerate character. Continual praise and repetition will help formerly irritating children become winsome and well-liked representatives of Christ.

A Hungry Heart

How hungry are you for the things and people of God? Our appetites are a clear indicator of the wisdom, or foolishness, of our hearts. As the verse below states, although all things are acceptable not all things are profitable. We must develop the wisdom to have an appetite for those things that are profitable. An appetite for anything that is not profitable in God's eyes must be put off and replaced with a hunger for those things that are well-pleasing to the Lord. Ask God to help you attain the wisdom to differentiate between what is acceptable and what is truly profitable.

I Corinthians 10:23

Parenting Point

Do your children get excited about spiritual things? Do they love to go to church and spend time with other believers? Spend some time evaluating their attitude toward spiritual things. If you recognize that they are indifferent, or even hostile, toward the things of God, you must begin to dig deep to find the root cause. Are they too involved in worldly activities? Have they developed friendships that discourage rather than encourage spiritual growth? Are they seeing hypocrisy in your home, and are, therefore, finding it difficult to be around other believers? Ask the hard questions. A spiritual appetite will not just happen. We need to excite the palate of our children. Evaluate your situation and seek God's help to make any needed changes.

Forgiveness

Developing Forgetfulness

No, we don't really need to develop a character of forgetfulness, but as today's verse reminds us, to be like God we must learn to choose not to remember. God doesn't forget our sins, but once we repent and confess He chooses not to bring them up to us again. We need to extend that same type of grace to our friends and even to ourselves. When we refuse to live as forgiven Christians by repeatedly grieving over sins that have already been dealt with, we lock ourselves into shackles of uselessness. Until we allow the forgiveness of God to free us from our past sins, we will be unfruitful in our service for the King. What do you need to "not remember" today?

Psalm 103:10-12

Parenting Point

I admit, as a parent it is very difficult for me to not hold onto the past wrongdoings of my children. Not only do I replay their disobedience or irresponsibility over and over in my mind, I sadly catch myself bringing up their sin as a "reminder" in times of conflict. We must carefully teach our children how to repent and seek forgiveness; however, once they have taken those steps, the onus is on us to graciously choose not to hold that sin over their heads as a weapon. Our children learn their picture of what God the Father is like through our example. I don't know about you, but I'm so very thankful that God doesn't continually club me over the head with my past failures. (I do enough of that to myself!) Because God is so gracious with me, I want my children to trust that He will be just as gracious with them. What if you've already slipped and used past sin against your children? Today is the day to seek their forgiveness! Tell them that you were wrong to keep a record of their wrongdoing (I Corinthians 13) and humbly ask them to forgive you for using that record against them. Our children are so quick to forgive! Commit to them and to the Lord that you will choose to "not remember" their forgiven sin anymore. Make sure you restore with a hug or a snuggle!

The Week in Review

Take some time to gather as a family and discuss the character qualities that you learned this week. Here are some questions to get the conversation started.

List the character qualities we studied this week.

Which character quality was the hardest for you to practice this week?

Did you see a family member consistently practicing one of this week's character qualities? Which family member?

Use your imagination and add questions of your own. After your time of discussion, spend some time praying together, thanking the Lord and sharing one another's burdens. Pray ahead of time for teachable hearts to incorporate and put into practice the character qualities your family will learn in the upcoming week.

A Wise Steward

What does your use of money say about your character? Are you a wise steward of the resources that God has provided, or do you spend however you wish, foolishly squandering your resources? The Word of God has much to say about wise stewardship. We must be careful, however, that our stewardship is directed by the Lord not a legalistic set of rules that binds us so tightly we cannot serve God generously. We can only live wisely in this area as we study and seek the Lord. So, commit yourself to know God's heart in this important area of wisdom. Then, as you grow in knowledge of the Lord's will, purpose to act on that knowledge in faithful obedience.

Mark 12:41-44

Parenting Point

Do your children know the things you do and the choices that you make to be a wise steward of God's gifts? Sometimes, as we are busy taking care of bills, obligations, and daily money choices, we forget to bring our children alongside to observe the decisions that we are making. Include them in the process and help them to learn, from the youngest ages, what it means to be a wise steward. An allowance is a personal family choice, but however your children receive money, teach them to give and save faithfully, as well as make wise choices in their purchases. When they are starting their own homes, they will be thankful for your good training!

Generosity • Stealing

Steal Not

I f stealing is a negative character quality that we should avoid, then "stealing not" would be the positive character quality. There are so many things that we can steal. I think all of us would recognize the wrongfulness of taking an item from a store, but how often have we stolen someone's time, reputation, or dignity? When we gossip about another person, we steal a part of their reputation that cannot be replaced. In the same way, when we publicly mock someone, we rob them of their dignity and self-worth. God wants us to be givers, not takers, so the character lesson for today is simple: Steal not!

Proverbs 20:17

Parenting Point

Have you taken the time to carefully instruct your children about the importance of not stealing? Sometimes, we just assume that our children know that something is wrong; then, we are shocked when they commit a wrongful act. Don't assume anything! Teach your children how important it is not to steal. Ask them what types of things can be stolen. Don't be surprised if they don't mention anything other than the "stuff" of life. For children, the idea that they can steal time, reputation, or dignity from someone else is a complex concept. As their parents, you must help them to take this complex concept and make it understandable and workable in their lives. Talk with them about the amount of time allotted to each person's day. Help them to list ways that they can steal time from a person's 24 hours. Some examples would be long-winded stories or dawdling over meals. Perhaps you would want to role-play what it looks like to steal time or to steal a reputation by gossiping. As your children get a visual picture of other ways that they can steal, they will begin to understand what it means to "steal not."

A "Friendly" Reminder

Today's scripture is once again found in I Corinthians and reminds us that wisdom is evidenced through our choice of friends. Do your friends encourage you to grow and glorify the Lord? Do you encourage your friends to grow and glorify the Lord? The fellowship of like-minded believers can be a powerful safety net when we are tempted to make bad choices; however, if all of our time is spent enjoying time with immature believers or the unsaved, our unwise choices will be encouraged, and we will grow in foolishness not wisdom. Be wise in your choice of close friendships.

I Corinthians 15:33

Parenting Point

With whom do your children spend the bulk of their time? Do you know their friends? Do you see positive fruit from their friendships? Friendships are far too important an area for us to be less than 100% involved. What about the offspring of your closest friends? Often, we so strongly desire to spend time with our own friends that we are not carefully paying attention to the influence that their children are exerting on our children. Be wise! Don't expose your children to bad influences simply because you want to spend time with another adult. Look for friends who are like-minded in their child training and make sure that even when you are enjoying fellowship your children are not simply left to their own devices (Proverbs 29:15).

Dependable Character

Dependability is defined simply as being reliable or trustworthy. Often, we think of dependability in terms of how someone performs a task or completes an assignment; however, our most important dependability is the trustworthiness or reliability of our character. People with dependable character can be counted on to make wise and trustworthy decisions regardless of their circumstances. How dependable is your character? A testimony of dependable character should be one of our most valued and well-guarded treasures. Read the scripture below to see the testimony of Noah, a man of dependable character.

Genesis 6:9

Parenting Point

Do your children have dependable character? Children who can "act the part" and display dependable character publicly but who are untrustworthy at home, do not have dependable character. Take the time to evaluate the characterization of your children's dependability. Do not settle for public compliance and private rebellion. The condition of our children's hearts is much more important than what others may think of them or us. If you see a disparity between their public and private behavior, pray and then spend some time dialoguing with them about this issue. A lack of dependable character will rob us of the ability to trust our children. It is important that our children realize just how precious our trust is and the painful consequences that a lack of trust can cause not only to them but to their whole family.

Thanksgiving

Each of us is designed by God to be obedient to Him and His Word. Obedience should grow into responsibility, and responsibility in turn develops into ownership; however, if we allow disobedience toward God to go unconfessed, we will eventually become irresponsible, and before too long the "entitlement" mentality takes control of our lives. Sadly, it is the entitlement mentality that rules and reigns in our current American culture. But wait, it gets even worse. According to Romans 1:21, if we refuse to give thanks to God for all things, at all times, in every circumstance, we run the risk of sliding down that hard slippery slope of Romans 1:18-28. The hard truths contained in Romans 1:18-28 start with *missing thanksgiving*. If you do not give God the thanks He is due, you will start down that slippery slope of Romans 1, and you may just end up being given over to a depraved mind. My hope and prayer for you today is that you, your friends, and family aren't missing thanksgiving.

Romans 1:21

Parenting Point

Are you thankful for Jesus? Are you thankful for the cross? Are you thankful for your job? Your school? Your pastor? Your church? Your friends? Do you model thankfulness to your children? Do they hear you grumble and complain? Do your kids know what it looks like to be truly thankful for all things? When was the last time you told any of the people in your life you were thankful for them? When was the last time you told God? Food for thought, prayer, and action!

Put-off Being Pugnacious

Although Pugs can be sweet little dogs, their crunched up faces make them appear angry and combative. People, on the other hand, may look sweet, but their characterization may be pugnacious. The dictionary defines pugnacious like this: combative in nature; belligerent. Unlike those poor little Pugs that can't help how they look, we can choose to discard a pugnacious character. Pugnacious people stir up trouble when there is no trouble to be found. Self-evaluate and determine if you are a pugnacious person. If so, replace that negative character quality with graciousness, kindness, and verbal restraint.

I Timothy 3:2-3

Parenting Point

Some children seem to be born with a pugnacious attitude, causing discord and strife within moments of walking into the room. Dealing with them is time consuming and often frustrating, as they will argue with us in the same way that they argue with other children. Do not lose heart! Though vexing in many ways, they desperately need our training and instruction. Call a family conference to enact a contentious argument. Ask your children dialog questions to gauge how they feel about what just transpired. Don't single out your pugnacious child, but include them with all of the other children. Have them give you words to describe what they saw (i.e., bickering, arguing, ugliness). Then, have them list positive character qualities that could replace arguing (i.e. kindness, encouragement, sharing). Teach into the put-on/put-off principle found in Ephesians 4:21-32. After you have discussed this principle, read Ephesians 4:29 and discuss what constitutes wholesome and unwholesome words. Spend time praying together that your family would develop a testimony of being gracious and kind-hearted. This may be all the encouragement your pugnacious child needs; however, if they continue in their argumentative attitude, take them aside and remind them of the need to change their manner of communication. If they refuse, you will have to bring correction into their life. I have found that often these children have just backed themselves into a bad habit, and my instruction and encouragement was all they needed to institute change. Remind them that you love them and that you don't want to see them lose their sibling and friend relationships because they are allowing themselves to be pugnacious. Praise them when you see them making good choices in their manner of communication.

The Week in Review

Take some time to gather as a family and discuss the character qualities that you learned this week. Here are some questions to get the conversation started.

- List the character qualities we studied this week.

- Which character quality was the hardest for you to practice this week?

- Did you see a family member consistently practicing one of this week's character qualities? Which family member?

Use your imagination and add questions of your own. After your time of discussion, spend some time praying together, thanking the Lord and sharing one another's burdens. Pray ahead of time for teachable hearts to incorporate and put into practice the character qualities your family will learn in the upcoming week.

The Blessing of a Pure Heart

Do you want to be blessed? Strive to have a pure heart. Sounds easy, doesn't it? However, having a pure heart is hard work. Our hearts are not naturally pure. Read Jeremiah 17:9 to get a biblical picture of the condition of our hearts. So, how are we to strive to have a pure heart? Scripture gives us some clear clues. Psalm 101 shows how David sought to maintain a pure heart through the things he did and did not allow in his home. Sometimes, it is hard to determine what is vile or defiling. Again, Scripture gives us guidance, as found in Philippians 4:8-9. As we think on things that are true, honorable, right, pure, lovely, of good repute, and excellent, the things of this world that are vile and defiling in God's eyes, will become vile and defiling in our eyes as well. Take inventory today. What are you willingly or inadvertently allowing to rob you of the blessing of a pure heart?

Matthew 5:8

Parenting Point

Until our children are mature enough in their own walk with the Lord to make wise decisions concerning what is and isn't acceptable, we must act as moral guardians for their protection. What books, movies, music, or internet sites are you allowing to influence your children? While many of these things are fine, any that are producing poor spiritual fruit should be plucked from our children's responsibility trees. Make wise decisions ahead of time. Instead of allowing something questionable to become a part of your child's life and then finding yourself being forced to remove the objectionable object or activity, look ahead and evaluate any potential danger. Yes, this is hard work; however, helping our children to protect the purity of their hearts until they are mature enough to ensure that protection on their own is well-worth any hard work that it takes.

The Blessings of a Good Appetite

Matthew 5:6 tells us that those who hunger and thirst after righteousness will be blessed. This begs a question for the follower of Christ, namely: How's your appetite? Are you hungry for the things of God? Unlike physical food, which leaves us full after a big meal, the Word of God will produce an even hungrier appetite. As you spend time studying, meditating on, and applying the Word of God to your life, you will find yourself wanting more and more; however, unlike a physical hunger which can only be satisfied by another meal, even as you are desiring more spiritual food, your hunger for righteousness will still provide satisfaction. That's the blessing of God-provided food and drink. Although you desire and seek after more food, you won't feel deprived in the process. So, build an appetite! This is the one time it's good to go back to the buffet!

Matthew 5:6

Parenting Point

Just like us, as they spend time in the Word of God, our children will naturally develop a deeper hunger for spiritual food. The best way to teach this discipline to your children is through modeling a hunger for God and His Word yourself. Let your children see you spending time in the Word. As well, make sure to share with them the truths that God has been revealing to you. Allow them to see the changes you make in your life as a result of the conviction and encouragement you find in your daily time with the Lord. One of the most important areas to remember is that: "More is *caught*, than *taught*." We don't want our children to simply "do" their devotions. We want time in the Word to transform their lives. Let your example of transformation be a catalyst for growth in their lives.

Compassion • Forgiveness • Mercy

Mercy

Mercy has many definitions. The first is kindness or forgiveness shown to an offender. A second definition, and the one that I desire the most, is a disposition to be compassionate or forgiving of others. As always, God is our example of this type of mercy. Ephesians 2:4-5 tells us, "But God, being rich in mercy, because of His great love with which He loved us, even when we were dead in our transgressions, made us alive together with Christ (by grace you have been saved)." While I was dead and undeserving, God graciously bestowed His mercy on me. How then, can I refuse to show that same mercy toward fellow sinners?

Matthew 5:7

Parenting Point

It is easy to be angry and vengeful toward those that have wronged us. It is even easier to have bitter feelings toward those who have wronged our children. First, we must work on our own hearts and attitudes, and then, we can teach our children how to respond with compassion, forgiveness, and with mercy. The first step toward becoming merciful is recognizing the hurts and needs in other's lives. Often, the bad behavior that other people exhibit is simply a reaction to the hard things they face in their own lives. We can't fix everyone else's problems, but we can extend mercy to them when we realize how often we need to receive that mercy ourselves. Help your children to recognize the hard and hurtful things in their friend's lives and to not only extend mercy, but to invest in prayer for those friends. A heart full of mercy will have no room for bitterness. Bitterness will rob us of our joy and will negate our positive testimony for the Lord. Bitterness left unchecked in our children's lives will show up in erratic behavior and disagreeable character. Remind your children often how merciful God has been toward them. May our families grow together in compassion, forgiveness, and mercy.

Others-oriented

Choosing to Prefer

What is the motivating force behind your character and behavior choices? Basically, we find ourselves with two choices: We can focus on our own interests, or we can be more concerned with the interests of others. Honestly, we can't do both because one or the other will suffer. Read today's verse. According to this scripture, there really is no choice. The Word of God instructs us to do nothing simply for our own personal interests, but instead to train ourselves to look out for the interests of others and, in fact, to consider others as more important than ourselves.

Philippians 2:3-4

Parenting Point

Children will not naturally choose to look out for the interests of others while subordinating their own desires and perceived rights. It is only through consistent training that they will learn to be concerned for others. Begin at home by encouraging your children to find ways to serve and encourage one another. When they are characterized by sacrificial love at home, find avenues for them to show that same concern outside the confines of your family. Perhaps you could "adopt" a needy child or family to whom you can display acts of kindness and concern. Encourage your children to look out for others, even when the "others" they are serving may not recognize their efforts. The encouragement of "well-done!" spoken by a loving parent is a wonderful reward all on its own.

Perseverance

I don't know that there is one character quality that stands out as more important than the others, but if there were one that I wish I could nail down, it would be the character quality of perseverance. The need for perseverance shows up in EVERY area of my Christian life. I need perseverance to continue praying. I need perseverance to extend forgiveness. I need perseverance to crucify my flesh. I need perseverance to serve, and the list goes on and on. The good news about perseverance is found in Galatians 6:9. Here, the Word of God reminds us that there is a reward for perseverance, and if we will just persevere, we will receive that reward. I'm not exactly sure when the due time to reap will come, but in light of God's promise that I will reap, I press on. Not growing weary, but instead persistently persevering!

Galatians 6:9

Parenting Point

Perseverance is hard for us, and it's no easier for our children. As we give our children attainable goals and tasks, then encourage them to keep going until those tasks are finished, we are helping them build the character quality of perseverance. Don't you appreciate when someone verbally encourages you that "YOU CAN DO IT!"? We can be those cheerleaders in our children's lives. Make sure that you are taking the time to encourage them that they can accomplish what they are trying to do. Don't just praise the well-finished job, but rather, spend time encouraging consistent effort and renewed attempts when something doesn't work out as planned. Children, who have learned to persevere, will be able to carry through and complete what is required, even when the going gets tough. Do your part and "persevere" in encouragement! Your whole family will reap in due time.

Love is Not Arrogant

Arrogant people are some of the most unpleasant people to spend time around. The dictionary defines arrogance as having or revealing an exaggerated sense of one's own importance or abilities. Arrogance is not self-confidence but rather an overconfidence that is unwarranted by an individual. Arrogance and humility cannot co-exist. Consider yourself soberly and be careful not to exaggerate your own importance. It is better for others to speak well of you than for you to toot your own horn and establish a reputation of arrogance!

I Corinthians 13:4

Parenting Point

Can our children exhibit arrogance? Even the small ones? I believe the answer is a resounding yes! While we wouldn't immediately recognize certain behaviors as arrogant, our children show us arrogance quite often. When they refuse to be taught, they are being arrogant. When they are wise in their own eyes, they are being arrogant. We had one daughter who responded to every instruction we gave her with a sweet, "Yeah, I know." Yes, her tone was sweet, but that answer just grated on me, and I couldn't figure out why. After praying about her response, I realized that her sweet, "Yeah, I know." was just a polite way of telling me to back off. She already knew what she wanted to do, and she certainly didn't need any instruction from me! It doesn't matter how sweetly an arrogant statement is made; arrogance is still unacceptable. Love isn't arrogant and none of us want to raise children who aren't loving, so arrogance must be dealt with each time it rears its ugly head. Use the word "arrogant" as you instruct your children. When they say something that is arrogant, stop them and repeat what they just said. Have your children explain, in their own words, what made their statement arrogant. As they begin to hear their own statements, they will begin to self-regulate and replace arrogance with a humble and teachable spirit.

The Week in Review

Take some time to gather as a family and discuss the character qualities that you learned this week. Here are some questions to get the conversation started.

- List the character qualities we studied this week.
- Which character quality was the hardest for you to practice this week?
- Did you see a family member consistently practicing one of this week's character qualities? Which family member?

Use your imagination and add questions of your own. After your time of discussion, spend some time praying together, thanking the Lord and sharing one another's burdens. Pray ahead of time for teachable hearts to incorporate and put into practice the character qualities your family will learn in the upcoming week.

Generous Character

The dictionary defines the word generous this way: Showing a readiness to give more of something than is strictly necessary or expected. Generosity is the difference between being willing and being eager. Often, we are willing to give when asked, but being generous means that we will look for opportunities to give and to give abundantly. Read today's verse. Our daily work is not simply for our own benefit; it is to provide what we need in order to be generous to others. Pray and ask God to increase your provision so that you can increase your generous giving!

Ephesians 4:28

Parenting Point

I am convinced that the reason we have been so blessed as a family is because my husband is such a generous man. He truly believes that we cannot out give God, and he demonstrates that belief through his generosity. Money is not the only means by which we can act generously. We can be generous with our time, our possessions, our praise, and our commitment. The root of generosity is found in a deep trust that God can, and will, supply all of our needs. Trusting that God can provide for us then frees us to act as His hands, providing for others. For me, there is no greater joy than seeing someone blessed through the generous provision of a joyful Christian. Generosity must begin at home. Our children are watching to see if we are as generous with each other, and them, as we are with those who are outside our home. Lavish one another with compassion, kind words, sacrificial time, and shared blessings. God will be glorified and your children will grow up knowing how wonderful it is to generously care for one another. Encourage them to find ways to share generously with their siblings and friends and praise them for unselfish acts of kindness. Without fail, whenever I have been generous in some way to someone else, God has blessed me by a generous act sent back my way. Whether a note of encouragement, a meal on a rough afternoon, or just a kind hug, God has used His children to bless me and I want to return that blessing by generously blessing others.

More Joy

J oy is defined as the emotion evoked by well-being, success, or good fortune or by the process of possessing what one desires; delight, a source or cause of great delight. If, as the dictionary definition states, joy is the process of possessing what one desires, we Christians have the greatest cause for joy. We possess joy not just for the present only but for eternity. As you would expect, Scripture has much to say about the topic of joy. Read the text below and describe the reaction of joy by the lame man, especially in verse 8.

Acts 3:1-9

Parenting Point

Do you have any "joy" routines? When days seem dark or the pressures of life are overwhelming, simple routines that bring us joy can be timely reminders not to doubt in the dark what we know to be true in the light. For myself, morning coffee and time with the Lord is a routine that brings me great joy. When my children were small, going in to check on them while they were sleeping not only brought me joy, but also reminded me that all of the hard work was well worth the effort. Let's live our lives intentionally and take the time needed to develop routines and daily habits that help us to return to the life of joy that God intends for His children.

Just Let Go

Do you enjoy rollercoasters? Nine out of our ten family members love to ride rollercoasters, the faster and scarier the better. For that tenth family member (me), rollercoasters are a nightmare. While my entire family squeals in delight, hands thrown high in the air, I desperately grip the handlebar, praying the ride will quickly end. Trusting God is often like riding that rollercoaster. When circumstances seem overwhelming, I'm tempted to hold on tight and to even manipulate those circumstances to make things go my way. Today's verses remind us to let go of the handlebar of control and to instead trust God to make our paths straight. Remember, it's more fun when you let go!

Proverbs 3:5-6

Parenting Point

Our homes are the best learning environment for our children to experience the blessing of a trusting relationship with the Lord. As they see us trusting God to provide for and protect our family, they will learn to confidently trust God as well; however, if we are characterized by worry, anxiety, or a general lack of trust, they will also begin to see God as untrustworthy. When we begin to manipulate circumstances in order to make sure things turn out the way we believe they should, we are teaching our children that God isn't able to care for us alone. He needs our help. Manipulation is nothing more than "leaning on our own understanding" as seen in today's verses. Children, who grow up in homes that are characterized by this type of manipulation and control, will soon become teens and young adults who use manipulation to make things go their way. Learning to trust God is a family adventure. When you are faced with hardships or troubling circumstances, take time as a family to pray and seek the Lord's direction. Encourage one another to trust and not fear. Learning to trust God wholeheartedly and seeing His provision for us makes for exciting family growth...especially when we take our hands off the handlebar and sit back to watch God at work!

Contentment

What's That You Said?

Read today's verse. Does doing everything without grumbling or complaining seem like an impossible goal? It certainly isn't something that comes easily, and simply containing my grumbling to the inner recesses of my heart isn't an option either. The King James Version translates this verse with the words "murmuring" and "disputing." Even what we secretly mumble under our breath falls under the scrutiny of God. Only through disciplined self-control and a heart controlled by the Holy Spirit can we attain to this godly standard. Remember, God is just as concerned with what is going on in our hearts and under our breath as He is with our outward and out loud behavior!

Philippians 2:14-16

Parenting Point

An alert parent listens closely not only to what their children say to their face, but to the mumbling and murmuring that goes on behind the scenes in their home. Sometimes, the children that seem to receive instruction with no outward expression are the same children that murmur words of complaint once they are out of our sight and earshot. Be careful to dig a little deeper with the silent children. Are they silent because they are contemplative and remorseful? Or is their silence simply a mask for anger or apathy? Ask good questions of your children and don't take anything for granted. Allowing sullenness or mumbled complaints will build bad habits that will cause damage in your children's future relationships.

Contentious Conversation

What does it mean to have a character that is contentious? The dictionary defines contentious this way: exhibiting an often perverse and wearisome tendency to quarrels and disputes. Yuck! What a terrible character quality, but how easy it is to slip into a character of contention. Examine your own life. Do you always have to have the last word? Do you disagree with whatever is being shared? Do you always have a better idea? Are you critical? If the answer to any of these questions is yes, it won't be long until you find yourself isolated and lonely. Ask the Lord to help you to HATE your contentious character and to love gentle and encouraging speech. It's hard work, but contention is a habit that can and must be discarded.

Proverbs 27:15

Parenting Point

Don't you hate repetitive and annoying noises? Anyone with young boys knows what it's like to hear constant drumming, humming, rapping, and other irritating and disruptive sounds. Read today's verse. Constant dripping is another one of those annoying and unnecessary sounds. For a parent, constant dripping looks like badgering, lecturing, threatening, and repeating. In the same way that we try to drown out and ignore annoying noises, our children will begin to drown out our contentious forms of communication. Although they may still be physically in our presence, out of self-preservation they will shut down mentally and tune us out. Be concise and precise in your communication with your children. Say what needs to be said in ten words or less. Lectures do nothing but demoralize our children, and they communicate a lack of respect for their personhood. Discipline and direction, stated calmly, concisely, and clearly, will be well received and more easily understood by our children. Contentious speech will build barriers in our communication that will prove hard to remove. As parents, hold one another accountable and help one another to put-off contentious speech, while at the same time putting-on clear and unambiguous communication.

Forgetfulness Causes Ungratefulness

Does thankfulness or an ungrateful heart mark your character? Today's verse speaks of people who "knew" God, but they did not give Him thanks. The longer we go with an ungrateful and unthankful heart, the harder it will become to give honor to God. It is only as we purposefully thank God and remind ourselves of His many acts of kindness toward us that our hearts will change from ungrateful to overflowing with gratitude, and out of that gratitude will flow honor to God. Stop and consider: What has God done for you today?

Romans 1:21

Parenting Point

Does your family keep a "Gratitude Journal?" One of the easiest ways to keep us, and our children, focused on the blessings of God is by writing those blessings down. Right now, we have a beautiful leather-bound notebook prominently displayed in our living room. Next to the notebook is a wooden cup with 6 different colored pens, one color for each family member living at home right now. As we individually recognize ways that God is blessing us, we each write down our observations in the notebook, numbering as we go along. About once a week, we bring the notebook to our family devotions and read aloud the numbered "thankfulnesses." What a blessing it has been to read what my children record! More importantly, they are learning to watch for God's workings all through the day. Sometimes, the recorded blessings were things that seemed hard at the time, but those same circumstances taught our family much-needed lessons. As all of us are learning to recognize God's continual provision in our family, we are all becoming more characterized by thankful and grateful hearts. What could you incorporate into your family routine to help yourself and your children develop hearts overflowing with thanksgiving?

The Week in Review

Take some time to gather as a family and discuss the character qualities that you learned this week. Here are some questions to get the conversation started.

- **List the character qualities we studied this week.**

- **Which character quality was the hardest for you to practice this week?**

- **Did you see a family member consistently practicing one of this week's character qualities? Which family member?**

Use your imagination and add questions of your own. After your time of discussion, spend some time praying together, thanking the Lord and sharing one another's burdens. Pray ahead of time for teachable hearts to incorporate and put into practice the character qualities your family will learn in the upcoming week.

The Week in Review

Putting Off Selfishness

The opposite of a self-sacrificing or a self-denying person is a selfish person. No one likes to be with a person who is focused entirely on their own wellbeing and their own desires. Read today's scripture. Seek God and ask Him to reveal the condition of your heart. For whom are you most concerned: yourself or others? Your calendar, checkbook, tweets, and status updates can give you a good indication of who or what dominates your thoughts. As today's scripture reminds us, we're not to "Look out for #1."

Philippians 2:3-4

Parenting Point

Children are naturally born selfish and self-centered, but the wise parent will take every opportunity to teach them to be others-oriented instead. It is sad to see a child who is excluded by friends or siblings because their selfishness has made them an undesirable playmate. Take every opportunity to encourage your children to think of practical ways to meet the needs of others. Several times we encouraged our children to gather toys to share with less fortunate children. Each time, our children eagerly picked out the "good stuff." To my shame there were times that I tried to convince them to keep certain toys because they seemed too valuable to give away. Shame on me! Don't deny your children the opportunity to give with open-handed abandon. The more often they give, share, or encourage others, the more they will learn to be selfless instead of selfish.

Encouragement

Don't Be Persnickety!

Do you know what it means to be persnickety? Persnickety people are those folks who seem to find something wrong with everything they encounter. Often, they totally overlook the wonderful teaching or blessing that they're receiving because they are too busy looking for something to be amiss. Another word for these folks would be "evaluators." Persnickety evaluators bring discouragement into other people's lives. The world has plenty of persnickety discouragers; use your influence to be a positive encourager instead!

Matthew 23:24

Parenting Point

Are you a persnickety parent? Persnickety parents will constantly discourage their children. When we can always be counted on to find an error or something out of order, our children will begin to lose heart. Instead of encouraging our children to even more good works, we will discourage them from even attempting to please us. It's so easy to get into the evaluator mindset. After all, we are constantly trying to teach them and train them in how to live biblically; however, constant evaluation will have the opposite effect of what we're trying to accomplish. Think about it... If God quickly pointed out every single mistake we made each day, life wouldn't be worth living. We would be scared to get out of bed for fear that we would mess up.

Even then, staying in bed would be a problem... Yes, we need to correct and train our children as we see them make poor choices, but may we encourage you to simply pick one or two areas to work on at a time. Spend time evaluating which major problems you are seeing in your children's lives and develop a plan to work on those areas. While you are concentrating on those specific areas, don't nit-pick the other problem areas in your children's lives. There will be plenty of time to deal with those other problem areas later. Praise your children for their positive choices without a "...but, you didn't..." added to the end of your praise. Persnickety-ism, (I made that one up myself!) will bring defeat and discouragement. Praise and encouragement will spawn more positive changes. It's hard to break the persnickety habit, but with prayer and self-control it can be done!

Love of Virtue
vs. Fear of Punishment

What governs your behavior? Most of the moral decisions we make each day come from one of two places: the love of virtue or the fear of punishment. When we operate from a fear of punishment, we lose the chance to elevate and glorify our God. Making choices based simply on whether or not we will be caught is evidence of a weak moral conscience. As we fill our hearts and minds with high quality biblical virtues, those virtues will guide our decision-making process, and in the end our God will look great!

I John 5:18

Parenting Point

What motivates your children's behavior? Are they making character choices from a deep and abiding love of virtue? Do the choices they make arise from a fear of punishment or a dread of disappointing their parents? Although we absolutely use the fear of punishment in a young child's life as a deterrent from wrong behavior, it is essential to persistently and consistently teach our children how to love doing right because they love God and His standards of virtue. Without a love of virtue, our children may behave circumspectly in our presence but have a totally different characterization when we are not available to coach and correct them. We cannot always have our eyes on our children, and it is in these times that a well-stocked heart, full to overflowing with Biblical virtues, will keep them from wrong choices and heartbreaking consequences. Keep planting those seeds of honesty, integrity, respect, compassion, etc. The long-term fruit is well worth the daily hard work. Help your children make the transition from a fear of punishment to a love of virtue by asking them good dialogue questions that will assist them to make the important self-discovery of what it is that truly guides their decision-making process.

Here Comes the Judge

Although it is essential for believers to be willing to be scrutinized by the Word of God, it is equally important that they not become scrutinizers of others. A Christian with a character that is known for judging others will be a Christian with limited impact. Read today's Scripture. It's pretty clear, isn't it? As Christ-followers, we are not to judge. It is a sobering thought to realize that we will be judged in the same way that we judge others. The world doesn't need more judges, so let's "put-off" judging others and instead spend time examining our own lives under the magnifying glass of God's Word.

Matthew 7:1-2

Parenting Point

It is so easy for our children to slip into the habit of judging others. Unfortunately, judging is an extremely difficult habit to break. Listen to the conversation your children engage in concerning others. If you hear them assigning a motive to other children's behaviors, or placing a value judgment on the choices of others, it is time to intervene. Share today's Scripture with your children. Often, judgment toward others comes from an inflated self-worth or a lack of mercy for someone else's unique circumstance. I often reminded my children that we had no idea what went on in anyone else's home. I asked them to consider what extenuating circumstances might be leading to a friend's behavior or choices. We may never know the hurts or difficulties that a friend might be experiencing, and when we allow ourselves the freedom to speak or act out in judgment, we lose the opportunity to be ministers of God's love.

Character with Eternity in Mind

What captures your thoughts? On what does your mind dwell? Do you find yourself distracted and consumed by the cares, pleasures, and distractions of the world? Take time to read today's verse and consider how you can proactively choose not to look at the things that are seen, but instead, to focus on those things that are unseen and eternal. An eye towards eternity will free your heart to experience joy in the midst of trouble, contentment in the midst of want, and hope when all seems dark. Remember, this world is not our home, and its distractions are temporary and fleeting.

II Corinthians 4:18

Parenting Point

Mom and Dad, are you feeling overwhelmed by the continual problems and discipline issues in your home? We understand! Raising children provides us with daily opportunities to see the unpleasant results of sinful choices, both our children's and our own. The necessity of dealing with one... more... argument... can seem overwhelming and discouraging; however, as we look toward eternity and remember the importance of our role as parents, we can face another day of parenting with hope and joy. It is imperative that we train ourselves to glance at the immediate problems facing our family and that we learn to gaze at the Lord. As we do so, we will see our children through God's eyes, and we can discipline them graciously, remembering that they are simply immature sinners in need of guidance and repetitive training. How do we train ourselves to gaze at the Lord? As we spend consistent time immersed in the Word of God and seeking the Lord in prayer, we will learn to turn our gaze toward God rather than staring with unbroken focus at our problems. As we are reminded in I Peter 5:7, we can cast our cares on Jesus simply because He cares for us.

Soft Spoken

What does it mean to be soft-spoken or to give a soft answer? Soft-spoken is an adjective that is defined in two different ways. When used to refer to people, soft-spoken is defined as speaking with a gentle voice. When used as an adjective describing words, soft-spoken means persuasive. Honestly, I think both definitions are bound together in today's verse. As we speak persuasive words with a gentle and soothing tone, we will become a winsome testimony of God's grace. Unlike harsh words, which incite anger, our soft-spoken words will turn away wrath and win other's hearts.

Proverbs 15:1

Parenting Point

Parents, what tone and type of words do you use when instructing and training your children? I am always surprised when someone shares with me that they are a "yeller." Experience has shown me that my children are much more willing to learn from me and obey my instructions when I speak to them with gentle and directive but also affirming, words. It is never my intention to incite my children to anger, and using harsh words to train them, according to today's scripture, would precipitate that result. Just this week, I needed to stand in line for an extended period of time with my son and many other young men and their parents. We were both surprised by the harsh words we heard other parents using about and to their boys. Many parents basically "monologued" in the line about their child's irresponsibility or in some sad cases, stupidity, to anyone who would listen. My son and I felt so sorry for those boys, and I was even more deeply convicted to be gentle and soft-spoken in tone and word choice. Don't be guilty of causing your children to become angry! We can and must train ourselves to speak words of healing and affirmation. Even when a conversation is difficult and corrective in nature, there is no place for harsh words and a harsh tone. Dad and Mom, hold one another accountable to making any necessary changes to your form of communication. Single parents, seek the Lord and ask Him to help you to hate a harsh tongue. Someday, we'll rejoice when we hear our children speaking to our grandchildren with the same soft-spoken tone and words that they learned at home.

The Week in Review

Take some time to gather as a family and discuss the character qualities that you learned this week. Here are some questions to get the conversation started.

- List the character qualities we studied this week.
- Which character quality was the hardest for you to practice this week?
- Did you see a family member consistently practicing one of this week's character qualities? Which family member?

Use your imagination and add questions of your own. After your time of discussion, spend some time praying together, thanking the Lord and sharing one another's burdens. Pray ahead of time for teachable hearts to incorporate and put into practice the character qualities your family will learn In the upcoming week.

Carefulness • Diligence

Don't Be Hasty

The dictionary defines hasty this way: done or made too quickly to be accurate or wise; rash. Does this definition characterize your decision-making process? While it is certainly possible to spend too much time deliberating before making a decision, being hasty is equally inappropriate. Read today's verse to discover the end result of making hasty decisions. According to Proverbs 21, that end result is "poverty." Poverty reveals itself in many ways including spiritual poverty, relational poverty, and physical poverty. Don't rush to make things happen! Instead, make your plans sure through diligent prayer, preparation, and counsel.

Proverbs 21:5

Parenting Point

Do you have hasty children in your home? Because we have such a large family, we have a smattering of both hasty children and hesitant children. Children who are hasty in their decision-making processes are often the same children who find themselves in trouble most often. Because these children tend to "leap before they look," they will routinely step over the boundaries of acceptable behavior. These are the children that recognize the standard that has been set in your home, but in the excitement of their hastily and poorly thought through decision, that standard becomes irrelevant. The joy of the moment outweighs any potential consequence that they may face. They will require your discipline, training, and correction multiple times throughout the day. These kids are tiring! However, don't miss the subtlety of the behavior of your more hesitant children. Often, the children who spend more time considering a course of action are the very children who quietly, but stealthily, step over the same line as their hastier sibling. Because they carry out those actions in such a deliberate and methodical manner, we often miss recognizing their disobedience. Be on the alert for both types of children. When our quiet children continually get away with inappropriate behavior with no consequences, they will begin to build habits of sneakiness and deceit. We can't allow our hasty children to distract us from recognizing what is going on behind the scenes, because they are so actively and constantly engaging our energies. Pray for discernment, and don't allow the "in your face" disobedience of one child to cause you to miss the subtle disobedience of another child.

Sacrificial • Self-Control

The Strength to Say "NO" to Self

Often, the hardest person to tell "no" is oneself. While self-denial may seem like an old-fashioned character quality or one that is relegated to a few fanatical Christians, self-denial is a cornerstone of godly Christian character. Those who have learned to say "no" to themselves are the same people that have been trained by righteousness as found in Hebrews 12:11. Self-denial is hard work, but it produces great fruit. What areas of needed self-denial is God bringing to your mind today?

John 12:24

Parenting Point

Don't you just love to delight your children with gifts and unexpected surprises? I know that I do! Unfortunately, the best way to teach our children self-denial is by sometimes practicing "child-denial" ourselves. Although we may have the means to provide everything that our children might desire, to always do so is harmful to their character. Strategically denying our children will help them learn to be thankful for their blessings and will assist them in avoiding the trap of entitlement. It isn't hard to see if your children feel entitled. Simply tell them "no" the next time they ask for an unnecessary item and watch their reaction. If they cheerfully submit to your decision, they are learning to practice self-denial; however, if they whine, complain, or argue about your decision, you can be confident that entitlement is rearing its ugly head. Entitled children will become entitled adults, and they will struggle to work for what they need and wait for what they want. As always, your example of self-denial will either underscore or undermine the lesson you are trying to teach!

Circumspection • Carefulness

Sandpaper Friendships

Do you have certain friends with whom you find yourself easily irritated? Being touchy and irritable is certainly not a positive testimony for a follower of Christ to earn. Read today's verse. The Lord knows we will all have relationships that are challenging and provoking, those "sandpaper" relationships; however, this scripture sets the standard high and reminds us that as we refuse to be easily irritated or simply rubbed the wrong way, we will attain a character that brings honor.

Proverbs 19:11

Parenting Point

Sometimes our family can just be so touchy! Something that seemed funny to a member of the family, just days before, is suddenly a big issue. My temptation is to just tell them to lighten up; however, honestly, at those times there are two different character qualities that are presenting themselves as teaching opportunities. First, it is important to encourage and teach our children to learn to laugh at themselves. Being easily irritated or touchy is simply a sign of an over-inflated focus on self. Learning to laugh at our own idiosyncrasies and foibles will serve to unite a family, while irritation and over-reaction will divide. However, it is equally important to teach our children to be sensitive to one another. There are certain topics and areas of personal vulnerability that should be off-limits when it comes to making family jokes. If something is offensive to our brother, it should be offensive to us as well. When both character qualities are intact, we can all laugh and enjoy family communication without offense. Easily irritated family members make the whole family feel as though they are walking on eggshells just waiting for the next issue to arise. Parents, make sure you aren't building an atmosphere of irritability in your home and help your children to not be irritable as well.

Wisdom • Gentleness • Kindness

A Wise Tongue

The tongue and its use, thereof, is one of the most obvious areas of wisdom or foolishness in a believer's life. Every day we are faced with opportunities to use our tongues for blessing or cursing. Often, we waste no time spewing harsh, hurtful, and impatient words, but find ourselves then spending great amounts of time trying to restore with those whom we have wounded. We must put off destructive communication and put on the "sweet as a honeycomb" words as described in Proverbs 16:24. Read the verses below. Do you want to be wise and understanding? The Scripture declares that the good behavior of our deeds will be outward evidence of the gentleness of wisdom that resides within us.

James 3:5-13

Parenting Point

Is your family characterized by "sweet as honeycomb" words or destructive tongues? In this area our example of kind communication will speak much louder than our many words of instruction. As parents, help one another to evaluate the tone and tempo that your words are setting in your home. If you have been characterized by a harsh tongue, don't waste anymore time. Seek your family's forgiveness today. Spend time searching scripture to see God's heart toward our tongues and memorize scripture that will help arm you to do battle with that restless evil residing in our mouths. Enlist your children to help you recognize when your tone is becoming harsh or hurtful. As you set a tone of kindness in your home, your example will help your children to desire to control their tongues as well.

Lying and the Put-Off Principle

L ying, half-truths, and exaggerations have been around since the Garden of Eden; however, just because lying has a long history doesn't make it any less repugnant to God. What is your attitude toward lying? There is a real difference between praying, "Lord, help me not to lie." and "Lord, help me to HATE my lying tongue." Until we learn to hate our lies, we will give wiggle-room in our lives for the occasional little lie, and we will stagnate in our walk with the Lord.

Ephesians 4:25

Parenting Point

As parents, we must help our children to develop an awareness of the gravity of lying. We begin teaching this by being disciplined in not allowing "little" lies to slip by unnoticed. There is a huge difference between make-believe and lying. When our children are playing imaginary games, they are not lying! Rather, they are using the imagination placed in them by their Creator; however, when our children are characterized by outright lies, or even half-truths, it is our job to help them learn to hate those lies. Begin by doing a search of scripture together with your child. Use a concordance to look up all of the scriptures that refer to lying and a lying tongue. In particular, draw your child's attention to the verses that share how God feels about lying. Pray with your child that they would learn to put-off lying and put-on honest speech. For some children lying is such an ingrained habit that they lie without even thinking about it. It is our job to cause them to stop and consider what they say. Sometimes lying shows itself as information that is withheld or understated. Discerning whether or not a child is lying is hard work, and we cannot do it alone! Seek the Lord diligently, and ask Him to help you have ears to hear any lies in your home and eyes to recognize any hidden deceit. Proverbs 6:16-17 tell us that God hates lying, and we need to view lying with the same contempt He does.

Love Doesn't Act Unbecomingly

What does it mean to act unbecomingly? The dictionary defines unbecomingly as not appropriate, attractive, or flattering; not in accordance with the standards appropriate to a situation. The opposite of unbecomingly would be circumspect. As Christians, we have the obligation to show love to others by behaving in a manner that draws attention not to ourselves but to Christ. To whom are you drawing attention today?

I Corinthians 13:5

Parenting Point

When our children do not behavior in a manner that is circumspect and appropriate to whatever situation they are in, they detract from their own personal testimony, our family testimony, and the testimony of Christ. Often, our children do not even realize what is appropriate or unbecoming in a given situation. Children running through a crowded room are not being circumspect. Children interrupting adult conversation to tell a story are not being circumspect. Children who announce that they don't like the food they are being served are not being circumspect. Children who grab products off the shelves in stores are not being circumspect. Don't expect your children to recognize these types of indiscretions on their own; they need your careful, consistent, and continual teaching. Role-play various situations that might tempt your children to exhibit unbecoming behavior. Your role-playing will build a foundation of circumspection, and then a simple reminder before entering a tempting environment will help your children to avoid trouble. Children, who are characterized by careful and appropriate behavior, will draw the attention of others who will often ask you why your children behave so nicely. Seize the opportunity to explain the reason you have trained them to embrace becoming behavior; it is because you love the Lord, and Christians who love the Lord are not to be unbecoming in their behavior. Your circumspect children will become the strongest link you have in your testimony for Christ.

The Week in Review

Take some time to gather as a family and discuss the character qualities that you learned this week. Here are some questions to get the conversation started.

List the character qualities we studied this week.

Which character quality was the hardest for you to practice this week?

Did you see a family member consistently practicing one of this week's character qualities? Which family member?

Use your imagination and add questions of your own. After your time of discussion, spend some time praying together, thanking the Lord and sharing one another's burdens. Pray ahead of time for teachable hearts to incorporate and put into practice the character qualities your family will learn in the upcoming week.

Character Construction

O ver and over in scripture, we see the truth that God doesn't simply ask us to initiate good behavior or alternately abandon bad behavior for our work to be done; rather, He requires that we examine and correct both sides of the equation. Yes, we must initiate good character choices, but if we don't discard the bad character choices that we are already making, our new paradigms will lack power and effectiveness. We will spend the next few weeks looking at both sides of the character equation; the good character that we are to "put-on" according to today's verse and the bad character that we must diligently "put-off." Each day will highlight either a put-on or a put-off principle. It's time to put our "putting" to work.

Ephesians 4:20-24

Parenting Point

Mom and Dad, which side of the equation do you tend to focus on when it comes to training and disciplining your children? While it is often easy to recognize and correct our children's bad choices, do we make as much of an effort to teach into the good character choices we want them to make instead? This is a good area for parents to help one another self-regulate. Ask your spouse to give you input regarding the focus of your training. If the answer comes back that you are one-sided in discipline, correcting the bad but not instilling the good, take positive steps to change that paradigm. Single parents, now is the time to seek the Lord in prayer asking Him to help you recognize your own parenting habits. As we diligently teach our children to both "put-off" and "put-on," we will see abundant character growth.

A Finisher's Attitude

Today's character quality can test the mettle of even the most committed believer. All of us have faced situations or circumstances where the easiest way out seemed to be quitting the course we were following and just hoping for the best. Christians, with the strong testimony of a finisher's attitude, are the ones who will make a difference in their homes, churches, and communities. We are barraged with well-meaning advice encouraging us to "cut our losses" and just walk away, but the character resolve to see a job, relationship, or difficulty through, will build the moral muscle necessary to "run with endurance the race that is set before us." (Hebrews 12:1)

Philippians 3:13-14

Parenting Point

Have you ever shared with your children any of the difficult times from your past that have shaped you into who you are today? While our children don't need to know the gory or offensive details of past sin, knowing the failures that their parents faced and overcame can help them to recognize the character-driven choices that you now make as a family. Share with your children how past difficulties do not define who you are now, but instead, have given you the strength to continue on and to reach for the prize of the upward call of Christ. Help them to understand that "forgetting the past" doesn't mean that past actions never come to mind, but instead, that past actions have no power to cripple your walk with the Lord now and in the future. If they are struggling with guilt over past actions, help them to seek the Lord's forgiveness and to allow Him to cover over their sin. When those past sins threaten to rear their ugly heads, reaffirm the forgiveness that they have already received because of Christ's sacrifice on their behalf.

Exuberant Thanksgiving

W hat comes to mind when you think of the word exuberant? For me, I picture an excited puppy, wagging its tail and jumping for joy over the presence of its master. Today's verse is a picture of one man who wasn't ashamed to express his thankfulness toward the Lord with exuberance and excitement. Too often we're just "thankful on the inside." Yes, the Lord sees our thankfulness, but as we are willing to discard our carefully constructed outer image and to instead bubble over with joy and thanksgiving to the Lord, others will witness and enjoy the bounty of the Lord as well.

Luke 17:15-16

Parenting Point

Are your children excited and exuberant about the workings of the Lord in your family? Perhaps an even more essential question is this: Do your children know that the Lord is working in your family? Sometimes, we allow the blessings of the Lord to go unrecognized, or we simply chalk them up to circumstances. Nothing good comes into our lives and into the lives of our children apart from the gracious hand of God. Help your children to recognize God's blessings and protection in their lives. Taking the time to record the gifts and workings of God in your family will provide a wonderful journal chronicling the faithfulness of God. In times of difficulty, returning to the entries in your journal will provide comfort for the day and hope for the future. When your children begin to see God personally involved in their lives each and every day, they will grow in their excitement and exuberance of thanksgiving. Don't squash that exuberance! Instead, learn from your children's example and become a family characterized by exuberant thanksgiving.

Good News!

Take some time to read today's verse. In every conversation we are given the opportunity to either make others glad or tear down and discourage. The world has plenty of gossips and talebearers. When we purposefully look for the good in someone else and then share our observations, we gain an incredible opportunity to make our God look great. When we are negative and intent on sharing the bad qualities we observe, we run the risk of making our God look small by giving the impression that Christians are judgmental and critical. What characterizes your conversations?

Proverbs 15:30

Parenting Point

I am always encouraged when someone takes the time to tell me of a good quality they observe in my children. Especially during our time as a pastor's family, it sometimes seemed as though folks were eagerly looking to share anything they perceived as negative. My poor children couldn't sneeze funny without someone making a comment! Although that time was often discouraging, it taught me an important lesson about communication with other parents. Yes, there are times that we need to share a particular child's problems and issues with their parent. Those would be times that their child is hurting or causing problems for others or when we observe their child engaged in dangerous (physical, emotional, or spiritual) behavior. Otherwise, we need to be so busy caring for our own children that we don't have any time to watch, judge, and report on someone else's child. At the same time, we can ask the Lord to give us eyes to see and recognize positive character in our own children and others. If we are characterized by sharing with other parents those positive traits that we observe, when a situation does arise that requires intervention, our intervention will be much more readily received and accepted. I think all parents experience moments of discouragement regarding their children and the parenting process. We can be messengers of doom and gloom, or we can be encouragers: helping them to see the positive qualities in their own children. Sometimes, that encouragement from an outsider is just what they need to change their view of their children. If you take the time to develop a character of encouragement, God will then be able to use you to help those hurting parents in times of discouragement and despair. Anyone can be the bearer of bad news; pray that God would make you a "glad tidings bringer" instead.

Hope

The dictionary defines hope as a feeling that something desirable is likely to happen, or a chance that somebody wants to have or do or wants to happen or be true. That definition just doesn't sound very hopeful to me! Romans 5:5 reassures the believer with this timeless truth: "...and hope does not disappoint because the love of God has been poured out within our hearts through the Holy Spirit who was given to us."

Psalm 62:5-6

Parenting Point

Is the cup half empty or half full? How would your children answer that question? Parents set the tempo in the home for the attitude of hope or hopelessness that prevails. We must build hope into our children's lives. One of the best ways to build hope for the future is to rehearse the past faithfulness of God. Take time this week to call a family conference table and use that time to simply list all of the ways that God has protected, blessed, grown, and encouraged your family. At the end of the conference, ask your children this question, "Looking at this list of all God has done, is there anything God can't do for this family?" Spend some time in prayer together thanking God for His abundant provision and seeking His will and guidance for the trials and decisions that loom ahead. Yes, trials will come, but as the past provision of God has made abundantly clear, no trial is greater than the blessing, protection, and grace of our God. When your family experiences doubt about the future, stop and once again rehearse the goodness of God in relation to your family. No one has more reason for hope than the family of God! Let's work today to build the muscle of hope in our families.

Contentment • Thankfulness

Contentment is Contagious

I s your character marked by contentment? Are you able to say that God has dealt bountifully with you? I don't know about you, but I love to be with people who are content with what God has provided for them. Their contentment is always a reminder to me of the goodness of God. Sometimes we forget that by simply living lives of contentment and gratitude, we say more about our great God than our words can adequately convey. What are you saying or doing to pass on the "Contentment Bug?"

Hebrews 13:5

Parenting Point

Discontent children are miserable children! It would seem that the answer to an unfulfilled and discontent child would be to provide more, but that's just the opposite of what they need. When our children exhibit a lack of contentment, what they are really showing is a lack of gratitude. In their minds, what you have provided just isn't enough. Sadly, those same children often grow up to be job and church hoppers. Their employment is never what they expected. Their church just doesn't seem to keep them as excited as they once were. Undoubtedly, this lack of contentment can be traced back to their childhood. It's fun to provide neat toys and opportunities for our children; however, be discerning! If you begin to see a lack of contentment and a continual desire for more, More, MORE...take the time to address this character issue. Help your children learn to be content by encouraging them to recognize all that they have to be thankful for each day.

The Week in Review

Take some time to gather as a family and discuss the character qualities that you learned this week. Here are some questions to get the conversation started.

- List the character qualities we studied this week.

- Which character quality was the hardest for you to practice this week?

- Did you see a family member consistently practicing one of this week's character qualities? Which family member?

Use your imagination and add questions of your own. After your time of discussion, spend some time praying together, thanking the Lord and sharing one another's burdens. Pray ahead of time for teachable hearts to incorporate and put into practice the character qualities your family will learn in the upcoming week.

Primary Priorities

W hat gave Jesus the courage to follow His Father in obedience all the way to the cross? I believe that courage was developed as Christ spent His entire earthly life committed to one primary priority-the priority of faithful obedience to the will of His Father. His every thought, action, and prayer was directed to His Father and submitted to His Father's will. It is so easy for our priorities to get out of whack and to be misaligned by the busyness and often crisis situations that our days offer. How can we keep our priorities straight? Like Christ, our priorities will be clear and manageable as we submit our every thought, action, and prayer to the Father. Set aside time this week and ask God to help you to clearly evaluate your daily priorities in light of His Word and direction. Just as it did in the life of Christ, priority living will help us to identify and accomplish the will of our Heavenly Father.

John 4:34, 5:30

Parenting Point

Do your children know that your primary priority is to fulfill the will of God? Whether the activity is training them, evaluating activities for your family, limiting friendships, or choosing an area of service, our children need to know that our first allegiance and obedience is to the Lord. Often, it is easier to simply go along with what everyone else is doing, but we must build the difficult practice of evaluation to ensure that our primary priority is in alignment with the Word of God and the will of God. As your children observe you carefully considering and discussing all areas of your life, they will assimilate the same Christ-like attitude of priority living in their own lives.

Becoming Circumspect

If you were asked to describe the character quality of being circumspect, how would you define the word? The dictionary defines being circumspect as being heedful of circumstance and potential consequences, prudent. We live in a world that has thrown out the character quality of being circumspect. In fact, the more rash and heedless our actions the more the watching world applauds and encourages such behavior. As Christians, it is our responsibility to be careful and watchful. We must behave in a circumspect manner to avoid the dangers that wait to ensnare us.

Proverbs 22:3

Parenting Point

It is important to teach your children to be circumspect. Take time today to read aloud the verse in Proverbs and discuss with your children what it means to "see the danger ahead." Role-play some scenarios to help them understand how to "hide themselves" from the danger ahead. Here is a simple tool to teach your children in starting them down the road to being circumspect. When your children enter a room, teach them to enter quietly and evaluate what is going on BEFORE they say anything. Your children will learn to be good observers and you will see a marked decrease in interruptions and thoughtless comments.

Contentment • Coveting

The Coveting Monster

Consider this definition of coveting: To feel *blameworthy* desire for that which is another's. Wow! Coveting isn't as simple as just strongly desiring to possess something that doesn't belong to us; that desire is described as blameworthy. In other words, no matter how we try to rationalize the legitimacy of our desire, that desire is still worthy of blame and is a blight on our character. Coveting is an ugly character flaw that must be put-off by whatever radical means are necessary.

Luke 12:15

Parenting Point

Children are natural coveters! Unfortunately, often their coveting happens so quickly that we don't even notice that they coveted. Every time their coveting goes unrecognized, and more importantly, unpunished, the habit of coveting is more deeply ingrained into their lives. Parents, work together as a team to catch coveting! Pray together that God would give you sensitive eyes and ears to recognize when your children are showing a blameworthy desire. For the single parent, God wants to be your ally and advocate. Ask Him to help you root out the ugly character flaw of coveting from your child's life. Because we are the daily example to our children, we must also be careful that we are not coveting what others possess. While we might not covet possessions, coveting relationships, position, or honor conveys just as poisonous a message to our children.

The Grand Finale

I don't know about you, but I'm an impatient learner. When God reveals an area of necessary growth or brings conviction into my life, I want it taken care of now, now, NOW! Because of this impatient character in my life, I often find myself discouraged or disparaging of the ability to ever change. Instead of allowing God to change me and then rejoicing in the growth He brings, I fuss, fret, and fume over what is left to accomplish in my growth. Aren't you thankful that God is patient with us? Today's verse is a wonderful promise to believers. Although we may see our daily failings, God will be faithful to complete what He's begun. We can't envision the end product, but He already knows what His good work in our lives will look like at the day of Christ Jesus. Now that's something to look forward to!

Philippians 1:6

Parenting Point

Parents, it is so easy to get discouraged by a lack of growth or maturity in our children's lives. Don't give in to that discouragement! The Word of God reminds us over and over that we don't know the end of the story; God does. Our responsibility is to be faithful stewards of the Word of God. We must diligently and patiently teach our children the ways of the Lord, but it is He, not us, who will bring about the necessary change in their lives. Too often, I find myself immersed in worry over their choices or seeming lack of good decision-making skills. At those times, it is tempting to step in and force the change that I see is so necessary. I must continually remind myself that God doesn't need me to act as the Holy Spirit in the lives of my children; in fact, His Holy Spirit does a much better job of convicting and bringing about change than I could ever hope to accomplish. Be diligent, be consistent, be transparent in your own growth; but most of all, be patient! If your children know Jesus as their personal Savior, God will be faithful to complete the good work that He has begun in their lives.

Hard Work and Generosity Go Hand in Hand

Do you desire to develop a character of generosity? According to today's verse, first developing a strong work ethic will make it possible for you to have what is necessary in order to generously share with others. In a world that is characterized by an attitude of "half-done" and "good enough," developing a consistent work ethic will cause you to stand out and will maximize your Christian testimony. Don't settle for less than 100% when it comes to working hard, and then you can enjoy the blessing of being able to share God's bounty with those in need.

Ephesians 4:28

Parenting Point

It would be easy to say that a strong work ethic comes simply by following the example of hardworking parents, but that isn't necessarily true. Although as parents we present a positive example of diligence and perseverance when it comes to working, our children can still choose the path of laziness and apathy. Don't allow this dynamic to fester in your home! As a mother, when I'm working hard each day, striving to serve our family, and I realize that I'm alone in those efforts, I'm tempted to become bitter and angry. At those times, it is so easy to lash out at my children and become a manipulative and martyr-type parent. Don't let it get to that point! Parents, and especially moms, you set the tempo for the work attitude in your home. Dad, lay out the vision for how you want your home to operate. Present your standards for chores and jobs in clear and unambiguous terms. Then, Mom, as the one at home most of the day, make sure your children fulfill their clearly explained duties. Chores, unsupervised and unverified, will soon become "good enough" or not completed at all. Take the time to encourage and exhort your children to do their assigned tasks diligently. When our children are faithful in completing their tasks and completing those tasks well, they build a character of diligence, faithfulness, and strong self-confidence. Teach your children the correlation between work and generosity. Find extra jobs, which they can perform for pay, in order to raise money to spend on someone else's needs. In our own home, our sons bind *CharacterHealth* books in order to raise money to support needy boys through Compassion ministries. As an added blessing, the fruit of hard work and generosity is a thankful heart. As our children give to others, they learn to be thankful for all that God has provided to them.

Love Rejoices with the Truth

Being someone who rejoices with the truth speaks to the inward condition of our hearts. Rejoicing with the truth means that we want to know what is true and right, regardless of the outcome. Much like Philippians 4:8, we must long for those things that are true, honorable, right, pure, lovely, and of good repute. Unlike those who rejoice in unrighteousness, those who rejoice with the truth share a love of righteousness with their Savior.

I Corinthians 13:6

Parenting Point

How do we demonstrate for our children what it means to rejoice with the truth? Unfortunately, rejoicing with the truth sometimes means that we must be committed to digging through layers of untruth in order to find what is actually truthful. When we avoid the easy road of taking everything at face value, and instead spend the time necessary to get to the bottom of stories and situations, we are teaching our children just how much we value the truth. If our children can count on us to check and double check facts, they will be careful to be accurate and honest; however, if we are sporadic in our commitment to verify facts, our children will become natural gamblers, hoping that this is another time that they can get away with half-truths or outright lies. From the time your children are babies, stress the importance of absolute truthfulness. Remind your children that the worst consequences often come from the cover-up not the crime. When we must doubt our children's words, we lose trust for them; and trust, once lost, is hard to reinstate. Do your part by building a home firmly planted in the truth of God's Word and a commitment to honest and reliable communication.

The Week in Review

Take some time to gather as a family and discuss the character qualities that you learned this week. Here are some questions to get the conversation started.

- List the character qualities we studied this week.

- Which character quality was the hardest for you to practice this week?

- Did you see a family member consistently practicing one of this week's character qualities? Which family member?

Use your imagination and add questions of your own. After your time of discussion, spend some time praying together, thanking the Lord and sharing one another's burdens. Pray ahead of time for teachable hearts to incorporate and put into practice the character qualities your family will learn in the upcoming week.

Protective Prayer

I t is an unfortunate truth that for all of us our flesh is weak. Thankfully, God has provided a means of protection for our weak flesh, and that means is through developing a consistent character of prayer. Read today's verse. Although temptations will come, we do not need to succumb to them. As we pray, persistently and consistently, we will be strengthened and able to resist entering into temptation. Persistence in prayer comes through daily practice. How's your practice of prayer, today?

Matthew 26:41

Parenting Point

Even the disciples, men who walked side by side with Jesus, dealt with the issue of their weak flesh. Yes, they had willing spirits, but they needed God's strength to resist temptation. The same is true for us today. Although we have a relationship with Christ, temptation still lures our weak flesh, and we know that temptation is seeking to draw our children into its nets as well. Prayer is a powerful and positive antidote to temptation. God delights to strengthen His children, but He is a gentleman, waiting and encouraging us to seek His help through prayer. It seems as though sometimes my children think that just because they are Christians, they will never give in to temptation. How far from the truth! It is essential to teach our children to recognize the weakness of their own flesh. It is when they feel confident in their own strength to face and conquer temptation that they are actually at their weakest. Begin when your children are very small to teach them how to seek God through prayer, asking Him to strengthen them and give them the courage to say "No" to sin. We often repeated the truth of Jeremiah 17:9 to our children. We wanted them to understand that their hearts were deceitful and would seek to deceive even them. Train your children to ask God for the discernment to recognize temptation *before* they are ensnared by it. It is important to remind ourselves that we are no better off than our children. Just like us, they want to do well, but their flesh wars against their good intentions. Remembering this truth will help us to maintain a merciful attitude, even when we may have to mete out consequences for their flesh-driven, poor decisions.

The Zeal of Repentance

Showing zeal in our relationship with the Lord is an outward manifestation of our personal relationship with Him; however, inward zeal is necessary to keep that relationship in a place of open and unbroken fellowship. In the same way that we show zeal about those things we find important, we must exhibit the same zeal in repenting of our sin. Today's scripture reminds us that God will do His part by reproving and disciplining His children; however, it is our responsibility to be zealous and repent. Repentance isn't simply a quick plea for forgiveness, but rather involves a conscious decision to change the wrong direction our hearts and actions are pursuing. Make it your goal to be zealous inside and out by asking God to search your heart and reveal your sin to you. Then, deal with that sin zealously through repentance and confession.

Revelation 3:19

Parenting Point

Teaching our children the importance of repentance is one of our primary parental responsibilities. Although we can train our children to seek forgiveness verbally, discerning the true intentions of their heart can be a difficult proposition. For example, if one of my children hit another child because they wanted a toy that the other child was holding, I would help them to recognize that the root issue of their behavior wasn't simply hitting, it was selfishness and unkindness. Then, when they asked for forgiveness they wouldn't simply say, "I'm sorry for hitting you." Instead, they would include a verbal acknowledgement of their wrong heart attitude. When the children were very young (under 5), I would often have to explain and help them to see their wrong heart attitude, but after age five I would ask them dialog questions to help them discover the wrong attitude on their own. When our children can self-diagnose their unbiblical attitudes, they are much more likely to take ownership of those wrong attitudes. Don't allow your children to just quickly parrot the words, "I'm sorry. Will you please forgive me?" Take the time to deal with the root heart issues and teach them to zealously and persistently seek forgiveness. If necessary, allow them adequate time to think about what is truly going on in their heart. Remind them that although God wants their outward behavior to be good, He is much more concerned with their heart, and that you, too, are more concerned with their heart than you are with their bad behavior.

Diligence

Diligence is defined as the persistent and hard-working effort involved in doing a task. Legally, diligence is the attention expected of all participants in fulfilling the terms of a contract. Due diligence is required for healthy relationships to thrive, especially our relationship with God. When I think of diligence, I usually think of the diligence I apply to my work outside of the home; however, diligence is just as important at home as it is away from home. Great relationships are not a matter of luck; they are a matter of persistent, hard-working diligence. Read and study the following text and take note of the reward for skillful diligence.

Proverbs 22:29

Parenting Point

What areas of diligence have you let slide? It is difficult to require your children to live up to a consistent standard of hard work that you are not willing to live up to yourself. As a family, do a word search study in the Bible on the character quality of diligence. Write down everything that you learn, and then make a list of things around the house that require your diligence. Don't forget about relationships, especially your relationship with God. Brainstorm together as a family ways that you can all be more diligent to grow in your relationships with the Lord. Decide what new practices you will implement to encourage that growth and make a plan to hold one another accountable. Spend time discussing chores and tasks. Discuss how important it is for the whole family to be characterized by a diligent work ethic. Use examples from business, the church, or even the human body to help your children see the importance of all members of a body functioning in a diligent manner. Just imagine what life would be like if your heart wasn't diligent. For some, that is the reality of life and they would be the first to say how hard it is to function well with a less than diligent body part. When we give them real life examples, our kids will quickly and easily assimilate the lessons we are trying to teach them. Have fun and role-play some instances of "Diligence Failure." After you have taught into this important character quality, a simple reminder now and then should help the whole family function as a diligent, well-ordered unit.

The Heart That Weeps

There are things that should cause us to embrace a heart and character of weeping. Jesus wept over the death of his friend Lazarus. In the same way, the plight of our friends, especially those who don't know Jesus, should cause weeping in our hearts. Do you have that type of care and compassion for your friends? If not, pray and ask the Lord to help you develop a tender heart and a winsome character that will draw your friends closer to Him.

Ecclesiastes 3:4

Parenting Point

It is essential to our children's character that we spend time instructing them in what is and what isn't a good reason for tears. Too often, our children will use their tears to avoid punishment, manipulate a situation, or register their displeasure with our decisions. None of these are legitimate reasons to cry and extending comfort and sympathy to our children at these times is simply counter-productive. By contrast, crying over a death or when in pain is to be expected. It's perfectly acceptable to instruct your children to stop crying when their tears do not have a legitimate cause. Sometimes simply sending them away from the situation until they have stopped crying delivers a powerful message. A couple of our boys were immediately reduced to tears whenever they received the slightest reprimand. Those tears weren't because they were sorry for whatever offense they had committed; rather, the tears were just to retaliate for their wounded pride. Wounded pride is not a good use of tears. We patiently reminded those boys to "Dry it up." Now their tears come less often and at more appropriate times. Yes, there are certainly times to cry, but our children need us to help them navigate what constitutes a good use of tears. Be the parent and help them use their tears wisely.

Loving Communication

I f your friends were asked to categorize your communication, what words would they use to describe how you communicate? Would you be recognized as a person who speaks carefully and gently? Or, would your testimony be one of harshness and a quick temper? Often, our thoughtless and ill-timed words build a reputation for us that we would never want to own. Gentle responses, in any situation, can help to heal, restore, or simply assist in meeting the needs of the moment. Harsh words, on the other hand, will take the same situation and produce anger and wrath. If you recognize that you are prone to sharp or harsh responses, take proactive steps to change your negative communication. Spend time with the Lord and ask Him to help you to hate your harsh words and to love speaking gentle words of healing.

Proverbs 15:1

Parenting Point

How we speak to one another and how our children speak to one another will build or destroy our family's testimony. I am shocked when I hear children speaking disrespectfully to their parents or in an unkind manner to their brothers and sisters. Rude or harsh communication is not a phase that our children should be allowed to go through. Instead, we must set high the standard of Christ-like communication in our home and then work diligently to enforce our standard. Take some time today to record the words that you use most frequently. Then, record the words that you hear your children using with one another as well. Are the words gentle, encouraging, and edifying? If they are, great! If not, spend time as a family talking about the direction of the conversation among family members and seeking forgiveness from one another for hurtful words that have been spoken. Next, help your children write out a list of positive and encouraging words that they can work to add to their vocabulary. As you hear them trying to change their form of communication, praise them! Set the standard high for yourself also, and let your children know that you are working just as hard as they are to speak in positive ways.

Decisiveness in Action

Generally speaking, decisive Christians are problem-solving Christians. Their ability to make quick and confident decisions makes them a natural choice to fill positions of leadership. This decisiveness can be a wonderful addition to any church or other organization; however, decisive leaders can have a down side as well. Because they are able to assess situations and act quickly, they often rob their less-confident brothers and sisters in Christ of the opportunity to grow in decisiveness and leadership. As today's verse reminds us, there are times to simply step back, mind our own business, and allow others to take the lead. Sometimes, deciding to do nothing is the best decision you can make.

I Thessalonians 4:11

Parenting Point

When our children are faced with decisions that are hard to make, it is so easy for us to rush in and make those decisions for them. Resist the urge! As parents, there are times we must exercise self-control. Often, the struggle to make a decision is the very lesson God wants to use to stimulate growth in our children's lives. Having to choose between two good opportunities will force our children to learn how to stop, think, and seek the Lord's guidance. Watch to see if your children simply assume that you will make all of their difficult decisions for them. If you see that this dynamic is at work in your home, set up some learning situations for your children to challenge them and help them develop their own decision-making skills.

The Week in Review

Take some time to gather as a family and discuss the character qualities that you learned this week. Here are some questions to get the conversation started.

- List the character qualities we studied this week.
- Which character quality was the hardest for you to practice this week?
- Did you see a family member consistently practicing one of this week's character qualities? Which family member?

Use your imagination and add questions of your own. After your time of discussion, spend some time praying together, thanking the Lord and sharing one another's burdens. Pray ahead of time for teachable hearts to incorporate and put into practice the character qualities your family will learn in the upcoming week.

Protecting Peace

H ow would you define peace? One of the dictionary definitions of peace is this: inner contentment or serenity. With that definition in mind, what do you find necessary to exist peacefully? Does peace come from conflict-free relationships? A balanced checkbook? A lack of strife or stress? No, true peace comes not through our circumstances but through a settled relationship with Jesus. Today's verse reminds us to simply be still, to stop striving, and to know that God is God. He can handle every situation with which we are confronted. While circumstances can never provide us with peace, they do have the ability to rob us of our peace. Spend some time today evaluating the "peace-robbers" in your life an, if needed, make necessary changes to protect the peace that your relationship with Christ provides.

Psalm 46:10

Parenting Point

Is your home a peaceful and peace-filled sanctuary for your children? As the adults in the home, it is our responsibility to act as the "door keepers" for our children. While most parents are careful to monitor movies and television shows, we often forget to protect our children from the "overheard" stresses of life. When we listen to talk radio with the children in the car or continually discuss the negative news about our world, economy, church, or relationships in their earshot, we are unwittingly robbing them of the peace of childhood. Soon enough, our children will be forced to deal with the painful realities of life. During their early years, invest your time sharing joys, blessings, and the workings of God. Build their peace and security by constantly reminding them of God's care and oversight on their behalf. Share their need for a Savior and the plan of salvation. Don't hand your children burdens that are too heavy for them to bear by exposing them to stresses that they can do nothing about. Shelter them now, in the peaceful sanctuary of your family, in order to strengthen them for the days to come.

The Character of a Cheerleader

Do you have the character of an "esteemer?" A person who esteems others will be beloved by all who come in contact with them. Unlike a backstabber, an esteeming person loves to point out the positive traits in someone else's life. It is so easy to be critical of, or even just uninterested in other people's lives. Learning to esteem others is simply a discipline that builds a positive habit for life. The more you train yourself to notice and affirm the positive character you see in others, the easier it will become. In fact, you will find yourself eagerly looking for someone to build up with your esteeming words!

I Thessalonians 5:12-13

Parenting Point

Although the normal course of life among children seems to be a tendency to "diss" one another and put each other down. Christian children need to live to a different, much higher, standard. Begin to teach the positive character quality of esteeming by carefully choosing the words you use in your home. Find every opportunity to build up others and to speak highly of the positive fruit you see in other people's lives. Under no circumstances should your children hear you gossiping, putting down others, or demeaning someone else's accomplishments. Help your children write notes of encouragement and esteem to their friends and siblings. Children who build the positive habit of esteeming others will find it easy to esteem their Lord in the presence of unbelievers.

Love Endures

Sometimes there are relationships or situations in our lives that seem absolutely unendurable. When we focus on those situations it is hard to feel anything but hopeless. For Christians, the key is to only allow the difficult situations to catch our glance while we keep our gaze firmly fixed on our Lord. He who endured pain, suffering, and humiliation for our salvation will certainly strengthen us to endure whatever hardships we are facing. Gaze at Him, glance at the problem; the answer is in your focus.

I Corinthians 13:7

Parenting Point

From the pain of childbirth, through sleeplessness, and into the uncertainty of the teen years, as parents we will endure many struggles and frustrations. How can we keep an attitude of Christ-like love in a way that brings glory to God as we struggle to endure? Several thoughts come to mind. First, the closer and more intimate that we are in our relationship with Christ, and the more aware we are of the struggles He endured on our behalf, the easier we will find it to imitate His attitude of endurance. I often ask myself this question: "After all He's done for me, is there anything I won't endure for Him?" The second thought is this: There is purpose in our endurance. We are not enduring frustration and hardships with our children with the goal of just getting by until tomorrow. No, we continue to strive with our children with the purpose of helping them to grow more like Christ. Galatians 6:9 presents our marching orders. "And let us not lose heart in doing good, for in due time we shall reap if we do not grow weary." The final encouragement is this: endurance builds spiritual muscle, not just in our own lives, but in the future lives of our children and grandchildren. As we share God's faithfulness toward us in our times of discouragement and trouble, we will be giving our children the courage they need to endure as the parents of our grandchildren. Don't grow weary; it **will** be worth it all!

Patience • Anger

Love is Not Provoked

A re you easily provoked? I know that sometimes I am. The dictionary defines provoked as being incited to anger or resentment. This isn't necessarily an abiding anger but rather a quick, knee-jerk reaction to a situation or circumstance. The book of James reminds us to be slow to speak and slow to anger; rushing to provocation is the antithesis of this teaching. Consider today what steps you must take to move from being reactively provoked to being proactively reasonable.

I Corinthians 13:5

Parenting Point

Do you have certain children that just seem to be always ready to respond with anger or resentment? These children fall into the biblical definition of being easily provoked. As today's verse reminds us, being provoked easily is one way of showing an unloving attitude. By contrast, being slow to speak and slow to respond angrily to others shows the precious character quality of love. Those people, who are continually upset, stressed, or provoked by the people and situations around them, are often truly unhappy people. Because they allow themselves to respond reactively, they cannot embrace a peaceful lifestyle. Begin today to help your reactive, easily provoked children to put-off their negative reactions and to put-on godly patience and long-suffering. As a family read James 1:19 and discuss what it means to listen quickly and give rise to anger slowly. If their reactivity is simply an echo of your own, now is the time to seek their forgiveness and as a family commit to responding to situations and one another with peaceable and proactive solutions, rather than provoked and angry retaliation. The results of your hard work in this area will be a calmer, more joyful home and proactive, problem-solving children.

The Character of Wisdom

Proverbs 1:7 says this, "The fear of the Lord is the beginning of knowledge; Fools despise wisdom and instruction." As faithful followers of the Lord Jesus Christ, we do not have the liberty to despise wisdom and remain fools. Instead, we must take whatever steps are necessary to become wise. This wisdom, or knowledge, begins with a reverential fear of the Lord. Let's consider some everyday areas where believers must grow and exhibit wisdom. Consider what attitudes and actions must be put-off and the converse put-on behaviors that will characterize a life of wisdom.

Proverbs 1:7

Parenting Point

Read today's scripture aloud with your children. Ask them what it looks like to "fear the Lord." Help them to understand the difference between an afraid or scared fear and a respectful and reverential fear. With my own children, I have encouraged them to consider fearing the Lord as being careful to know what the Lord desires and then acting on those desires in a way that would never disappoint our Lord. Ask your children what it looks like, on a daily basis, to despise wisdom and instruction. Help them to understand that disregarding your instruction is the same as despising the wisdom you are trying to build into their lives. If appropriate, or necessary, help them to seek your forgiveness for despising your instruction, and therefore, the Lord's. Pray together that your family will be characterized by fearing the Lord and growing in wisdom.

Spirit Saturated

Developing the character quality of being filled, or saturated, with the Spirit can only be accomplished by believers in the Lord Jesus Christ. Although the world can mimic the behavior of Christians, only those who have trusted Christ as their Savior can be changed and transformed by the Spirit. As today's Scripture reminds us, it is only as we walk by the Spirit that we will be able to stop carrying out the desires of our flesh. Walking is an active verb. It is not enough to ingest Scripture, sermons, and good teaching, we must actively engage in, and never forget, what the Spirit teaches us. That active engagement will change us from forgetful flesh-lovers to Spirit-saturated soldiers for Christ.

Galatians 5:16-17

Parenting Point

Each of our children experience different fleshly desires or sin appetites. Take some time this week to consider what causes temptation in each of your children's lives. For yourself, make a prayer notebook, recording what you observe. Then, commit to spending time seeking the Lord on behalf of your children. After you have recorded their sin appetites, look up appropriate Scriptures with which to address those areas and set some memorization goals for each child. Perhaps, you will want to join them in memorizing these Scriptures. The co-memorization with Mom or Dad will be a great incentive for your child to be successful. These targeted verses will bear fruit as the Word of God brings conviction and strength to overcome areas of temptation. Obviously, parents face various areas of temptation and sinful appetites as well. The memorized Word of God will also help us to build spiritual muscle and avoid falling into temptation.

The Week in Review

Take some time to gather as a family and discuss the character qualities that you learned this week. Here are some questions to get the conversation started.

- List the character qualities we studied this week.
- Which character quality was the hardest for you to practice this week?
- Did you see a family member consistently practicing one of this week's character qualities? Which family member?

Use your imagination and add questions of your own. After your time of discussion, spend some time praying together, thanking the Lord and sharing one another's burdens. Pray ahead of time for teachable hearts to incorporate and put into practice the character qualities your family will learn in the upcoming week.

The Sluggish Sluggard

To be completely honest with you, when I was in college I lived by the "Why do today what I can put off until tomorrow?" axiom of life. Today's scripture makes it clear that such an attitude will only lead to begging and need in our lives. Are you characterized by a diligent and hard-working attitude? Or, do you sluggishly move through your day hoping that someone else will pick up the slack or bail you out when you find yourself in a time of need? Although being a sluggard is a hard habit to break, it can be done! Spend some time tonight listing your priority activities for tomorrow and then work hard to complete those necessary tasks. Sluggishness in our spiritual lives will lead to spiritual need and poverty as well, so be careful to include your spiritual priorities on that to-do list!

Proverbs 20:4

Parenting Point

Sluggards aren't born; they're trained! Just this week as I was looking over our plans for the second half of the school year, I realized just how sluggardly our whole family had become over the Christmas vacation. I've got my work cut out for me! Although sleeping in during vacation is a welcome treat, it is easy to slip into permanent habits of sluggardly behavior. Take some time to evaluate your home routine. Is sleeping in, skipping chores, and staying up late watching television a treat or the expected norm in your home? If we don't train our children to be hard-working and diligent in their normal day-to-day lives, we can expect that they will drift into habits of undisciplined and lazy behavior. For us, when we allow ourselves to be sluggardly in training and disciplining our children, the results will show up in poor behavior, disrespectful attitudes, and a lack of obedience in our children's lives. If this is the case in your home, seek your children's forgiveness for your own lack of discipline in training them and then push the reset button on family priorities. As they see you willing to take ownership for your own lack of discipline, it will be much easier for your children to take ownership for their part of the problem. Set the example of working hard when it is time to work. Make discipline and diligence the characterization of your home and everyone will enjoy vacation breaks so much more. When diligence becomes the characterization in your home, vacation won't be a bad habit that needs to be broken but rather a special break from the normal busyness of a hard-working family.

Trials: God's Path to Patience

Are you a patient person? If you asked me that same question, I'm afraid my answer would have to be, "It depends." Sadly, my patience, or impatience in many cases, depends on how my day is going. When all is going smoothly, I can be patient and long-suffering. However, when my plans have been rearranged or life throws me a curveball, my patience is the first character quality to go. Today's verse reminds us that those very curveballs, or "various trials," are the building blocks God uses to build patience in our lives. Don't despise the curveballs; welcome them as an opportunity to build your character of patience.

James 1:2-4

Parenting Point

Whenever we are facing a particularly trying day, my husband and I accuse one another of praying for patience. We both realize that out of whack days are fertile soil for growth, but it's sometimes easier to blame each other for our circumstances! Patience is not a once-learned-never-forgotten character quality. Rather, patience is built slowly, and sometimes painfully, into our lives through repeated opportunities to endure trials with perseverance. For our children, those trials are just as important when it comes to learning patience. Don't try to protect or extricate your children from those various trials. God uses their multi-colored trials to hone and perfect His character of patience in our children's lives. Even when it is possible for us to keep them from the trial, doing so is counter-productive when it comes to their character development. Share your trials with your children and encourage them as they face trials of their own. As a family, pray for the courage to welcome your trials and become skilled at hitting those patience-building curveballs out of the park!!

Love is Not Jealous

Have you ever experienced jealousy? Unfortunately, I think that we all have succumbed to the stomach-churning, heart-wrenching emotion of jealousy at one time or another. Sadly, some people spend their whole lives rotting away with jealousy over relationships, possessions, or even position. For the Christian, jealousy must be replaced by an attitude of happiness for others. When we focus on the well being of others, we are forced to turn the spotlight off of our own desires and to instead show care and consideration for the advancement of someone else.

I Corinthians 13:4

Parenting Point

Jealousy is one emotion that we must never tolerate or encourage in our children. When they are hurt, we should sympathize with them. When they are frustrated, we should help them. When they are lonely, we can offer them companionship or proactive solutions to their loneliness. However, when we recognize that they are exhibiting the negative character quality of jealousy, we must be diligent to teach them to abandon their jealous attitudes and actions. Jealousy shown by our children should never elicit a response from us that would encourage further jealousy. Teach your children to be happy for one another and insist that they practice the actions of selflessness and others-orientation. Actions may precede belief in this area, but the actions you teach will help them to embrace a character that is free from jealousy. You can help your children learn this habit of happiness for others by not always making sure that every child receives the same things. It is important for our children to rejoice with others, even when they aren't directly receiving anything themselves. Be quick to squash signs of jealousy and encourage attitudes that show joy in the well being of others. Jealousy is a joy-robber; don't let it rob your children.

Gentleness • Graciousness

The Blessing of Gentleness

What do you think of when you picture gentleness? Perhaps, you picture a mother tenderly caring for her child or a nurse caring for an elderly patient. Although gentleness most often shows itself through action, I would challenge you today to consider the gentleness of your thoughts. Matthew 5 reminds us that the gentle will be blessed, and I certainly don't want to miss out on that blessing because of a less than gentle thought life. Sometimes, I am shocked by the ungentle words that come out of my mouth! Scripture reminds me that what comes out of my mouth is a direct representation of what is abiding in my heart. If I allow ungentle or ungracious thoughts towards others to reign in my heart, these thoughts will eventually find their way out of my mouth. There is no blessing for that kind of attitude. Taking our thoughts captive is hard work! How gentle is your heart today?

Matthew 5:5

Parenting Point

Teaching our children to be gentle takes patience, persistence, and a long-term attitude. In the hurriedness of their day, it is much easier for our children to run rough-shod over one another, both physically and emotionally. Take the time to teach and re-teach the need to be gentle. Role-play and model gentleness for your children. There is nothing sweeter than seeing an older sibling take the time to gently comfort a wounded younger child. In fact, one of my earliest childhood memories is of my oldest brother, Andy, carrying me inside after I fell off my new pink bike and sprained my ankle. This memory has stayed with me for 45 years. Don't underestimate the impact that a child's gentleness can have on a younger sibling! The hard work is well worth the end result.

An Honest Man

How would you define an honest man? Psalm 15:2-3 uses some very descriptive words to paint the picture of what God seeks in an honest man. According to these verses, an honest man possesses integrity and righteousness. An honest man speaks the truth with his heart, and he doesn't slander. An honest man doesn't act with evil intention toward his neighbor. None of these qualities are optional; an honest man works hard to be found complete in all of these aspects. It is much easier to define honesty as simply the words that we choose to speak, but, as always, God digs deeper and evaluates not only our words but our actions and heart intentions as well.

Psalm 15:1-3

Parenting Point

How would your children define honesty? If they are only concerned with the truthfulness of the words that they speak, their understanding of honesty is limited. Often, our children exhibit dishonesty through their actions, or perhaps even more often, through their lack of words. Leaving out the pertinent details of any situation, when those details might not shine a favorable light in their direction, is just as dishonest as an outright lie. Be careful to evaluate your children's honest, or dishonest, actions. In our home, regardless of whatever other character qualities we are working to develop, we ALWAYS pay close attention to areas of honesty. If you require truthfulness in all areas of your children's lives, you will be equipping them for successful living as adults. Pray for discernment to recognize when you aren't being told the truth, the whole truth, and nothing but the truth!

Respect

Respect is defined this way: to feel or show admiration and deference toward somebody or something. Another definition is to pay due attention to and refrain from violating something. All throughout our days, we have the opportunity to show respect by our obedience and subjection to rules and regulations and also to extend respect to others through our admiration and esteem. Respect, it seems, is an almost forgotten character quality. Instructions such as "Respect your elders." and "Be respectful." have virtually disappeared from our conversations. Even the dictionary definition seems to make respect optional, contingent on whether we consider a person or object worthy of our respect. What does respect look like in your life? Do you show proper respect to those close to you? Do you respect strangers more than your friends and family? And what about self-respect? Do you make God-honoring choices that demonstrate respect for self? Your choice of words, friends, activities, even clothing, all speak to the quality of your self- respect or lack thereof. Read the following passage and write down any insights you gain regarding respect.

I Peter 2:18-20

Parenting Point

Have you ever considered all of the different people and areas that require our respect? Gather your children and compile a list of all of the "respect" areas they should recognize (i.e., the elderly, possessions, authority, etc.) Have fun with the list. You could take time to role-play what different types of respect would entail. For example, the respect that you show toward someone else's time is quite different than the respect that you show toward the police. Make respect among family members a high priority in your home. It is easy to slip into disrespectful patterns of speech and behavior within our homes. Don't allow this paradigm to take root. If necessary, call a halt to all outside activities and relationships until a Biblical standard of respect has been reestablished in your home. Respectful children will stand out in their neighborhoods and schools. Teach your children how to show the highest levels of respect and watch them shine!

The Week in Review

Take some time to gather as a family and discuss the character qualities that you learned this week. Here are some questions to get the conversation started.

- List the character qualities we studied this week.

- Which character quality was the hardest for you to practice this week?

- Did you see a family member consistently practicing one of this week's character qualities? Which family member?

Use your imagination and add questions of your own. After your time of discussion, spend some time praying together, thanking the Lord and sharing one another's burdens. Pray ahead of time for teachable hearts to incorporate and put into practice the character qualities your family will learn in the upcoming week.

The Glad Game

Do you remember the movie *Pollyanna*? In the old Disney classic, the lead character, Pollyanna, taught an entire town to change their attitude from one of cynicism and criticism to an attitude of gladness. She did this by helping them to first look for the good things in their lives and then to share those good things with others. It's easy to notice what's wrong and even easier to share those things; purpose to be a sharer of gladness instead. Not only will others be blessed by your example, but you'll begin to recognize God's goodness in your own life, as well.

Ephesians 4:29

Parenting Point

What types of conversations does your family engage in around the dinner table or when you are spending family time? It is so easy to slip into the habit of negative conversations. There is much to bemoan regarding our government, schools, money, the neighbor's dog, and the list goes on and on. Although it's easy to have those conversations, they do nothing to build up and encourage one another. In fact, often we walk away from family conversations feeling even more discouraged and downhearted. That definitely shouldn't be the characterization of our Christian families! It's easy to put-off a negative conversation habit and to replace it with uplifting and edifying habit of conversation. Spend time asking each family member to share three "encouragements" from their day. Spend time thanking God for His blessings to your family. Have each family member share what they think is especially neat about the person sitting next to them. Be creative, but purposeful, in finding avenues of positive conversation. Once your family has developed a taste for uplifting and positive conversation, they will crave it more and more. Soon, you're family will be addicted to the "Glad Game," and in the process God will be honored and glorified by your edifying and uplifting words!

Love Doesn't Brag

Consider these words that are synonymous with brag: boast, vaunt, swagger, bluster, and big talk. I don't think anyone would want to be known by any of these labels, but how often do we choose the way of the braggart? When we feel the need to "one up" our friends or when we always have to have the last word, we are making the choice to show a lack of love in our words and actions. It is the rare friend who will tell us that we are characterized by bragging, so in this area, we must be self-regulating. Ask the Lord to expose any bragging ways that you have adopted and abandon them as unloving.

I Corinthians 13:4

Parenting Point

Are your children characterized by bragging? Spend some time inconspicuously listening to the conversation that goes on between your children. Do they seem to always have to possess the biggest, best, or most outrageous stories and situations? The habit of bragging and boasting is easily built and very hard to break. If you sense that your children have started down the road to a braggart's life, intervene today. The book of James tells us that God is opposed to the proud but gives grace to the humble. There is nothing humble about a boastful or bragging child. Really, there is nothing humble about a boastful or bragging adult, either. When you hear your children bragging, stop them and correct their self-inflated boasting immediately. When you observe them being good listeners or encouraging and applauding the exploits of others, praise them. This is an instance where punishing bragging will discourage more bragging and encouraging humility will reap great and positive fruit in your children's lives. As always, make sure that they aren't learning the habit of bragging from you! If they are, humble yourself and ask them to forgive you and to help you to not be a braggart as well.

Love Hopes

Are you a hopeful person? One of the standout qualities of a person characterized by Christ-like love is the hopeful way that they approach life. For the Christian, this world is not our home, and our hope must be placed in the promise of our eternal life through Christ Jesus. That type of hope can help us to love the unlovely and undeserving. Hope is what brings beauty to the scarred and ugly situations in our lives. Allow God's hope to fill you today with love for the unlovely.

I Corinthians 13:7

Parenting Point

As parents, and maybe especially as mothers, it is easy to lose heart and feel the utmost certainty that all of our parenting hopes are in vain. Those are the very thoughts that Scripture encourages us to take captive. It is the deceiver who wants us to become so mired in hopelessness that we cannot see any light in our present situation. If you are feeling hopeless in your parenting, take some time today to make a list of all of the positive character qualities your children exhibit. Sometimes it is hard to even begin such a list, but as you pray and ask the Lord to reveal successes in your home, He will be faithful to encourage you. Thankfulness for what is already evident and prayer for future growth are our greatest allies in reviving a hopeless spirit. God is not done with us or our children, and only He knows the end of the story. He is ever hopeful for our change and maturity, and we can share that same hope regarding our own children. Love always hopes! Don't grow weary of well doing, in the end, although it may look very different than you expected, God will reward your hopes.

Hope

G race and hope are very closely connected in the Scriptures. It is God's grace directed toward us that gives us the necessary hope to tackle the difficulties each day brings our way. Without hope, cynicism takes control of our lives. Once cynicism takes root we live lives of unbelief. We begin to live for that which is temporary. Living in the moment robs us of the blessing of God's grace. Hope is bound up in godly, eternal things not carnal, temporal things. What are you hoping for? Not sure? Your calendar and checkbook know for sure!

Titus 3:7

Parenting Point

What is the difference between coveting and a wish list? Especially during the Christmas season, all of our children have hopes for what treats and gifts might come their way. Help your children realize when they are too focused on what they will receive. Constant requests and too much conversation about their desired gifts is a good indication of your child's heart attitude. What is the antidote for coveting? Help your children find opportunities to serve and give to others. As they receive the blessing of giving to others, the "I want its" of life will lose their mesmerizing appeal.

Love is Patient

How would you define patience? The dictionary defines patience as the capacity to accept or tolerate delay, trouble, or suffering without getting angry or upset. I don't know about you, but to me that seems like an impossible task at times. Today's verse makes it clear that God desires His people to be patient people. Do you struggle with patience? Ask a trusted friend to help you recognize the times that you exhibit an impatient attitude. Developing the character quality of patience will build a positive attitude of contentment and perseverance.

I Corinthians 13:4

Parenting Point

Many times, I have had people tell me that they think God gave us so many children because we must be exceptionally patient. Every time I hear that, I just want to laugh. God didn't give us children because we **were** patient; He gave us children to develop our patience. Slow moving, easily distracted children can push my patience to the breaking point, but as I remember that scripture says, "Love is patient." I am forced to slow down and control my own impatient attitudes. When I grumble and complain because I need to get up off the couch and deal with a disobedient or disrespectful child, I show my lack of patience, and at those times, God must deal with me before I can effectively deal with my children. Make a list of "patience robbers" in your life. Commit those challenging circumstances to prayer and ask God to help you to put off impatience and to embrace patience. Our children grow up so quickly! Some of their actions that caused me such impatience when they were small are the very things I miss the most with no young children in our home today.

Don't Forget Forgiveness

Because of Christ's death, burial, and resurrection, we can experience forgiveness for our sin. Because we are forgiven, we can freely forgive as well. In preparation for worship, may we encourage you to make sure that, as far as it is in your power, you have forgiven and sought forgiveness in any troubled relationships. Don't underestimate the power of forgiveness to restore a broken relationship and to make new what seems ruined or destroyed. Purchasing our forgiveness cost Jesus His life. Pursuing and extending forgiveness costs us nothing but our pride.

Luke 17:1-10

Parenting Point

Do your children know how to extend and receive forgiveness? Teaching them how to properly assimilate the forgiveness model in their lives will provide them with the medication necessary to restore and heal broken relationships. Take the time to insist on the forgiveness model in your home. As your children learn to habitually seek and proffer forgiveness in your home, they will be building the spiritual muscle necessary to live winsome and forgiving lives outside of your home. Christians who seek and extend forgiveness frequently and fervently are the Christians who will draw others to Christ. Let your example of incorporating forgiveness with your spouse and children be a model they can imitate.

The Week in Review

Take some time to gather as a family and discuss the character qualities that you learned this week. Here are some questions to get the conversation started.

- **List the character qualities we studied this week.**
- **Which character quality was the hardest for you to practice this week?**
- **Did you see a family member consistently practicing one of this week's character qualities? Which family member?**

Use your imagination and add questions of your own. After your time of discussion, spend some time praying together, thanking the Lord and sharing one another's burdens. Pray ahead of time for teachable hearts to incorporate and put into practice the character qualities your family will learn in the upcoming week.

Respect

Who's The Boss?

How much respect do you exhibit toward those who hold a place of authority in your life? It has become the cultural norm to mock and ridicule those who would be seen as authority figures, but such an attitude should not be evidenced in the life of a Christian. Read today's verse. Even though Paul disagreed strongly with Ananias, he still held himself to the standard set by God. Paul did not continue to speak disrespectfully of the high priest once he recognized his title of authority. Be careful of the jokes and loose humor you exhibit about police officers, judges, pastors, and others who hold positions of authority. An untoward comment can damage your testimony and limit your influence for God.

Acts 23:5

Parenting Point

We teach our children, "Be careful little ears what you hear!" How often are we, as their parents, guilty of causing their little ears to hear things that they shouldn't? Our children are tuned into everything we say, and if the normal order of things involves jokes about police officers or disrespect towards the pastor, our precious little sponges will grow up thinking such disrespect is acceptable. Is it any surprise that those same children struggle to show respect to the authority of their parents? Be careful of the example that you are setting! A momentary laugh at the expense of our children's character is never the right choice. For us it must become, "Be careful little lips what you say!"

The Blessing of Mourning

Although I believe God blesses our efforts to grow into Christ-likeness by exhibiting godly character, not all character qualities come with a promise of blessing; however, Matthew 5:3-11 provides us with a list of character qualities that God describes as being blessed. This week, we will spend time looking at the Beatitudes and discovering the character that God desires for His children. We'll begin with the character quality of mourning. Obviously, we all mourn deaths, tragedies, and injustice, but for the believer, the most important question is this: Do we mourn over our sin? Recognizing the depths of our sinfulness should cause us to mourn each time we choose the momentary pleasure of sin over faithful obedience and allegiance to the Lord. Mourning is more than simply "feeling" sorry and is clearly defined in II Corinthians 7:10 as godly sorrow. Would God consider you a "blessed mourner?"

Matthew 5:4

Parenting Point

How do we teach our children to mourn appropriately? For our children there are really two types of mourning. First is the mourning over things, relationships, hurts, etc. To help our children learn how to mourn in an appropriate way, we must show sympathy for their hurts and disappointments, but then, as good coaches, we must teach them to deal with the hurt and move on. Allowing them to hold onto past hurts and disappointments will, in essence, teach them how to become bitter. More importantly, however, we must help them learn how to mourn over their own sin. Our children will often be quick to say that they are sorry, but this is not always the same as mourning over sin. Only as you patiently and persistently teach your children how God feels about sin, can they learn to truly mourn the destructiveness of their own sin. Spend time in the Word, helping them to discover God's heart toward sin and toward those who choose to continue in sin. Also, show them how freely God extends compassion to those who exhibit godly sorrow. Don't allow a quick "I'm sorry." to replace true mourning over sin.

Joy

What does it take to bring you joy? As I think about my own answer to this question, I am confronted with the reality that it should require very little to bring joy into my life. Joy ought to be a deliberate state of mind rather than the result of a certain set of circumstances; however, joy has been an elusive character quality in my life, and I find that joy has also eluded many who call themselves Christians. Much like any other character quality, joy can be developed. What are you doing to develop joy in your life? Consistent time spent in God's Word, encouraging words shared with the people in your life, and time spent daily thanking God for His goodness are all ways to develop joy.

Galatians 5:22

Parenting Point

Joy and thankfulness are two sides of the same coin. In my own life, and in the lives of my children, when the overwhelming attitude being displayed is negative and critical, I can usually trace it back to a lack of thankfulness. Noticing and thanking God for the little blessings we receive throughout the day will help us to regain our joy and discard our negativity. Together with your children begin a notebook of daily blessings. Record both the big and little joys that God brings into your life. Whether it is a beautiful rainbow, a surprise ice cream cone, or the first smile of a newborn, recognizing our blessings will bring us joy, and then our joy will overflow to bless the lives of others.

The Faith Formula

Read today's scripture. Are you confident that the Lord wants to reward you? Often, we base our understanding of how God feels about us on what we have done for Him or on how faithful we have shown ourselves. Today's scriptures remind us that God doesn't base our reward on our actions but on our belief. He desires to see us seeking Him and rewards us for that seeking. Sometimes the reward is hard to see, but faith reminds us that though we can't see it, we can trust God who is our rewarder. The more consistently and persistently we seek God, the more assurance we will have to trust Him for those things that are unseen. Have you diligently sought God today?

Hebrews 11:1,6

Parenting Point

Faith can be a difficult concept for our children to grasp. They are used to placing their trust in the people and things that they can see, touch, and understand, but faith requires them to trust what they cannot see. Your example of steadfast faith will be your strongest teaching tool in this area. As they see you trusting God to provide, protect, and reward, and as they join with you in rejoicing over answered prayer, they will begin to understand how to trust Someone they cannot see. A simple object lesson about gravity can help them to visualize how we can trust what we don't see. To further show them the power of something unseen, take them outside after a storm and together look at the changes that the wind can bring about. Remind them that although they can't see the wind, they can see its effect on its surroundings. In the same way, God has a powerful effect in the lives of His people. Point out to them the way that God works in your own life and remind them of how He has intervened on their behalf. Seeing the works of God will help them to develop a strong foundation of faith and trust. As a family, spend time seeking God, developing a strong assurance of those things which cannot be seen. Remember to record how God rewards your family through blessings and through His faithful watch care over you.

Circumspection • Carefulness • Orderliness

Carefulness

To be careful means to exercise caution and to pay attention to something so as to avoid damage or potential problems. The careful person pays painstaking attention to detail. In our culture it seems that carefulness is a forgotten virtue. The disposable, materialistic, consumer culture we live in has destroyed the careful attention to detail of yesteryear. Are you careful with your things, even if they are easy to replace? Are you careful with your relationships? Do you mistakenly believe that those relationships are expendable and easily replaced? Read and study the following Scripture on carefulness.

Ephesians 5:15

Parenting Point

Ask your children to define carefulness. Next, ask them to list those things that they are careful with and to list those things with which they could be more careful. Finally, ask them what it means to be careful with people. Moms, is your house cluttered and messy? If so, you can expect careless behavior from your children. I Corinthians 14:40 clearly exhorts believers to manage their lives in a way that is decent and orderly. Do your children see that scriptural dynamic played out in your home and schedule? Take some time to evaluate your daily calendar and routine. Is there a clear order and purpose to the way you spend your time? Although it is easy to commit to many worthwhile activities, is the time spent on those activities adding to the overall peace and stability of your home life? Often, when we are overcommitted and rushing from one activity to another, our relational and home priorities suffer from a lack of carefulness. Don't allow busyness to replace your established priorities. Examine your home. Is there a sense of decency and order in the way your home is maintained? A well-ordered home could provide a sanctuary for family members and a safe haven for friends and neighbors. If, after evaluating your calendar and home, you sense the need for change, don't become overwhelmed! Enlist the help of all family members and work together to develop a home and routine that are characterized by decency, order, and careful attention to detail.

Love Bears All Things

What unbearable things are you being called upon to bear today? As followers of Christ who desire to grow in His character of love, God will give us daily opportunities to grow in love through bearing up under what seems like unbearable situations. Don't lose heart! Hebrews 4:15 reminds us that Christ Himself sympathizes with our difficulties and disappointments. Embrace the unbearable; it is the very tool that God will use to form His character of love in your life.

I Corinthians 13:7

Parenting Point

Is there a parenting trial that you are struggling to bear up under? Perhaps it is an unhealthy child, a rebellious teen, or a lack of like-minded friends for your family. Don't despair; God sees your burden and He will use it to perfect in you His character of love. Often, our children need our help to realize that the burdens of today won't necessarily be the burdens of tomorrow. Because they lack the ability to understand the passage of time, when they feel crushed by a circumstance they begin to think the crushing will never come to an end. Mom and Dad, tag you're it! Our children need us to help to carry the unbearable circumstances in their lives; they need us to lift the load. We often told our children that a situation or problematic relationship was too heavy for them to carry, and we would ask them to let us carry it for them until they were spiritually stronger. This always brought relief to their burdened hearts. For each child, we role-played what handing over their burden looked like by asking them to pick up a too heavy suitcase. We told them that in the same way that they couldn't lift the suitcase, that particular burden was unable to be lifted by them as well. It brought them security to know that what was too heavy for them was manageable for Mom and Dad. When they were older, we transferred some of those "too heavy" circumstances back to their ownership, but often the situation was over and they were free to move on without concern. Carrying our children's heavy burdens helped them to understand how God can carry our burdens as well. Just as we can do with God, our children can cast their cares on us simply because we care for them.

The Week in Review

Take some time to gather as a family and discuss the character qualities that you learned this week. Here are some questions to get the conversation started.

- List the character qualities we studied this week.
- Which character quality was the hardest for you to practice this week?
- Did you see a family member consistently practicing one of this week's character qualities? Which family member?

Use your imagination and add questions of your own. After your time of discussion, spend some time praying together, thanking the Lord and sharing one another's burdens. Pray ahead of time for teachable hearts to incorporate and put into practice the character qualities your family will learn in the upcoming week.

Sacrificial • Others-oriented

Love is Not Self-Seeking

What does it mean to not be self-seeking? In our "me first," "look out for #1" society, we are encouraged daily to seek our own good and to trust that others can take care of themselves. Jesus Christ never lived by that paradigm. Instead, He calls His followers to an others-oriented, self-sacrificing lifestyle. Don't allow society to squeeze you into its mold. Going with the flow will produce nothing but self-centeredness; choose today to care for others in a loving and Christ-centered manner.

I Corinthians 13:5

Parenting Point

Anyone who has parented for any significant amount of time realizes that our children are born self-centered. In the beginning, that self-centeredness is important to their survival, but it doesn't take long for their inward focus to become a well-established habit of living. So, how do we help our children learn to deny their own desires and instead focus on meeting the needs of others? Teaching an others-orientation will not happen by accident, we must be very intentional as we teach our children to recognize and meet the needs of their family, friends, and even strangers. A first step in teaching this important character quality is to teach your children what it means to prefer one another. We show preference to others when we willingly give up something that we have a legitimate right to in order to use that right to bless someone else. Help your children list things that they could give up to bless another sibling. Some examples might be: the front seat of the car, the last muffin at dinner, time alone with a parent. Assist your children in making their list, but don't make it for them. Throughout the day, encourage and exhort them when they miss an opportunity to prefer another, and praise them when they show preference to another. Be an example yourself, and soon you'll teach your children how blessed it is to give up our rights in order to uplift and encourage someone else.

Long-Suffering or Quick Tempered?

Two character qualities that cannot co-exist are the quality of being long-suffering and the opposite quality of being quick-tempered. We never hear people described as being both; therefore, to develop the character quality of long-suffering, the opposite poor quality of quick-temperedness must be put-off. Only through diligent prayer and consistent self-control can we develop the practice of long suffering. A quick, thoughtless reply can negate our efforts to put-on God-honoring long-suffering. As believers, we must not allow ourselves wiggle room in this area. Our responses to all people, and especially those in our family, must show patience, kindness, and an attitude of long-suffering. How are you doing today?

Galatians 5:22-23

Parenting Point

Have you ever spoken to your children and they responded with quick, harsh words? Where do they learn to talk that way? I am afraid, that too often, that example comes from Mom and Dad. Impatience, at the end of a busy day or even at the start of an activity-filled day, can cause us to respond in a quick-tempered way. The more often we are characterized by this type of communication, the more natural it will be for our children to imitate and emulate our poor example. If this is you, take time to seek your children's forgiveness each and every time that you respond in a quick-tempered manner. Yes, this will take time and will be an interruption to your day; however, the more often you stop and restore, the more sensitive you will become to your harsh responses and the sooner you will be able to put-off quick-temperedness and develop sweet long-suffering. Your children will benefit from your growth and example.

Sacrificial • Generosity

What Makes a Sacrifice a Sacrifice?

I f you could choose one word to describe the death of Christ on the cross of Calvary, what would that word be? For me, the word would be sacrifice. Christ gave up everything that He already possessed to become a sacrifice for you and for me. How does the character quality of sacrifice show itself in your life? Are you willing to sacrifice your time, money, possessions, free time, _____ (you fill in the blank) for the cause of Christ? As we consider the sacrifice of our Lord, take some time to evaluate your own life and your attitude toward sacrifice. In the words of Jim Elliot, "He is no fool who gives up what he cannot keep, to gain what he cannot lose."

Ephesians 5:1-2

Parenting Point

I cannot count the number of times we have told our children, "For a sacrifice to be a sacrifice, it has to be a sacrifice!" Too often, our children are willing to give up something to which they have no emotional or physical attachment, but when it comes to making a true sacrifice, they are unwilling or distraught at the very thought. Take the time to teach your children to give their BEST to others. Whether they are donating toys to a family in need or giving up their time to serve a sibling or another family member, learning to sacrifice what they think they have a right to possess for the good of someone else is a necessary lesson for all believers. Be an observer of your children. Praise them for generosity and cheerful giving; coach and encourage them when you observe selfish or self-centered attitudes. Remember, they are watching your example all of the time. Be careful to not only sacrifice for those outside the family; make sure your children see you willing to sacrifice for them as well.

Boasting vs. Humility

D o you desire to be humble? I think most Christians would agree that humility is an important character quality. Sometimes, however, we derail our efforts to be humble simply because we have forgotten the "put-off" principle found in Ephesians 4. Humility and boasting cannot co-exist! Search your heart, or better yet, ask a trusted friend to evaluate your level of self-promotion or boasting. As you work to put-off boasting, humility will become a more natural put-on in replacement. The book of James reminds us that God is opposed to the proud but gives grace to the humble. I certainly want God's grace not His opposition!

Proverbs 27:2

Parenting Point

Help your children to evaluate how much they boast and speak of themselves. A valuable lesson can be found in simply recording how many "I" and "me" phrases they incorporate throughout their day. Gently remind them of the need to uplift and encourage others, rather than boasting about themselves. Be patient, it is natural for children (and many adults) to extol their own virtues, but patient teaching will bear great fruit. Perhaps, you and your children would want to memorize Proverbs 27:2 together. Make sure you are praising your children's good character, both to them and to others.

Coveting Consumes Contentment

C oveting is a nasty little character quality. All of the sudden, out of the blue, we can find ourselves no longer content with what God has provided simply because we are coveting something we see, hear about, or know someone else possesses. For a believer, a heart characterized by coveting is an affront to our God. Coveting is a decision to regard what the Lord has given us as inadequate, unacceptable, and incomplete. We must replace coveting with contentment. Take your thoughts of coveting captive, confess them as ingratitude to the Lord, and begin to recall the many blessings that God has bestowed on you. Then, like Paul, you can say that you are content in all circumstances.

Philippians 4:11-12

Parenting Point

Are your children thankful? The first step to developing a contented heart is learning to be thankful for what has already been provided. Take some time to observe your children's level of thankfulness. Do they naturally and spontaneously thank you and others for what is provided or must they always be reminded and prodded? Teaching your children to be thankful will go far in teaching them to be content. Content children will be eager to be generous instead of being envious and coveting what others possess.

Are You a Worrywart?

The word worry is defined as a state of anxiety and uncertainty over actual or potential problems. Synonyms for worry are: trouble, bother, and harass, which is exactly what worry does...It bothers and harasses our heart. Today's verses remind us that we have no need to worry. Our Heavenly Father knows what we need, and He holds our concerns and us close to His heart. Spend time today seeking Him and His righteousness and watch how He displays His love for you!

Matthew 6:25-34

Parenting Point

Have you learned to hand your worries over to God and to simply trust Him to care for you and your family? One of the saddest side effects of a worrying parent is the residual stress it places on their children. When our children sense that we, their parents, are worried, they begin to feel insecure and frightened. While they know in their hearts that something is wrong, they lack the ability to do anything to solve our problems. Our worries become their fears. That's one reason it is so important for us to learn to put-off worry and put-on trust. Only then will we be able to appropriately model God-trusting behavior to our children. When our family faced situations that were troubling, and quite honestly tempted us to worry, we purposefully included our children in prayer for those situations as was appropriate. Joining us in prayer helped to allay their fears and forced us to be consistent in taking our worries to the Lord, transforming those worries into areas of trust and faith-building growth. Don't allow worry to dwell unchecked in your home. Seek God and His righteousness and allow Him to carry the burden of your troubling circumstances.

The Week in Review

Take some time to gather as a family and discuss the character qualities that you learned this week. Here are some questions to get the conversation started.

- **List the character qualities we studied this week.**

- **Which character quality was the hardest for you to practice this week?**

- **Did you see a family member consistently practicing one of this week's character qualities? Which family member?**

Use your imagination and add questions of your own. After your time of discussion, spend some time praying together, thanking the Lord and sharing one another's burdens. Pray ahead of time for teachable hearts to incorporate and put into practice the character qualities your family will learn in the upcoming week.

What is Your Loving Saying About You?

Are there people in your life that you have granted yourself the freedom to not love? We all have folks in our lives that have wounded us, deserted us, or just plain annoyed us. Still, God's Word makes it clear that regardless of their poor behavior, as followers of His Son, we must show them love. Read today's Scripture. What does your love say about your relationship with Christ? It is one thing to recognize Christ; it is quite another thing to know Him in a relationship of obedience. The scripture is clear: If you know God, you will love your brother.

I John 4:8, 20

Parenting Point

Do your children know God? One of the clearest evidences of a love relationship with Christ will be shown through your children's words to one another. Children who lash out with harsh words such as: "I hate you!" or "I don't like you!" are clearly giving you a glimpse into their heart condition. It is tempting to simply instruct them of the need to speak kindly, but it is imperative to dig deeper and discern what is truly going on in their hearts. Take them to I John 4 and ask them if their actions point to a love relationship with the Lord. Help them to understand His love for them, even when they are less than loveable. Without lecturing, gently instruct them and help them find ways to deal with others in a loving way. If, after examining the Scriptures, they don't feel that they know the Lord, take this opportunity to help them begin a relationship with the One who loves them.

Stability Provides Security

Consider these words that are used to define stability: constancy of character or purpose, steadfastness, reliability, dependability. All of these words denote a firm and confident foundation. How stable is your relationship with Christ? The stability of your faith will speak volumes to a lost world that is always watching to see if your God can be trusted all the time and in all ways. As today's verse reminds us, we must learn to seek God in faith with no wavering. As we "firm up" our foundation in Christ, we will become the stable Christians that our families and friends can turn to with confidence.

James 1:5-8

Parenting Point

Have you ever considered that the stability of your own faith can provide security for your children? I believe that it certainly can! While our children need not be exposed to *all* of the difficulties that we face in our adult lives, it is important that they see how their parents handle troubling situations. As they see you walking faithfully with God and trusting Him for wisdom and discernment, regardless of your circumstances, they will feel safe and secure. The storms of life will come, and we must teach our children how to ride out the storm; however, of more importance, we must teach our children that their stability and security comes from the God who is never surprised or overcome by the storms they face. Parents who are easily dismayed by hard situations can inadvertently undermine their children's security. The more time we spend in the Word and in developing our own stable relationship with Christ, the more easily we will be able to pass on that stability to our children. What can you do today to firm up your foundation of faith?

The Heart of a Planter

As today's scripture tells us, there is a time in everyone's life to be a planter. What are you planting today? We have so many options of what to plant. We can plant seeds of reconciliation or seeds of disintegration. We can plant harmony or discord. We can plant unity or strife. Examine your life and relationships to discern what seeds you are planting. Don't waste your time as a planter planting anything but godly seeds.

Ecclesiastes 3:2

Parenting Point

As parents, I don't think that there is ever a time when we aren't called to be planters. Whether we are planting the budding seeds of early responsibilities or the simple seeds of the Gospel, we are always to be at work planting multiple seeds into the rich soil of our children's hearts. The busier we are about planting those seeds, the easier it will be to work the soil. If we are inconsistent planters, the soil of our children's hearts will become hardened and baked by the world. We must consistently plant seeds of character. Think about the character qualities that you would like to see exhibited in your children's lives and then begin to intentionally teach and train your children by sowing the seeds of that character. Sow honesty, and diligence, and compassion, and respect, and courage, and commitment. At times, the list of seeds waiting to be sown may seem endless, but as planters that is our responsibility. We must also be careful not to sow seeds of discontent, disrespect, or dishonesty. The example we exhibit in our own lives will plant seeds, whether we intend for that to happen or not. Someday we will reap, but even in the reaping new plantings will continue. Embrace the character of a planter with the future harvest of your children's good character as the goal of your hard work.

Spiritual Hunger • Diligence

Practice, Practice, Practice

S everal of my children are serious athletes. Because they take their chosen sport so seriously, they are willing to practice simple and somewhat mundane moves over and over. Whether it is a batting swing or a swimming stroke, they are training themselves to recognize and perform the necessary action correctly. Today's verse reminds us that only through the diligent practice of studying the Word of God can we become proficient in discerning good and evil. We are either practicing to succeed or practicing to fail. What does your practice schedule say about you?

Hebrews 5:14

Parenting Point

Every day we end our email with a simple reminder to not grow weary of doing well. When it comes to parenting, there are no quick fixes. It is only as we train our children over and over again that we will begin to see fruit. Just like skipping a stone on water, the more active we are to "stir-up" the water of our children's moral conscience, the more quickly they will learn the lessons that we are trying to impart. If we don't take the time to stir-up our children, we run the risk of watching their moral conscience become hardened and unwilling to receive instruction. I know it's tiring. I know it's frustrating. I know that sometimes it seems fruitless and pointless. However, don't grow weary! Pray and ask God to give you a moment of encouragement with your children each day. Although there will be some days that the encouragement is small, little by little those small encouragements will bring about big changes and strong Christ-like character!

The Time is Now

King Solomon reminds us in the book of Ecclesiastes that there is an appropriate time for everything. When we do not complete what is necessary in the appropriate time, we are guilty of procrastination. The dictionary defines procrastination this way: to put off doing something, especially out of habitual carelessness or laziness, to postpone or delay needlessly. Good character requires careful attention to timely completion of tasks. Don't allow procrastination to destroy your testimony of good character.

Proverbs 10:5

Parenting Point

Can you trust your children to complete their tasks in a timely manner? If not, what is causing that lack of completion? Children, who are allowed to embrace habits of procrastination, will struggle as adults in the workplace. We do our children a grave disservice when we do not insist that they complete what is necessary in an appropriate amount of time. Whether it's eating their meals, or completing their homework, or doing their chores, procrastination is never an option. If necessary, use a timer to help your children manage their time more wisely. If something needs to be completed before they can leave for a fun activity, do not allow them to rush through the necessary work in a sloppy manner just to get it done. Missing out on a fun option because they procrastinated and didn't complete their work is a powerful lesson. Tell them that you are sorry they can't go this time, but that you are confident they won't procrastinate next time. Although most of the tasks and activities our children must complete do not seem to have any urgency attached to them, it is important that our children learn to do their work in an appropriate manner. It is not the importance of the task that is the issue at stake, but the careful character training of our children.

Integrity

I ntegrity is not simply a stand-alone character quality. Rather, integrity is the sum total of all of the character qualities working together. Picture a ship. You would not want to set sail in a ship that lacked integrity! If even one part of the ship were to fail, you would find yourself in a precarious position. If a ship needs integrity, how much more does a Christian man, woman, or child? Are there areas of your life that would fail the "integrity test"? If so, in humility, seek the Lord's forgiveness and make a positive plan to implement change in your daily life.

Psalm 15:1-2

Parenting Point

Often, you will hear integrity defined as "Who you are when no one is looking." Is your family characterized by a testimony of integrity? Are you the same person regardless of your surroundings? What is the report about your children? Sometimes, my children would be causing discord and strife in our own home but receiving praise and accolades for their outstanding behavior at church and in other arenas. When this happened, I knew I needed to challenge their integrity and help them to rise to the same standard of character, regardless of where they were and with whom they were spending their time. Don't allow your children to receive praise outside of the home as a replacement for good character in the home! Teach into the hypocrisy with your children, and if necessary, ask their coaches or teachers to withhold public praise until they are characterized by the same attitudes and actions at home. This is not harsh; it is a necessary tool to teach our children to have the same testimony at all times and in all places. When I have had to approach a coach or teacher about my child's hypocritical behavior and attitudes, they have always been helpful and more than willing to help me train them in the character quality of integrity. Integrity is one of the clearest areas that our example will speak much louder than our words. Make sure that you are consistently elevating integrity in your own life and confidently encourage your children to do the same. A testimony of integrity is vital to our ministry for the Lord.

The Week in Review

Take some time to gather as a family and discuss the character qualities that you learned this week. Here are some questions to get the conversation started.

- **List the character qualities we studied this week.**

- **Which character quality was the hardest for you to practice this week?**

- **Did you see a family member consistently practicing one of this week's character qualities? Which family member?**

Use your imagination and add questions of your own. After your time of discussion, spend some time praying together, thanking the Lord and sharing one another's burdens. Pray ahead of time for teachable hearts to incorporate and put into practice the character qualities your family will learn in the upcoming week.

Pleasing Character of Faith

W ould you like to be rewarded by God? Read today's verses. Verse 6 assures us that God will reward those who seek Him; however, in order to seek God, we must first have faith that He is who He claims to be. Although we cannot see God, we can know Him through faith and through an abiding relationship with Him. What are you doing on a daily basis to know God more and to increase your faith in Him?

Hebrew 11:1, 6

Parenting Point

It is important to help our children understand what it "looks like" to have faith in Someone whom they cannot see. Take the time to plan some object lessons that help your children understand what it means to place their trust and faith in something that isn't visible. Air, gravity, and the wind are just a few examples of unseen things that we know are real. Although we don't view the germination process of a seed planted in the soil, we trust for the vegetables that will someday appear. Every day events provide a myriad of opportunities to teach into the concept of faith. When you pick up your children at the door after Sunday School or nursery, talk about how they could trust that you would come, even though they didn't see you coming. Because you told them that you would arrive, they could believe your words. Make sure they know that you completely trust the Word of God in the same way that they can trust you. Prove yourself faithful in living up to your promises to your children. Your faithfulness paints a picture of God's faithfulness, and they will easily understand how to trust and seek God. As they grow up trusting and seeking Him, they will become people of great assurance who find their reward in God.

A Healer's Heart

Many in our world try to offer help and healing to hurting souls; however, it is the Christian who holds the key to the ultimate healing for the deep hurts that so many people endure. What are you doing to develop the heart of a healer? In order to be characterized as an effective healer, we must be intimate with Christ and well-studied in the Scriptures; only then will we be equipped to lead our friends to the Great Healer. Don't miss a God-ordained opportunity; make the necessary preparations to have the character and heart of a healer.

Ecclesiastes 3:3

Parenting Point

I don't know about your children, but when my kids were little they thought that a kiss from Mom and a smiley face band-aid could make any hurt better. It wasn't until they began to experience heart hurts rather than skinned knees, that they lost faith in the band-aids. In many instances, our presence, prayers, and counsel are the first line of healing that our children need to make it through the pitfalls of their busy lives; however, we can never replace the ultimate healer in their lives. Our children need to have an intimate relationship with Christ to find healing from their sin and healing from the daily hurts they experience in our sinful world. When we lead them to believe that we can fix all of their problems or heal all of their hurts, we are doing them a great disservice. Christ alone can heal their every pain. We must be quick to lead our children to Him and to help them learn to cast their cares and concerns into His arms. When our children have learned to trust Christ as their Great Healer, they will be equipped to help their friends find the same source of help and healing. A prayerful, loving, Christian teen can often provide the counsel that another young person is searching for in their life. Model for your children how to turn to Christ for help and healing and you will be blessed to see them imitate what you have taught them as they minister to their needy friends. It's nice to be needed by our little children, but it's wonderful to see them confidently run to the One who can truly meet their every need.

Keeping It Clean

I n the same way that Philippians 4:8 provides us with a wonderful standard to guard our speech, this same verse also helps us to monitor our thought life. Although no one else may ever be able to see what is going on in our thoughts, unbridled and unguarded thoughts will produce negative fruit that will eventually be obvious in our lives. On what do you allow your thoughts to dwell? Inappropriate input through television, books, magazines, or websites can cause us to fill our minds with destructive and filthy thoughts. Take action today and safeguard your thoughts by running them through the Philippians 4:8 cleansing filter.

Philippians 4:8

Parenting Point

Parents, we are responsible to be the standard-bearers in our home as well as the doorkeepers who monitor what comes into our homes. Whatever is allowed in our homes will become the food for what our children's thoughts feed upon. Be careful and discerning. Just because everyone else, even everyone else in the church, is doing something doesn't mean that it is beneficial for your family or children. Once our children have been exposed to certain defiling and harmful influences, it is very difficult to get those thoughts out of their heads. Be aggressive in protecting your children from those harmful inputs. This does not mean that our children can never leave the home! Yet, while they are young, shield them diligently. As they mature and begin to spend more time outside of your home, spend time training and preparing them to independently protect their hearts, minds, and thoughts. Don't be afraid to ask your teens how they are doing with their thought life. Good communication and resisting the urge to over-react will build strong relationships and an ability to offer counsel that will be gratefully received. Our thoughts need protection just as much as our children's thoughts need protection. If there is anything in your home that is causing you to harbor unbiblical thoughts, take whatever radical steps are necessary to rid your home of those things.

A Wrecker's Heart

Have you ever watched a building being torn down? What once stood tall can quickly be reduced to nothing but a pile of rubble with a wrecking ball still swinging overhead. Sometimes we are called to have that wrecker's heart and character about our own lives. When we realize that we have been building our lives, hopes, or dreams on any foundation other than Christ, it is time to pull out the wrecking ball, reduce our efforts to rubble, and begin anew with Christ as the only sure foundation. On what is your foundation laid today?

Ecclesiastes 3:3

Parenting Point

It is important to periodically examine the activities and relationships in which our children are involved. Are their activities drawing them closer to the Lord and encouraging them to live in a way that points them to Christ, or are their activities self-focused and working as a distraction from Christ? Different activities may produce a different outcome in different children's lives; therefore, what is acceptable for one child in your family may be unacceptable for another. The difference is found in the individual children's heart appetites. If you find that an activity or relationship is built on a foundation of worldliness or carnality, is it time to become the "wrecker parent?" No! We don't go in and demand that our children destroy what they have just built. Instead, we teach into the character and spiritual lack in their activities and relationships. As we spend time with our children and in the Word of God, it is He who will bring about the necessary change in their lives. We fill the role of the foreman on the job: pointing out what must be accomplished and helping the workers get the job done but not doing it for them. Be the wrecking ball in your own life, and your children will see how the destruction of faulty foundation process works!

Disrespect Leads to Death

Too many times, as we follow the crowd in showing disrespect to those in authority over us, we put to death our own testimony. We lead others into harmful disrespect and kill our opportunity to show others the difference Christ has made in our lives. Can you think of a time that your lack of respect led a younger brother or sister in Christ to go even further down the road of disrespect? If so, what were the consequences? Recognizing that, as believers, we are all slaves of the Lord Jesus Christ will help us to render respect with the right attitude. Read Ephesians 6:5-6 and answer this question: From where should our respect for others emanate?

Ephesians 6:5-6

Parenting Point

How respectful are your children toward you and toward their siblings? Notice, I didn't ask how respectful they are toward others. Respect is one of those character qualities that we too often concentrate on requiring outside of our home, while allowing disrespect within our homes. Children, who are disrespectful verbally through words or tone or non-verbally through their actions toward their own family members, are not children who have embraced the character quality of respect. When we allow, or even encourage, our children to be respectful toward outsiders, while allowing them to be disrespectful at home, we are teaching them to be hypocrites. These hypocritical children will grow up to become spouses and parents that treat others outside the home with esteem, while disregarding the preciousness of their own families. True respect begins at home and overflows to those outside our homes. Begin today to build a home atmosphere of mutual respect!

Leadership

Leadership is commonly defined as the ability to guide, direct, or influence people. Who better than the community of Christ to take over the leadership needs in our homes, communities, and country? Leaders are not just born that way; they must be developed and matured through consistent and diligent character training. We all have the responsibility to fulfill a leadership role in someone else's life. Think of the people who look to you for leadership. Are you taking advantage of the opportunities that God is providing for you to lead others? Are you working consistently and diligently to develop your own character in such a way that you will earn the right to be a leader?

Matthew 4:18-22

Parenting Point

Do you think Peter, Andrew, James, and John saw themselves as natural leaders? I doubt it! However, the Lord took these humble fishermen and developed them into leaders who would turn the world upside down by introducing the Gospel of the Lord Jesus Christ. Begin today to talk to your children about the leadership possibilities in their futures. Even a four-year old can be a positive leader to a younger sibling. As you bestow more leadership responsibilities on your children, they will eagerly rise to the occasion, wanting to show that the trust you put in them is deserved. Humble leadership is a worthy goal for any Christian. Build excitement for that goal by bestowing responsibility, rewarding faithfulness, and praising progress. You'll be blessed as you see your children embracing their rightful roles in the church and community. Oftentimes, the "hyper" children, who seem to cause the most turmoil and trouble in our homes, are the very children that God is preparing to take on mighty roles of leadership. As you pray for the patience to deal with those children, also pray that God will turn their stubborn self-wills into courageous "Christ-wills." Adults, characterized by stubborn adherence to the Word of God, will be greatly used for His glory.

The Week in Review

Take some time to gather as a family and discuss the character qualities that you learned this week. Here are some questions to get the conversation started.

- List the character qualities we studied this week.
- Which character quality was the hardest for you to practice this week?
- Did you see a family member consistently practicing one of this week's character qualities? Which family member?

Use your imagination and add questions of your own. After your time of discussion, spend some time praying together, thanking the Lord and sharing one another's burdens. Pray ahead of time for teachable hearts to incorporate and put into practice the character qualities your family will learn in the upcoming week.

Obtaining Orderliness

I recently saw a plaque that read, "Boring women keep clean houses." While this saying may be good for a laugh or a sarcastic roll of the eyes, is it really an accurate picture of the Christian life? Is orderliness boring, or is it a character quality that must be evidenced in each believer's life? From the Genesis account of creation, through the painstaking and meticulous measurements and adornments of the Temple, all the way to Paul's admonition to the church in I Corinthians, we are presented with the picture of a God of order and structure. While orderliness certainly comes easier to some than others, we don't have the freedom to declare ourselves unable to obtain this character quality. What steps are you taking to present a testimony that emulates our God? A testimony of a life devoted to step-by-step growth in obtaining orderliness.

Genesis 1:1-31

Parenting Point

Do your children think that orderliness is the normal way of life, or are they growing up surrounded by clutter and disorder? To teach our children to appreciate orderliness in all areas of their lives, we must be working consistently to model this character quality in our own lives. Spend some time evaluating your home and routines. Are your actions undermining your teaching on this subject? If so, enlist the entire family to make the changes necessary to build your family testimony of structure and order. Begin with a family purge of unnecessary items and activities. You will be surprised how much stress is relieved for your family just by this simple step. Orderly homes and schedules provide security for our children.

A Greedy Character

Have you ever overindulged in something that was just really yummy? Did you feel awful afterwards? Temperance is an old-fashioned word that simply means the ability to practice self-restraint. The opposite character quality would be greediness or over-indulgence. Today's verse reminds us of the danger of greediness and the unpleasant consequences that often follow.

Proverbs 25:16

Parenting Point

Sadly, watching children proceed through the line at a church fellowship is often a picture of greed and over-indulgence. As they fill their plates to overflowing, these children are not learning the important character quality of temperance. Temperance is necessary in so many areas of our lives. Whether it is eating, or drinking, or working, or playing, intemperance can cause damage to ourselves and to those with whom we are connected. Too much of a good thing is just that...too much. Teach your children to practice self-restraint and to limit themselves, regardless of what everyone else is doing. Until our children can regulate themselves in this area, it is important to oversee the choices they are making. It is the prudent parent who stops their child from over-indulging. Consider your child's day. Do they practice temperance when it comes to television viewing? Eating? Time spent on social media? If not, spend some time discussing your observations with your child and help them to develop good habits of self-control and temperance. Remember, your own example is paramount. If they never see you telling yourself "No." and meaning it, they will have no reason to think it is necessary to deny themselves either. If this is an area of struggle for you, be transparent with your child, and, if appropriate, ask them to help you to be accountable to the practice of temperance.

Maximizing Your Potential

What does it mean to be faithful to the trust that God has given to each of us? Every believer has certain talents and abilities that God wants to use for the furtherance of His kingdom. Although He equips us with those talents, He does not force us to use them. Instead, we must make the choice to harness our potential and then to expend it in kingdom work. Take some time today to consider how God has gifted you. Are you using those gifts for Him?

1 Corinthians 4:2

Parenting Point

Sometimes the talents that God gives us don't seem very glamorous or of much value in kingdom work; however, in God's economy, every gift we possess is given to be used for the glory of God. We must help our children learn how to embrace and maximize their God-given talents and gifts. Often, children will long to possess someone else's talent, thinking that their contribution isn't as valuable as other people's contributions. Nothing could be further from the truth. With every gift given, God knows exactly how that talent or gift can be used for His glory. Just as each person's individualized testimony is special and can be used to point to Christ, each different talent or gift can be used to meet specific needs in the body of Christ. Encourage your children to think of practical ways that they can use their strengths to bring blessing and encouragement into the life of someone else. Are they musicians? Perhaps they could bring the ministry of music to a nursing home. Are they talented writers? Letters of encouragement can bring hope to a soldier far from home. Are they athletes? Playing soccer or kickball with special needs children can bring joy to a child's heart. Help them to be creative and challenge them to list ways to use their talents in a God-glorifying manner.

Patience • Perseverance

Patience of the Savior

C.S. Lewis once said, *"We ought to give thanks for all fortune: if it is good, because it is good, if bad, because it works in us patience, humility and the contempt of this world and the hope of our eternal country."* We must not confuse God's patience with us for His approval of our sinful appetites. God's grace and mercy are often manifested through His infinite patience. We too, can show God's grace and mercy to others through our acts of patient forbearance. Read the verses below noting the purpose behind God's patience with us.

1 Timothy 1:15-16

Parenting Point

Wouldn't it be nice if our children only presented us with one parenting issue at a time? Unfortunately, in our home, my children often have multiple areas of sin that need to be addressed. Remembering God's patience toward my own sin helps me to parent my children with a forbearing and patient attitude. I often remind myself how wretched I would feel if the Lord dealt with all of my areas of failure at once. Instead, God gently works in my heart and life to change me one area at a time. Don't try to address every one of your children's problems at once. Focus on one, or at the most, two areas at a time. Your children will have a better chance to succeed, and you won't be as frustrated and impatient. When your children have had some measure of success in a formerly troubling area, take the time to praise and encourage them. Too often, our children show positive fruit, and then we immediately raise the standard of behavioral expectation. Once again, they are plunged into areas of failure with no time to celebrate success. Stop and celebrate. Make a note of the positive changes you see and refer back to that note when your children are feeling discouraged, defeated, or unable to accomplish more change. Remind them how God worked to help them achieve success in a sin area and reaffirm that He is still working in their lives. Initiate the same practice in your own life. Don't become overwhelmed with the need to change every area of your life all at once. Instead, ask the Lord to show you what priority areas He would have you address and then make a plan to bring about Biblical change.

Diligence • Perseverance • Focused

Laser Focus

Everyone can develop habits and practices that will enable them to remain more focused, but as followers of Christ, it is imperative that we don't simply develop better focus but that we learn to focus on the right priorities. It is easy for me to stay focused on the things I find enjoyable, but how is my focus on things that are necessary but not as easy or fun? Evaluate your priorities today. Is your focus in the right direction? If not, rearrange your thinking to focus on God's priorities for you and enjoy the peace that comes from a proper focus in the proper areas.

I Corinthians 9:24-27

Parenting Point

How can we teach our children to become more focused? One easy tool that we have used, especially with our more distracted children, is the implementation of verbal lists. Give your child a simple list of instructions to follow, perhaps two or three different items to put away or tasks to complete. Have your children repeat the list back to you, word-for-word. Then, send them off to accomplish what you have directed. If they are successful, praise them!! If not, have them repeat the list (again, word for word) and try again. As they become more proficient, add more tasks to the list. Your children will gradually learn to be more careful listeners and successfully focused achievers.

Lovingly Truthful

W hat does it mean to speak the truth in love? In our part of the country, many folks pride themselves on "telling it like it is." The more brutal the truth, the more acceptable, it seems. However, Scripture makes it clear that the character quality of truthfulness is of no quality at all if it is not loving. So, again I ask, what does it mean to speak the truth in love? I believe this character quality has three prongs to its application: 1. We must speak. 2. We must speak the truth. 3. We must speak the truth in love. We do not have the freedom to remain silent, when speaking the truth is in order. The end goal of our speaking must be love, edification, encouragement, and growth of the person to whom we are speaking. How are you doing? One or two out of three isn't good enough. To fully embrace this character quality, we must embrace all three prongs. Begin your day with prayer that today you might be lovingly truthful.

Ephesians 4:15

Parenting Point

Our children will not choose naturally to speak the truth in love. Instead, the easiest choice is often to lie, to speak the truth in an unloving manner, or to simply not speak at all. None of these options should be acceptable in our homes. Take some time today to role-play what it looks like to speak the truth in love. Set up some scenarios where your children have the choice to speak the truth or to choose to do otherwise. Have them act the part of the parent as they watch you making the same types of choices. Refer back to this role-playing time as you deal with times of dishonesty, unloving truth, or stubborn silence. Just as a reminder, when something is obviously wrong and you ask your child to tell you what is going on, an answer of "nothing" is just as untruthful as an outright lie. Don't set your children up to lie by your untimely question. Instead, tell them that you know something is wrong and that you want them to prepare their heart to tell you the truth. Sometimes, just that few moments of preparation will give them the courage they need to speak truthfully.

The Week in Review

Take some time to gather as a family and discuss the character qualities that you learned this week. Here are some questions to get the conversation started.

- List the character qualities we studied this week.
- Which character quality was the hardest for you to practice this week?
- Did you see a family member consistently practicing one of this week's character qualities? Which family member?

Use your imagination and add questions of your own. After your time of discussion, spend some time praying together, thanking the Lord and sharing one another's burdens. Pray ahead of time for teachable hearts to incorporate and put into practice the character qualities your family will learn in the upcoming week.

A Missionary Heart

Do you love your friends and family? True love shows itself through a heartfelt desire to see all of our friends and family come to a saving knowledge of the Lord Jesus Christ. Read today's verse and ask God to give you a heart that is prepared to be a witness for Him. Everyone has a different Judea, Samaria, and remotest part of the earth... What is yours?

Acts 1:8

Parenting Point

When my children were young, they were so eager to be missionaries for Jesus! In fact, my daughter Emma used to, as she said, "Get them ready." Then she would bring her little friends and acquaintances to me, fully expecting that I would lead them to the Lord. It was only as they got older that my children became more nervous about witnessing. I wonder if they learned that nervousness from me? I know the Lord would be honored if we all had that child-like enthusiasm about sharing Christ with others. As a family, we can work together to develop missionaries' hearts and character. As we pray together as a family for unsaved friends and relatives, we will gain excitement about seeing others come to Christ. In training our children, we encouraged them to develop a 10 Most Wanted List of unsaved friends for whom they were praying. As we saw people get saved off our individual lists, the entire family was encouraged to stay faithful in prayer. Speaking of the Lord and His workings on our behalf in a natural way in our homes will make speaking of Him to others much less intimidating. Our families have the opportunity to shine more brightly for the Lord together than we can each shine independently. Take the time to develop and grow as a family with the character and hearts of missionaries.

Broken and Contrite

What does it mean to have a character of brokenness? Although the dictionary offers many definitions for the word "broken," one in particular seems to reveal a clear picture of brokenness in a believer's life: tamed, trained, or reduced to submission. Just as a horse can be "broken" to a halter, the Christian must be "broken" to submission. Only as we recognize our sinful state and respond to God with a contrite heart can we become truly broken, and that brokenness will exhibit itself as complete submission to the authority of God. Unlike the proud heart of a stubborn man, a broken man will be moldable and malleable in the Master's hand.

Psalm 51:17

Parenting Point

Do your children exhibit brokenness over their sin and disobedience? Too often, we allow our children to mouth the words, "I'm sorry." when sorrow over sin is the furthest thing from their minds. When you are training your children and bring correction into their lives, SLOW DOWN! Take the time to discern what is going on in their hearts. If you sense that they are simply upset that they got caught or just wanting the punishment to get over and done with, enforce some contemplative time to consider their wrongdoing. Parents, we provide the strongest model of brokenness that our children can see. Do they see you contrite and grieving over sin in your own life? If not, what are they learning from you? God can accomplish much with a heart that is broken and malleable; don't allow the deceitfulness of sin to harden your heart or the hearts of your children.

A Studious Character

What type of student are you? Do you love to learn or must you be dragged, kicking and screaming, to your studies? When it comes to the Word of God, we are all to be students of the Word. Spend some time reading today's verse and consider what our attitude should be concerning time spent in the scriptures. What changes could you incorporate to make study time a time of delight?

Psalm 1:2

Parenting Point

If we want our children to learn to love spending time in the Word, it is absolutely essential that they see us spending time there ourselves. Do your children know that the scriptures are a delight to you? In different seasons of parenting, it may become more difficult to spend time lingering over the scripture; however, no matter how tired we are or how busy our days become, it is absolutely essential to spend time studying and meditating on the Word of God. Unlike a heavy meal, which will fills us up and kills our appetite, time spent filling our hearts with God's Word will give us a hunger for more. Mom and Dad, do whatever it takes to guarantee you have daily time with the Lord. Share what you are learning with your children, not in a "lesson" type of way but just as one excited follower of Christ to another. Start this habit when your children are young, and when they are teens, ingesting the Word of God independently of your directions, they will naturally and easily share their daily growth with you as well. Meditating on God's Word day and night will give our families the strength and encouragement they need to face each day's challenges with courage.

A Careful Watchman

I s your good character under close watch? Even areas of character that we have worked hard to develop can be compromised and lessened, if we don't take steps to guard and protect them. Read today's verse. Watching over our life and character choices isn't an easy proposition. Rather, it takes diligent and persistent effort on our part. Take time to seek the Lord, as King David did, and ask Him to show you any areas that need to be cleaned up or even fine-tuned. Diligent guardianship of our character will not only keep it safe but will give us opportunities to grow and develop even more godly character.

Proverbs 4:23

Parenting Point

While our children are young, it is our responsibility and privilege to act as watchmen, guarding their hearts and character. Often, what is going on in our children's hearts will be evident in their speech, actions, and eyes. A diligent parent is prayerfully on the watch for anything detrimental that is harming their children or bringing about poor character choices; however, as our children enter their teen and early adult years, the watch care for their character becomes their own responsibility. If we continue to constantly point out questionable areas and then we instruct them in the necessary changes, our children will never develop the ability to recognize those areas themselves. Instead, we must become good question-askers. There is a huge difference between asking our children to help us understand a choice they just made and telling our children that their choice was lousy. When we ask good questions our children discover and discern for themselves what kind of choices they are making. Then, they can take ownership of those choices. Children who feel respected in the decision making process will be much more likely to seek our advice. Advice that is handed out without being requested will become a roadblock to open and useful communication. Pray diligently for your children during this transitional period. Yes, they will make mistakes, but if you have carefully planted seeds of godly character, they will have the internal resources they need to guard their own hearts and make right choices.

Compassionate Care

The dictionary defines compassion as sympathetic pity and concern for the sufferings or misfortunes of others; mercy, sympathy, or commiseration. How does this character quality fit into a sarcastic and cynical world? Those who choose to encourage and comfort others will stand in sharp contrast to those who follow the culture's normal "dissing" and cut-down behaviors. Do not allow the world to squeeze you into its mold; instead, be an example of compassionate care toward all.

Philippians 2:1-2

Parenting Point

We begin to teach our children how to be compassionate from the moment they are born. As they experience our compassion toward them, compassion will become a normal pattern for life. Homes that are filled with kind words, sympathetic listening ears, and tender physical care will be a powerful breeding ground for more of that type of compassionate behavior. As our children mature, we can encourage them to show compassion to their brothers and sisters by praying for them and sharing in their times of pain. Emphasize to your children that when one family member is hurting, the whole family hurts. If this isn't true in your family, why isn't it? Evaluate what is missing. Are you intentionally building a family identity where each family member feels interconnected with all other family members? A strong family identity now will build the foundation necessary for strong relationships outside of your home. Take the time necessary to build those strong and compassionate ties in your family.

All Grown Up

In J.M. Barrie's classic work of children's literature, *Peter Pan*, Peter is a boy who never wants to grow up. His idea of a fulfilled life centers on staying a boy and enjoying child-like pursuits. It is Wendy, the main female character in the story, who is forced to make responsible and grown-up decisions. Read today's scripture. The world is full of plenty of immaturity. God's desire for His followers is that we would grow up, in all ways, in order to become more like Christ.

Ephesians 4:15

Parenting Point

Are you trying to raise children or adults? Today, in our child-centered world, the emphasis is on keeping our children immature and self-centered. As Christian parents, in all of our parenting decisions we must keep the end goal of our children's growth as our focus. Obviously, there is no rush to have our children develop adult appetites and habits while they are young, but it is a misunderstanding of childhood to think that our children should engage in all play and no responsibilities until they are older. Young children crave responsibility. They want to be like their older siblings. They want to feel like an important and necessary part of the family. As we assign chores and responsibilities within their abilities, we will help our children to develop self-confidence, self-worth, and self-respect - three very important character qualities. When you assign jobs, make sure that you are challenging your children. Don't make the jobs too easy or unnecessary to the wellbeing of your family. It is good to stretch our children outside of their comfort zones, and knowing that their job is essential within the family will encourage them to perform it with carefulness and diligence. Waiting too long to include our children in the family responsibilities will only serve to make them irresponsible and entitled. Start young! Don't expect perfection. Praise your children heartily for work well done. **Do not** undo and redo their work! If you have a job that must be done perfectly, by all means, do it yourself. As our children embrace more responsibility, they will more easily make the transition from obedient children to responsible adults.

The Week in Review

Take some time to gather as a family and discuss the character qualities that you learned this week. Here are some questions to get the conversation started.

- **List the character qualities we studied this week.**

- **Which character quality was the hardest for you to practice this week?**

- **Did you see a family member consistently practicing one of this week's character qualities? Which family member?**

Use your imagination and add questions of your own. After your time of discussion, spend some time praying together, thanking the Lord and sharing one another's burdens. Pray ahead of time for teachable hearts to incorporate and put into practice the character qualities your family will learn in the upcoming week.

Appropriateness • Respect

Reverent Character

We love God, we worship God, we honor God, and we praise God. But do we reverence God? The dictionary defines reverence this way: a feeling of profound awe, respect, and veneration. This goes much deeper than a casual feeling of closeness and shows itself through respect and awe. While many have lost their reverence toward God and replaced it with a "buddy" relationship, today's verse reminds us that God is awesome and worthy to be greatly feared.

Psalm 89:7

Parenting Point

Just as important as teaching our children that Jesus loves them, is teaching them that God is awesome, awe-inspiring, and worthy of our reverence. Teaching reverence for God begins by teaching respect for all who hold positions of authority over our children. Beginning with their parents and continuing on through pastors, teachers, grandparents, and babysitters, it is important for our children to learn how to show respect through their words and actions. I took any report of my children acting disrespectfully toward authority with great seriousness. Occasionally, my children would share that a friend's family made it a practice to mimic and mock the pastors in the church. How sad. I taught into those moments with my own children, while recognizing that their friends were being trained in how to disrespect authority. Undoubtedly, those parents will be unhappy with the level of respect they receive from their children, but they will be responsible for training their children to respond that way. Children who are habitual in responding with respect will find it easy to respect God. Then, as we share the scriptures describing the awesome attributes of God, their respect will begin to transition to reverence. As they, and we, become more aware of our own sinful condition and the absolutely sinless nature of God, we cannot help but reverence Him. Don't worry about those who would say your family is too serious about God. Obey Him, reverence Him, and focus only on pleasing Him.

Love Never Fails

What an encouragement to know that the love of Christ will never fail us. He will be faithful to perform all of the promises that He has laid out for us in the Bible. People may fail us, dreams may fail us, plans may fail us, but Jesus Christ will never fail us! If you are having trouble embracing Christ's unfailing love, may I encourage you to take a note card and record at least ten of His promises to you? In times of discouragement, refer to the note card to remind you of your unfailing Savior and His unfailing love for you.

I Corinthians 13:8

Parenting Point

Isn't it difficult to watch our children struggle with the disappointment of failed friendships, plans, or expectations? At those times, it is important to sympathize with our children, but it is also a great opportunity to teach them about the unfailing love of God. The Bible is full of references to the God who never leaves or forsakes us. Spend some time with your children helping them to make their own "Bible Promises" notebook. Let each child decorate their own notebook with drawings, stickers, or sayings, then help them to begin to fill the pages with the promises found in Scripture. Perhaps as you are doing daily devotions with your children they can keep their notebooks handy to record new promises that you discover together. These notebooks will become cherished friends as your children refer to them over and over. Encourage your children to share what they have written in their notebooks with their friends who may not know about the God who never fails. Even we, their parents, sometimes fail our children. It is a safeguard and a security for them to know, without a shadow of a doubt, that the God they serve will never fail them.

A Life of Conviction

In 21st century America we often confuse independence with conviction. Christian conviction brings with it strong emotions. When I was a young believer, I was convicted about so much and rightly so, but I was equally sure that everybody else should be convicted about the same issue at the exact same time, and so I sometimes wore out my welcome. Strong convictions are different than strong opinions. The independent spirit is strong on opinions, but short on conviction. Be careful in today's "feelings" driven world to check your opinions at the door. A life of conviction is a life surrendered to the supremacy of God's Word. How's your time in His Word?

I Corinthians 3:1-4

Parenting Point

Are you a convicted parent? It is so important to spend time studying the Word of God and settling the convictions you will uphold in your home and parenting. Without the strength of your convictions, it is easy to be drawn to one different standard or type of parenting after another. This distracted "sheep parenting" is detrimental to our children's spiritual growth. Children, who live their lives unsure of what standard will be the next standard in their home, are children who will lack security and the strength to develop and stand on their own convictions. Choose carefully what you will allow and disallow in your home; then work hard to uphold those convictions consistently. When we demonstrate a life of peer dependence to our children, we have no reason to be surprised when we see them living lives that are peer influenced as well. Together, as a family, build strong boundaries of conviction in your home and then encourage one another to honor and uphold those family convictions.

Adam, the Onlooker

Adam is no different than many of us. As today's Scripture indicates, he stood by and watched Eve make the devastating decision to eat the fruit, and then he joined her in her bad choice by taking the fruit for himself. Adam lacked courage in his character. Courageous Christians step in when they see a friend about to make a catastrophic mistake, and they certainly don't join them in their bad choices. Does someone in your life need you to make the courageous decision to intervene today?

Genesis 3:6

Parenting Point

All of our children, whether they attend public or private school or they are home educated, are indoctrinated with the virtue of "not being a tattletale." Yes, our children need to learn to not run to others in a gossiping and self-righteous way, but there are times that our children need to intervene for a friend by telling an adult what is truly happening. No child wants to be known as a "snitch," but there are actions and activities that they or their friends can become involved in that have life-threatening or life-changing consequences. Talk with your teens about what situations are appropriate or necessary to bring to the attention of an adult. We need to be a safe place where they and their friends can come for counsel and help. If they are afraid that we will over-react or punish them for telling, they will never open up to us. Many teens want to help their friends, but they are simply too young and ill-prepared to offer counsel. Help your children learn to recognize danger signs that mean a friend needs help (i.e. drug use, continual lies, sudden weight loss, etc.). The more openly you communicate with your own teens the more they will see you as a trusted counselor and friend, and the more influence you will have with your children's friends as well. Caring Christian parents have the unique opportunity to influence not only their own children but other needy children as well. What are you doing to take advantage of this opportunity?

Characterized by Insolence

Read today's verse. The word translated "pride" in the King James and New International versions is also translated "insolent" in other versions. What does it mean to be insolent? The dictionary defines insolence as: rude, impertinent, and inclined to take liberties. Sadly, insolence has become the mark of much of the communication in our society. We find ourselves dealing with rudeness and impertinence on a daily basis. In fact, such a manner of speaking is often considered to be funny, or a more intelligent use of language. Only through diligent self-control and an accurate understanding of biblical communication can we avoid the "Insolence Trap." Remember, how you speak is often the only testimony your friends will see. Don't allow insolence to be the characterization of your speech.

Proverbs 13:10

Parenting Point

We are often appalled by the way we hear children speak to their parents and other adults. Rude and impertinent communication is never appropriate and must be recognized and discouraged immediately. Remember, if a form of speaking would be inappropriate for an adult, it is equally inappropriate for children. Too often, we laugh at the "precocious" statements of a young child, while to hear the same comments from a teen would be considered rude and blameworthy. Our children will not outgrow this type of inappropriate speech, and at some point people will no longer consider their impertinent comments as cute but rather as offensive. Suddenly, these "Wise in their own eyes" children will find themselves ostracized and disliked by the same folks who thought they were so funny just a short time before. Don't allow your children to develop this negative character quality. Each time they speak inappropriately, stop them and have them slowly repeat what they just said. Ask them to explain to you what made their statement unacceptable; then, have them replace what they previously stated with an appropriate and uplifting comment. Repeated practice will help our children to put-off insolence and put-on God-honoring speech.

Trust

A Character of Casting

When you are overwhelmed with circumstances or reeling from one problem or another, where do you take your troubles? Read today's verse. Not only are we told to cast our many cares on Jesus, but also, we are reminded why we may do so. We can cast our cares on Him because He cares for us! We are not bothering or inconveniencing the Lord when we come to Him with our problems. We are simply obeying His wishes, and He is delighted to carry our load because of His deep and abiding love for us!

I Peter 5:7

Parenting Point

When our children are young, they need the absolute security of knowing that they can run to us with their problems, and we will be available to help them. Knowing that they do not have to carry their burdens alone is a great relief for our children; however, as they mature, it is important to teach them how to run to Jesus with their cares and concerns. Beginning when my children were elementary age, when they came to me with a problem I tried to first point them to the Lord. Although it was tempting to simply solve their dilemma, I would instead ask them to join me in taking their question or problem before the Lord. After praying, I would ask them what they thought God would have them do to solve the problem. Sometimes, simply helping them think through the process by asking good questions was the only help they needed. At other times, I would help them look in Scripture to see what the Word of God had to say concerning their issue. They always knew that I was aware and involved in the process, but I wanted them to realize that God was much more competent than I at solving their problems. I also tried to model, by my example, what it looked like to hand over sticky situations to the Lord. When I was facing a decision or dealing with a problem, I would often ask the children to join me in praying and asking for wisdom. As they saw me stop what I was doing in order to seek the Lord's direction, they learned to go to God first, without hesitation and without gathering lots of opinions. We can't always be there to help our children, but God is always there, and He

The Week in Review

Take some time to gather as a family and discuss the character qualities that you learned this week. Here are some questions to get the conversation started.

- List the character qualities we studied this week.

- Which character quality was the hardest for you to practice this week?

- Did you see a family member consistently practicing one of this week's character qualities? Which family member?

Use your imagination and add questions of your own. After your time of discussion, spend some time praying together, thanking the Lord and sharing one another's burdens. Pray ahead of time for teachable hearts to incorporate and put into practice the character qualities your family will learn in the upcoming week.

The Compassion Put-On

When you hear the expression "put-on," does it elicit a positive or negative response in your heart? As today's Scripture instructs us, there are character qualities that must be "put-on," and compassion is one of those qualities. It is easy to be compassionate toward our friends and family, but Christians must be prepared to show compassion to all without partiality. Ask the Lord to give you eyes of compassion to see the needs of others.

Colossians 3:12-14

Parenting Point

Children who are normally kind and compassionate at home often neglect to practice that same level of compassion outside the security of their family sanctuary. As parents, we must diligently train our children to not only see the needs of others but to also learn how to effectively and compassionately meet the needs of others. Take time to research a need that your family could compassionately fill. Some ideas would be: stocking the freezer with meals for a single working mom, shoveling snow for elderly neighbors, writing encouraging cards to shut-ins, etc. The opportunities are endless. Give your children some ideas to get them started. Then, spend time together brainstorming how you will meet the chosen need. After planning, make sure to actually do the hard work necessary to complete your family mission. As your children learn to extend compassion outside their home but still within the safety of the family, they will be building the spiritual muscle necessary to continue a commitment to living a life of compassionate acts on their own.

Overflowing or Stingy

To be thankful is to express gratitude toward someone or something. It is to be grateful or appreciative. Being thankful costs us nothing, and yet on a daily basis we too often hold on stingily to the words or actions of thankfulness. As forgiven believers, our thankful attitudes should overflow and set us apart as a grateful people. How grateful are you? Are you characterized by thankful, appreciative gratitude toward others and God? Or are you discontent, impatient and envious of others and God? Read Hebrews 12:28 and ask yourself what you offer God when you are thankful.

Hebrews 12:28

Parenting Point

Are your children thankful? Often, we are careful to ensure that our children express gratitude and thankfulness to those outside our homes, but are we as careful within our home and family? On a daily basis our children have many opportunities to express gratitude. Do not miss those opportunities to train your children to verbally express thankfulness to you as well as to their siblings. The busyness of our days can oftentimes tempt us to overlook a lack of thankfulness from our children, but resist the temptation to ignore this character lack. What you train today in your home will become the ingrained habits that your children carry into adulthood.

Humility • Encouragement

Honor

To honor someone is to afford them great respect and admiration; to recognize someone publicly or to elevate their status, usually by giving them a title or an award. As Christians, we are to show honor to others and to purposefully humble ourselves. Too often, the converse is true in our lives; we seek honor for ourselves and neglect to extend the honor to those whom honor is due. When we honor others we have the opportunity to encourage and build them up. What a wonderful opportunity!

I Peter 2:17

Parenting Point

Honor doesn't cost us anything except our pride. We should be extravagant with the honor we show to others, and we should encourage our children to do the same. Our children can show us honor through their words, their actions, and their obedience. Children, who are unwilling to honor their parents, will become young adults who are unwilling to show honor to their God. Do not allow your children to dishonor you. Dads, listen to how your children speak to their mother. Do their words show honor or contempt? Don't be afraid to step up and be your wife's defender; your children will appreciate your timely lesson when they are older. How can we, as parents, show honor to our children? One easy way is through the use of a "You did great plate!" Use the plate to honor a child who has shown great effort in character or in overcoming a difficult task. Make it an occasion and your children will strive to please you with their efforts. It's easy to award the "You did great plate" when our children have some recognizable academic or athletic success; however, the real value of the "You did great plate!" is found in using the plate to reward actions of Christ-like character. When a child shows compassion, or mercy, or kindness, encourage more of that great character by the public bestowing of the "You did great plate." Mom and Dad, look for opportunities to reward one another with the "You did great plate!" as well. Your kids will love to cheer for your successes and you'll go far in building and strengthening your family identity.

Patience of Spirit

G eorge Savile, an English statesman, writer, and politician once said, *"A man who is a master of patience is master of everything else."* True words indeed! Patience is a spiritual condition. If our spirit is well fed by the Word of God, we tend to be more patient (in mastery of) with the minor and major frustrations that life presents. By contrast, when our spirits are not well fed, we tend to grow anxious, impatient, and even judgmental of people and circumstances. Haughtiness is the expression used in Ecclesiastes 7:8 to describe those who are impatient. Read the following verses and note the side effects of impatience.

Ecclesiastes 7:8-10

Parenting Point

What steps are you taking to prepare yourself to avoid impatience and irritability? Late nights, irregular schedules, and a lack of time in the Word of God can cause us to respond impatiently toward those who deserve it the least. What are you encouraging your children to do to avoid frustration and impatience? When you see your children headed down the road to frustration and a lack of patience, step in and help them to avoid the danger that lies ahead of them. Rather than punishing them AFTER they step over the line, encourage them to sit quietly for a few moments and consider the road they are choosing. Often, these few moments of reflection can ward off trouble and unpleasant consequences and redirect our children's attitudes and behavior. Consider the context of your days. Are you spending too much time in the car? Children need plentiful times of large muscle activity to maintain a healthy attitude. Are you allowing your children to stay up too late? Children need much more sleep than we adults; make sure they have an appropriate and consistent bedtime. Are you permitting your children to spend unlimited amounts of time with friends and those outside your immediate family? Differing standards and an overabundance of free time will cause our children to feel unstable and insecure. Help your children to succeed by helping to direct their environment. The result will be peaceful, pleasant, and teachable young people.

Inclusive Integrity

A few years ago Megan and I went to one of those all-inclusive resorts in the Caribbean. For one price, everything you would or could ever possibly want was covered for the week. When it comes to character, we ought to be like an all-inclusive resort. God wants our Christian character to have integrity. Look at the following Scripture and pay close attention to the use of the word ALL. Just like the all-inclusive resort, a character healthy believer holds nothing back when it comes to character excellence. He or she can be counted on to be honest, faithful, trustworthy, dependable, humble, etc. How inclusive is your moral character? Is your character more like an all-inclusive resort or an a la carte buffet?

1 Chronicles 29:17

Parenting Point

When it comes to character, teach your children to put it ALL together. Kindness is not a means to an end, for example, when you want something. Likewise, trust is something that is earned ALL of the time.. Too often, we wrongly approach character as a means to an end, rather than a morally and God pleasing end in itself! Lovingly, yet firmly, show your children how character is a complete package. Do not allow them to neglect areas of character because of their personality, physical limitations, or personal likes and dislikes. Although any of these areas of difficulty may make raising the standard of character more challenging, none of them are an excuse for a lower standard of character. Encourage your children that any challenge they meet is already well known by God, and He will enable them to rise to and overcome those challenges. The challenges that God allows to enter our lives are perfectly formed to cause the greatest growth and maturity in our lives. As appropriate, share some of the challenges you face when it comes to consistently elevating character in your own life. Share with your children the positive and pro-active changes you have made to ensure that you are elevating character and not allowing yourself to skimp in the challenging areas. When you see your children making an effort to show character in the areas they find the most challenging, praise them and let them know that you notice their good effort. Praise will bring about more positive character, so be generous with your uplifting words.

Initiative

Initiative is defined as the quality of possessing and steadfastly adhering to high moral principles or professional standards. Initiative is the prerequisite character quality necessary in the life of anyone who would aspire to be a true leader. Leaders don't wait to be called upon. Rather, leaders are busy looking for jobs to be done, goals to be accomplished, and people to encourage and lead.

Proverbs 6:6-8

Parenting Point

I don't believe that there is a parent alive who doesn't want their children to show initiative. In fact, in our home, the lack of initiative I see in my children is the thing that makes me the most frustrated! We can help our children to grow in the area of initiative, or we can prevent their growth, even as we think we are helping them. What do I mean? When we do too much for our children, picking up after them, remembering their homework for them, solving their every problem, we are in fact, hindering our children from becoming skilled in the character quality of initiative. Instead, teach your children to faithfully fulfill what is required of them and then to look for what else could be done. I know it is tempting to "help" them out, but don't rob them of the moral training opportunity of a forgotten backpack or missed bus. It is through these hardships that our children will learn to take responsibility for their own lives, and they can then become the leaders our world so desperately needs. Yes, it can all begin with a chore well done, a bed well made, or a consistently used manner. God doesn't despise small beginnings and neither should we! You can rest assured that George Washington's mom didn't remind him to take his musket to Valley Forge!

The Week in Review

Take some time to gather as a family and discuss the character qualities that you learned this week. Here are some questions to get the conversation started.

- **List the character qualities we studied this week.**

- **Which character quality was the hardest for you to practice this week?**

- **Did you see a family member consistently practicing one of this week's character qualities? Which family member?**

Use your imagination and add questions of your own. After your time of discussion, spend some time praying together, thanking the Lord and sharing one another's burdens. Pray ahead of time for teachable hearts to incorporate and put into practice the character qualities your family will learn in the upcoming week.

Diligence • Perseverance • Focused

Keeping in Focus

H ave you ever considered the ability to remain focused as a character quality? The diligence to remain focused on our many tasks, responsibilities, and relationships is a key component of the character quality of self-control. In a society that seems to expect a lack of focus and finds excuses for those who are constantly distracted, people who have trained themselves to be self-controlled and to stay focused on the task at hand will stand out from the crowd. Although focus is harder for some than others, all can work diligently to be more self-controlled. If you struggle with staying focused, begin today to incorporate habits of self-control that will translate into a more focused and productive lifestyle.

Proverbs 25:28

Parenting Point

Begin at the earliest age to teach your children the important character quality of "focus." The best way to begin the process of helping our children learn how to be more focused is by considering our home environment. Too many toys or clutter is distracting and will encourage our children to be less focused and less self-controlled. Ask your children to help you declutter your home by gathering up unnecessary possessions and donating them to someone less fortunate. Besides helping them to make their environment "focus-friendly," you will be teaching them important lessons about generosity and giving. Tomorrow we will look at more tools to help our children learn to stay focused.

Appropriateness • Encouragement

The Character of a Cannibal

Read today's verse. What a graphic picture of what we do to one another when our critical words are out of control. What began as a single critical comment can soon become slander, gossip, and all out backbiting. As today's scripture reminds us, when we bite and devour one another, we run the risk of being consumed by one another. As Christians waste time criticizing one another, both in the church and in the world, we draw attention to our sinfulness and we detract from the beauty of Christ. Is it any wonder that the unsaved world has no desire to be like us?

Galatians 5:15

Parenting Point

Do your children hungrily devour one another with their words? As parents we must be diligently observant of the direction of our children's communication with one another. It is wonderful to hear our children laughing and joking with one another; however, when joking gives way to critical comments and sarcastic put-downs, it is time to step in and give some clear instruction. It is important to teach our children the importance of kind speech. Role-playing various communication scenarios with them can help them practice how to build one another up with their words rather than using their words as weapons. Sarcasm and sarcastic jokes have no place in the home. The word sarcasm literally means "to tear flesh," and that is exactly what we do when we allow this form of communication as an acceptable alternative in our homes. It is easy to see the discouragement and hurt on our children's faces when they have been torn down by sarcasm. Mom and Dad, make sure that you are not the initiators of sarcastic and hurtful speech in your home! Your example is the strongest model of training for your children, so be careful to exhibit kind, encouraging, biblical communication.

Responsibility in Action

Responsibility can be broken into three basic categories: Budding Responsibilities, Primary Responsibilities, and Secondary Responsibilities. In the simplest terms, budding responsibilities are focused on self, primary responsibilities are focused on others within the security of the home environment, and secondary responsibilities are oriented outside the home and with the highest level of ownership. Where are you on the responsibility continuum? As adults, it would seem obvious that we should all be well-established in the realm of secondary responsibilities. Sadly, often this is not the case. A quick flip through the daily regime of reality shows will reveal adults who are unable to fulfill secondary responsibilities, neglectful of their primary responsibilities, and still dependent on others to help them or remind them to fulfill their simplest budding responsibilities. A sad state indeed!

Luke 12:48

Parenting Point

Parents, unless you want your children to be living with you and depending upon you completely well into their 30's and 40's, it is absolutely imperative to teach them to take ownership of the character quality of responsibility! The transition from obedience to responsibility needs to be at the forefront of your teaching; however, to make the transition from obedience to responsibility, your children must first be *characterized* by obedience to your directions. How are they doing? Do your children obey immediately? Do they obey with complete fulfillment of what you are requiring? Do they obey with a joyful spirit? If you can't answer yes to these questions, now is the time to work on training your children in obedience, so that soon, you can begin the transition to teaching your children to take on responsibility. Spend the next week to ten days focusing on your children's level of obedience and taking the necessary steps to deal with disobedience. If you are diligent and consistent, soon you will see great fruit in your home. Your children, once characterized by obedience, will be eager to begin to take on their character-building, budding responsibilities.

Gentleness

A Brawler or a Peacemaker

How would your friends characterize your behavior? Are you known for stirring up brawls, or does your calm demeanor promote peace? Today's verse makes it clear that those who quarrel easily are nothing more than fools. There is no dishonor in avoiding strife; in fact, to do so is honorable. Ask a trusted friend to share their opinion of your behavior and, if necessary, take steps to put-off brawling and put-on peace.

Proverbs 20:3

Parenting Point

I think we all know children who are spring-loaded to brawl. They are the children that seem to have a chip on their shoulder, and they are quick to take offense. Perhaps one of those children lives in your home. How do we help those children put-off a brawling attitude? Our first line of defense is to take our children to Scripture and show them what God has to say about hot-tempered brawlers. Next, encourage them to memorize Scripture about choosing to be peaceful instead of angry. Boys seem to be more prone to get into physical brawls quickly, but their gender is not an excuse for inappropriate anger. Although girls may not get into a physical brawl, there are young ladies who are quick to anger; they do their fighting with their tongues. Brawling anger is inappropriate regardless of the age, sex, or personality of a child. Do not allow a brawler to continue down the road of strife. Persistently and consistently rebuke, correct, and punish as necessary. Break the habit of brawling while they are young, and they will not be characterized as a brawler when they reach adulthood.

Faithfulness as the Foundation

When you consider what it means to be faithful to God, what thoughts come to mind? Too often, we consider our faithfulness as a list of required to-do's that must be checked off in order for us to be successfully faithful. Although Bible reading, prayer, fellowship, service, and more are all important aspects of our Christian life, they, by themselves, are not a clear indication of our faithfulness. Faithfulness to God, much like faithfulness in marriage, is all about relationship. As we daily draw near to God and learn to walk in the Spirit, all of the above activities will then flow naturally from a faithful and heart-full relationship with the Lord. It's less about doing and all about "being." God, Himself, is faithful, and as we walk faithfully with Him, we'll overflow with the actions of a faithful heart.

Psalm 101:6

Parenting Point

Do you have children that are struggling to obey, struggling to complete their chores, or struggling to show respect? Perhaps the struggle is coming because of a lack of close relationship. Yes, our children need to obey our clear and unambiguous instruction, but we are responsible to make that instruction palatable to them. How do we do that? We make our instructions easy to follow by making sure that our relationship with each child is close, intimate, and as much as possible, without strife. When our children know that they are loved and that we are purposefully seeking to build and strengthen our relationship with them, they will want to obey and please us. When the basis of our relationship is disinterest, strife, or harsh words towards one another, our children will balk at obedience, and find it difficult to respect and honor us. If you are struggling with one child in particular, take some time to evaluate your relationship with that child. Think about what makes them feel loved and spend some time investing in that love relationship. For one of my children, it is important to share encouraging words. When all of my communication with her has been directive or corrective, she begins to wilt. Often, just a simple note of encouragement, sharing the positives I see in her life, is all that is needed to get her back on the right track. You know your children better than anyone else. Use that knowledge to build relationship and to train and guide them out of love. When we have won our children's hearts, obedience and honor will be the natural outflow of that love relationship.

Compassionate Character

The dictionary defines compassion this way: a feeling of deep sympathy and sorrow for another who is stricken by misfortune, accompanied by a strong desire to alleviate the suffering. Today's verses remind us that this type of compassionate heart is to be "put-on" by followers of Christ. The implication is clear, we don't naturally have compassionate hearts, but as we strive to be like Jesus, we can put on a heart like His. What emotion does the suffering of others invoke in your heart? Seek the Lord in prayer. Ask Him to show you your heart condition. If there is a lack of compassion, pray for the courage to compassionately care for others.

Colossians 3:12-14

Parenting Point

Although it is hard work, teaching our children to be compassionate toward others is one of the most rewarding tasks of parenting. As we encourage our children to observe and respond to needs, we will grow to be more compassionate ourselves. Teaching compassion, like most other character qualities, begins at home. When one child or parent is suffering, help your other children learn to minister compassionately. If you have a sick child, ask your other children to think of things they could do to help the sick child to be more comfortable. Perhaps they could play quiet games together, or take the sick child a cold drink, or even straighten the bedroom so that the sick child is more comfortable. Once your children have practiced being compassionate at home, begin to help them see needy people outside the home. As they notice needs around them, be available to assist them in meeting those needs. Don't be surprised if your children push you outside of your own comfort zone. My youngest son noticed an extremely disheveled and dirty man standing outside of the grocery store several times while we were shopping. After the third time of seeing the man, Taylor asked me if he could walk over and give the man his allowance money. My first thought was to just give the man some money myself, but Taylor was eager to serve. When he handed the man his hard-earned money, the man was so thankful and told Taylor that he was a good boy. Taylor just glowed with happiness! We spent some time praying for the man, and I told Taylor how proud God was of his servant heart. As our families pray for eyes to see the needs around us, we will find more and more opportunities to extend Christian compassion.

The Week in Review

Take some time to gather as a family and discuss the character qualities that you learned this week. Here are some questions to get the conversation started.

- **List the character qualities we studied this week.**
- **Which character quality was the hardest for you to practice this week?**
- **Did you see a family member consistently practicing one of this week's character qualities? Which family member?**

Use your imagination and add questions of your own. After your time of discussion, spend some time praying together, thanking the Lord and sharing one another's burdens. Pray ahead of time for teachable hearts to incorporate and put into practice the character qualities your family will learn in the upcoming week.

Sanctification

D o you think of sanctification as a character quality? Really, it is an accumulation of many character qualities working together to change the believer into the likeness of Christ. Sanctification involves self-control. Sanctification involves purity. Sanctification involves rejecting old paradigms and embracing new, Christ-like paradigms. Sanctification isn't like magic. We aren't zapped with it, and suddenly we're new. No, sanctification is the process of faithful obedience and-self sacrifice carried out over time to produce change in a believer's life.

Ephesians 4:22-24

Parenting Point

Take some time to read today's Scripture as a family. Discuss with your children what it means to "lay aside the old life." Often, when our children are confronted with an area of sin in their lives, their first response is to "do" something different in order to please God or Mom and Dad. Simply doing something different is not the essence of laying aside. Our children need to understand that true change in their lives will only come from a mind that is renewed by the Holy Spirit and the Word of God. Anyone can "put on" a change for a short time, it is the renewed mind that is sanctified and conformed to the image of Christ. Help your children understand the difference between a renewed mind and the self-atonement that comes from a "to do" list of more desirable behaviors. Finally, as a family, discuss the proactive steps you can take to daily renew your minds. For example, practices such as family devotions, personal times of prayer and study, and service to others will build a foundation of biblical living that will provide a positive environment for spiritual change.

Compassion • Others-Oriented

Does Your Heart Need to be Tenderized?

Does being tenderhearted seem like a weak or vulnerable character quality? Consider this definition of tenderhearted: Easily moved by another's distress, compassionate. What a wonderful character quality for a Christian to possess! In a world that is focused on self-distress and self-compassion, a Christian intent on loving others in a tenderhearted manner will have a tremendous testimony for Christ. While others worry about themselves, the tenderhearted Christian can extend Christ-like compassion to those in need. All it takes is an others-orientation and a deliberate decision to not focus on self.

Ephesians 4:32

Parenting Point

Teaching our children to be tenderhearted is one of the most joyous teaching experiences of a Christian parent! From the earliest days, as you teach your little ones to stop and pray for siblings, friends, and strangers, you will be teaching them to notice and care for the distresses of others. One of our children, with no prior instruction from us, would enter the nursery and stop to lay her hand on her little crying friends, and then she would pray for them to be happy in the nursery. Her prayers weren't deep and theological, but they came from a tender heart. Be alert to recognize children who show great compassion to their friends outside your home, while exhibiting harsh or uncaring attitudes toward the members of your family. Such behavior is not becoming in a Christian family. Remind your children that God chose them to be brothers and sisters. We often told our children that they would never be kinder husbands or wives than they were brothers and sisters. Help your children find opportunities to minister in practical and helpful ways to others, and you will be well on the way to developing a household of tender hearts.

Hearty and Wholehearted

When I read today's verse, my mind tells me to just do "a really good job." Upon closer reflection, however, this word means so much more. Hearty is a synonym for being wholehearted, and both words are defined as: expressed unrestrainedly. I don't know about you, but when it comes to relationships with my husband and children, I don't want them to just do a "good job." I want them to love me wholeheartedly and unrestrainedly. As well, I want their actions of love to be shown in a wholehearted not just "good enough" manner. So, the question becomes this: Do you serve the Lord with your whole heart because of your deep love for Him, or does working heartily look like a good effort but not necessarily giving it your all? Take time today to evaluate yourself and ask the Lord to reveal the intent of your heart in respect to your work ethic.

Colossians 3:23

Parenting Point

Although sometimes it makes our life easier to simply allow our children to do their work with a "check in the box" or "half-done is good enough" attitude, we are doing them a disservice when we allow this type of work ethic to become their characterization. We must continually teach and encourage our children to do their work with a hearty and wholehearted attitude. Whether it is a job or assignment that they enjoy or one they just need to get done, teaching them to approach everything with unrestrained heartiness will help them to build a strong character of wholeheartedness. When they can incorporate the truth that no matter what they are doing, their efforts are to be focused on pleasing the Lord, they will be able to embrace hard and unpleasant jobs with the same joy they feel when beginning exciting jobs and opportunities. Wholeheartedness in everything we do builds contentment and thankfulness, regardless of our circumstances. Lives characterized by contentment and thankfulness provide a compelling testimony to a watching world. Don't be afraid to send children back to redo a poorly or sloppily completed job. The time you spend training them now will pay off in huge character dividends in the future!

Encouragement

To encourage means to hearten or embolden. It means to fill another with courage or strength of purpose. To encourage someone means to raise their confidence, giving them hope and promise. Whom have you encouraged recently? Would your circle of friends and relatives consider you a source of strength and courage? What role do your words play in emboldening others to confident action and hope in Christ? Simply stated, do your words build others up or tear others down? Remember, God is aching for His children to become encouragers of each other. Christians especially need to fill each other with courage. Just think what the world would look like if our words were always aimed at building up, instead of tearing down.

Ephesians 4:29

Parenting Point

All of our children receive encouragement through different means. For one child a word of praise will infuse them with courage, while for another child a loving hug or a hot cup of cocoa and a prayer will fill the encouragement need. It is easy to try to encourage our children in a "one size fits all" manner but resist the temptation to take the easy road. Spend time studying your children, each with their unique personalities and temperaments, and you will be well-equipped to provide them with the encouragement they need to face whatever situations come their way.

Diligence • Perseverance

Decision Depot

A ccording to 2 Peter 1:5, diligence is the key to success inside the doors of the Decision Depot. When heart, mind, and moral conscience meet, diligence is required to consistently elevate virtues above feelings. If we don't exercise due diligence to our Christian walk, we risk being ruled by our emotions, which Jeremiah 17:9 reminds us are deceitful, desperate, sick, and impossible to understand. So let's be diligent... diligent Bible readers, diligent church attendees, diligent servants, and diligent slaves of our Lord Jesus Christ.

2 Peter 1:5-8

Parenting Point

In what areas do you lack diligence? Simple things like dirty dishes left over night in the sink communicate a subtle message about diligence. How many projects have you started and never finished? Unfinished work communicates a poor message to your children regarding the importance of diligence. Sit down today, as a family, and have each person pick a project that they plan to complete by the end of the week. Mom and Dad, this includes you! At the end of the week throw a diligence dessert party and celebrate your accomplishments, remembering to thank God in the process. Do it all again next week, and pretty soon diligence will be part of your family's moral fabric.

Appropriateness • Diligence • Faithfulness

A Well-Earned Rest

Do you enjoy a day off? I know that I certainly do! However, what is our attitude toward our days off, or perhaps more importantly, what is our attitude toward our work? We live in a culture that seems to be teetering on the edge of two extremes. One extreme lives for the weekend, seeing work as a hindrance to their real life. The other extreme are the folks we label as "workaholics," those people who find their greatest fulfillment in completing more and more and more work. I believe God wants us to land somewhere in the middle. Today's scripture makes it clear that work is commanded by God, however, so is rest. Both are the plan and gift of our loving God and both are simply avenues to bring glory to Him.

Exodus 23:12

Parenting Point

When it comes to teaching our children how to be diligent workers, often we parents are their biggest stumbling block. It is always easier, quicker, and more efficient to do the necessary work ourselves, but when we don't allow our children to learn how to work, we are robbing them of the important character quality of a consistent work ethic. Children who have never been trained to work hard will become adults who feel as though they should be taken care of by others. Teach your children how to complete the tasks necessary to keep your home running smoothly. Encourage them that fun activities will be even more enjoyable against the backdrop of jobs well done. Set attainable work goals and standards for your children and then monitor their progress. As you see them developing faithfulness in what has been required, reward them with increased responsibilities and freedoms. Children who feel like they are a necessary part of the family's wellbeing will have a strong and secure family identity.

The Week in Review

Take some time to gather as a family and discuss the character qualities that you learned this week. Here are some questions to get the conversation started.

- List the character qualities we studied this week.

- Which character quality was the hardest for you to practice this week?

- Did you see a family member consistently practicing one of this week's character qualities? Which family member?

Use your imagination and add questions of your own. After your time of discussion, spend some time praying together, thanking the Lord and sharing one another's burdens. Pray ahead of time for teachable hearts to incorporate and put into practice the character qualities your family will learn in the upcoming week.

Others-Oriented

Concerned Christians

Are you a concerned Christian? I'm not referring to a busybody or someone who entangles themselves in the affairs of others, but a Christian who is concerned for the *welfare* of others. We live in a world that promotes the attitude of "whatever." This attitude stands in stark juxtaposition to the care and concern that Christians should show for other people's needs, possessions, problems, and most importantly, salvation. A "whatever" attitude may be "cool," but it is aloof. Our Lord was winsome and cared deeply for each and every person He met. True concern for the needs of others will often earn us the right to share the good news about our Lord.

Luke 10:25-37

Parenting Point

Teaching our children to be concerned for others is really just teaching them to be others-oriented. Take some time today to read the story of the Good Samaritan. Ask your children to describe the Samaritan's actions and attitudes as he ministered to the injured man. Now, ask them how they can show concern for others with the same actions and attitudes. Help them to develop practical ways to show their concern for others. Don't allow them to simply settle for the correct "Sunday School answer." Encourage them to learn to show concern at home by caring for their brothers and sisters. As you see them exhibit good actions and attitudes of concern, take the time to praise and encourage your children. When your children are characterized by showing concern for the other members of their family, begin to reach out to those outside of the family. Ministering together will provide your children with opportunities to grow and mature while still working within the security of their family unit.

Encouragement

True encouragement goes well beyond mere words. It is easy to share kind words that flatter, but the heart of encouragement is bound up in serving others. A *gossip* is willing to say something behind your back that they will not say to your face. A *flatterer* will say something to your face that they are unwilling to say behind your back. But an *encourager* will say to your face what they are willingly saying behind your back. Think about it. Words can be hollow but actions speak loudly. Go back and read Ephesians 4:29-32 and ask yourself the hard question: Which am I a gossip, flatterer, or encourager?

Ephesians 4:29-32

Parenting Point

What are you doing to cultivate an environment of encouragement in your home? It is not enough to simply correct our children when they speak words of discouragement or words that tear down one another. Rather, we must actively teach and train our children to use words that build up and encourage each other. Help your children to recognize the times that they could use their words to build up and instill courage into their sibling's lives. Mom and Dad, make sure that you are making the most of every opportunity to dispense encouraging words as well. Your positive example will speak volumes to your children and will become the building block for a home overflowing with encouraging words!

Be Careful What You Say

In the same way that we can build a reputation for being kind and gentle, we can build a reputation for being a gossip or slanderer. Having a character that is defined by gossip will estrange us and alienate us from our friends. Most people understand that if we gossip about others, we will be just as likely to gossip about them. Guard your reputation and testimony by refusing to fall into the gossip trap.

Titus 3.2:

Parenting Point

There is so much written in the Bible about the deadly effects of gossip and slander. Take some time today to talk as a family about this issue. If you have older children, teach them how to use a concordance and have them list all of the verses they can find concerning gossip. Ask them to define gossip and explain what it looks like within a family. Help your children to understand that tattling on one another is nothing more than gossip in its simplest form. If your family has been struggling with tattle-tales, walk your children through the process of seeking one another's forgiveness. Be careful that you aren't encouraging your children to build the habit of gossiping by allowing them to run to you with stories about one another. Define for your children what is appropriate and necessary to report (I.e., fire, imminent injury, etc.) and what shouldn't be tattled. We taught our children to confront the erring sibling and encourage them to tell on themselves. If that wasn't effective, we told the children to offer to come with the erring sibling to us. Finally, if the sibling just wouldn't repent, we gave the children permission to come tell us that "_____, has something they don't want to tell you." Doing it this way took away the joy of sharing those nasty little tidbits, and we saw the tattling drop off dramatically. We've all been wounded by gossip. Let's be careful not to train our children to be wounding gossips themselves.

Irresponsible Stewardship

Stewardship is defined as the careful and responsible management of something entrusted to one's care; however, for the Christian, our most important area of stewardship is the stewardship we exercise over our testimony and the reputation of our Lord Jesus Christ. Poor stewardship of our testimony can take our great God and make Him look less great. To many, we are the only pictures of Christ they will ever see, so our testimony needs to be a clear and accurate reflection of our great God. In fact, careful stewardship of our testimony should make us so transparent that people look through us and only see Christ. Don't squander your most precious possession: your testimony.

Luke 16:1-2

Parenting Point

Do your children know and can they articulate their personal testimony of faith in Jesus Christ? For many children raised in Christian homes, they came to know Christ as their personal Savior while they were still young and the details may become dim in their memory. To help your children, we would encourage you to take a couple of very practical steps. First, record all of the events surrounding your child's conversion. For example: Where were they? What prompted their decision? What did they pray? Whom did they tell? Secondly, we made a "Birth Certificate" for each of our children and placed it in a new Bible purchased at the time of their decision for Christ. The Birth Certificate was a simple document stating when and where they committed themselves to Christ and included several scriptures reminding them of God's permanent commitment to them (i.e., I John 5:13, John 20:31, and Galatians 2:20). Both of us would sign the Birth Certificate as witnesses to their new commitment. When our children were older and faced times of doubt, looking back at the certificate was a reassuring reminder of the decision they had made to surrender their hearts to Christ. As well, I would often rehearse the details of their conversion, especially on their spiritual birthday each year. Not always, but often, we celebrated their spiritual birthday with a cake and candles, just like we celebrated their natural birthday. Teach your children how important their testimony is and how carefully they must guard that testimony. Also, make sure to share your own testimony with them and let them know how your testimony has been a protection in your life and a tool to lead others to Christ.

Ignoring the Truth

As Christians, we have some "nice" words to define our disobedience. We speak of stumbling or backsliding, or we pray about "getting around to" obedience. Today's Scripture gives us God's definition for disobedience. As the Scripture states, "If we know what is right, and we choose not to do what is right, we are sinning." If we want to have the moral authority to teach others how to live the Christian life, we cannot be characterized as having a disregard for the clearly revealed truths of God. Spend some time today asking God to reveal any areas of disobedience you have allowed to remain in your life and make a concrete plan to change those areas.

James 4:17

Parenting Point

Let us encourage you to call sin, sin. Too often, as merciful parents, we want to candy coat the small and large disobediences in our children's lives. We are doing them no favors when we give in to this impulse. Rather than protecting them, we are helping them to build a hardened heart. The Word of God defines sin in our lives, and we must help our children recognize that their ungodly choices and acts of disobedience are sin. Once they can recognize that they sin and, therefore, are sinners, they will easily understand their need for a Savior to forgive them for that sin. Don't let a momentary desire to be merciful undermine the long-term and eternal goal of salvation for your children. At the same time, teach your children how to take their sins to the Lord in order to seek forgiveness and receive cleansing from their sins, as seen in I John 1:9.

Practicing Preference

While serving others and encouraging others are actions that we can "do," preferring others is an inward attitude that cuts deeply at the roots of our own self-centeredness. Practicing preference as a family will build strong character and an environment of others-orientation in your home. Children will most easily learn to practice preferring others if they see that attitude of preference in their parent's lives. Who can you prefer, today?

Philippians 2:5-7

Parenting Point

Teaching our children to prefer others may be one of our hardest tasks, as parents. When we prefer others, we willingly give up something that belongs to us or that we have a right to possess. Preferring requires us to make a sacrifice of our time, possessions, and sometimes, relationships. Take time today to teach your children the importance of preferring others. Next, have each family member share some way that they could show preference to another family member. Some examples of preferring could be: giving up the front seat for a sibling, including a younger sibling when friends are visiting, or taking time to play a game when you would rather sit and read a book. Each family's preferences will be different because each family considers certain "rights" as more important than others. After sharing your ideas, spend time praying for one another and then commit to preferring one another with your actions. Praise your children when you observe them preferring one another. The more you praise their acts of preference, the more preference you will see! Preferring one another teaches us to hold on to everything loosely. Children who learn this important character quality will be free to serve God, whenever and however He calls.

The Week in Review

Take some time to gather as a family and discuss the character qualities that you learned this week. Here are some questions to get the conversation started.

- **List the character qualities we studied this week.**

- **Which character quality was the hardest for you to practice this week?**

- **Did you see a family member consistently practicing one of this week's character qualities? Which family member?**

Use your imagination and add questions of your own. After your time of discussion, spend some time praying together, thanking the Lord and sharing one another's burdens. Pray ahead of time for teachable hearts to incorporate and put into practice the character qualities your family will learn in the upcoming week.

Confidence

K nowledge dispels fear. Oppressed people throughout history were held captive by ignorance that fed their fears. God wants us to be confident (free) in Christ. Where other religions seek to contain followers via uncertainty and doubt, Christians are told that they can know with certainty that they are bound for Heaven, according to 1 John 5:11-14. Verse 13 reminds us, with confidence, that those who have surrendered to the Son have eternal life. Do you know with certainty where you will spend eternity? Christian confidence is not arrogance, Christian confidence is freedom... freedom from fear.

1 John 5:11-14

Parenting Point

Read 1 John 5:11-14 to your children today. Ask them if they know where they will spend eternity. Based upon their answer, help them to build confidence in God's promise to them in 1 John 5, or help them to understand their need to surrender to Jesus according to the same verses. Throughout their childhoods, our children had times of doubt regarding their salvation. Whether it was because of sinful choices they were making or simply the fear that perhaps they hadn't "done it right," it was important for us to address their fears with tenderness and compassion. As your children come to you with their fears and doubts, take the time to redirect them to God's Word and allow the scripture to remind and comfort them. Never belittle their fears! For each of our children, we took the time to make a "Birth Certificate" to place in their Bible when they trusted Christ for salvation. On that birth certificate we included the date of their conversion, a short recitation of the events leading up to their salvation, and some key verses to remind them of the permanence of their salvation. When doubts assailed, we always took the children back to that birth certificate and rehearsed with them, once again, how God had drawn them to Himself.

Compassion

The dictionary defines compassion as sympathy for the sufferings of others, which often includes the desire to help. True compassion goes well beyond a sense of pity. It is better thought of as a verb than a noun. True compassion results in action, not just sympathy. Simply feeling badly for a person is not compassion; rather, doing something about their plight is compassionate. What are you doing this week that will demonstrate true, actionable, make-a-difference compassion in the life of another? Study the following Scripture. Make a list of other character traits that accompany compassion.

Colossians 3:12

Parenting Point

Although our heart's desire may be to show compassion to those in need, unless we make a concrete plan to exercise that compassion, we will miss a multitude of opportunities. Call a family conference. Read the definition of compassion and then spend time looking at the Scripture listed above. Ask your children to list ways your family could show compassion to others. Help them get started by listing activities such as: delivering a meal, raking someone's leaves, running errands for an elderly friend, etc. Don't rush this activity. Encourage them to use their imaginations and to think creatively about ways to show compassion to others. Then, spend time praying as a family that you would develop compassionate hearts. The next day ask your children to list people that could use the blessing of compassionate service. Write down each person's name and a possible service that your family could perform for him or her. Now, grab your family calendar and write in some of the people that your children have listed. Often, my children would come home from church with an idea of someone who needed help. I had to train myself to take their suggestions seriously and to act on the need that was presented. Don't disregard your children's ability to discern need. Several of my children have very tender and compassionate hearts. Many times, they have been the impetus for the compassionate service our family provided to others. I'm afraid that if we always waited for me to notice the needs of others, my task-oriented mind would handicap us and thwart our desire to show compassion. Work as a team; use the gifts of tenderness and compassion that God has given to certain family members to increase your testimony for Christ through compassionate care and service to others.

Creeping Complacency

Complacency is simply defined as: an instance of usually unaware or uninformed self-satisfaction. Complacency leads us to disregard oncoming dangers or deficiencies in light of the comfort of our present situation. Spiritual complacency is a slippery slope and often takes us further and costs us more than we could have ever imagined. We don't jump into complacency; rather we slowly creep down the complacent road until we find ourselves looking back and wondering how we ever got so far away from our starting point. Only you can accurately diagnose your spiritual condition. Has complacency crept into your life? If so, seek the Lord's forgiveness and change direction today.

Revelation 3:15-16

Parenting Point

If it is hard to diagnose our own complacency, sometimes it can be nearly impossible to recognize an attitude of complacency in our children. For many of our children, because they have been raised in a Christian home the correct biblical answer at the correct time is always on their tongue; however, just knowing the right answer is not a clear sign of a dynamic spiritual life. Take some time to observe your children's attitudes. While they may be saying and doing the right thing, a lack of spiritual energy will quickly show up in their attitudes. Discuss with your children the goal of making the right choices. It isn't simply to have a "Christian" exterior. Instead, those right choices should come from the overflow of a full spiritual cup. Ask them what you can do to help them from becoming complacent. In your home, don't allow spiritual activities such as family devotions and prayer to become dull and dreary times of correction and duty. Instead, mix it up! Use your God-given creativity to make your family's spiritual life as vibrant and exciting as the Lord we serve. It is so easy to become complacent, but complacency is the thief of joy and growth-spurring excitement. Parents, encourage one another's spiritual exuberance and watch the contagious effect that your excitement will produce in your children.

Why Patience?

I t is no surprise that the very day that I decide to write about PA-TIENCE as a character quality, God will test my PATIENCE. So, you can guess the kind of day I have had so far, trapped behind slow, aimless, vacation bound motorists, in line behind people that were apparently SURPRISED they actually had to pay once their items were scanned, and oh yes, my favorite, the counter worker who continually answers the phone instead of waiting on me, the living, breathing, person standing right in front of them! Yikes!!! Ahhh, now I feel better. I know you understand. Why patience? Why is God patient with us? Read Romans 2:4 and you will learn the answer, and, hopefully, you will gain the motivation to be more patient next time with the poor chap behind the counter!

Romans 2:4

Parenting Point

When it comes to patience, is your home a "do as I say, not as I do" type of environment? When I notice my children being impatient and short-tempered with one another, often I need look no further than myself to find the source of their attitude. It is so easy to recognize impatience in others, but do we take the time to self-evaluate and deal with our own impatience? If you have been impatient with your children, spouse, or even the checkout person, stop and ask their forgiveness. Your impatience is **not** their fault! We all have the choice to deal patiently or impatiently; no one forces us into that decision. Asking forgiveness will go far in repairing the damage our impatience may have already caused, and it will often provide us a chance to share about the Savior, Who models such patience toward us. In the same way that we pre-activity our children before they enter an area of temptation or struggle, we can pre-activity ourselves regarding patience. If you know that certain circumstances or situations will cause your level of patience to plummet, spend a few moments preparing your heart ahead of time to deal with that situation with patience, gentleness, and a Christ-like attitude.

Shopping at the Moral Mart

Every choice we make involves a meeting between our mind, our heart, and our moral conscience. I call this meeting place the Decision Depot. Think of the Decision Depot as a sort of giant Moral Mart where there are well stocked shelves, plenty of customers, and high quality merchandise. Our Decision Depot should be full of all sorts of high quality values and virtues such as honesty, integrity, respect, love, diligence, and compassion, just to name a few. How well stocked is your Decision Depot? And, how successful have you been at stocking the shelves in your children's Moral Mart?

2 Peter 1:5-8

Parenting Point

Mom and Dad, what plan do you have to add virtue to your child's faith? True knowledge, according to 2 Peter 1:5, is the product of faith and virtue (moral excellence) combined. Virtue training ought to be a casual part of your regular routine, in the spirit of Deuteronomy 6:7. Megan and I created the Characterhealth ministry to help you stock the shelves in your children's hearts. Take some time today to visit Characterhealth. com WITH your children and watch a Parenting Point Video or two. Also, you may want to purchase a copy of Studies In Character for each family member. We wrote Studies In Character to help you stock their shelves in a casual, yet effective, way.

Trust • Faith

The Worry Bandit

According to the dictionary, to worry is to give way to anxiety or unease, to allow one's mind to dwell on difficulty or troubles. It is a state of anxiety and uncertainty over actual or potential problems. Worry doesn't accomplish any positive outcome in our lives! In fact, worry robs us of the opportunity to experience daily joy and replaces that joy with stress, tension, and dread. Today's verses remind us that we have no need to worry; our faithful Father is always concerned for our wellbeing, and He knows just what we need.

Matthew 6:25-32

Parenting Point

Do you have any worriers in your home? Worry doesn't just rob adults of their joy; it will have the same effect on children. With my own children, I realized that many of their worries surrounded the "what ifs?" of life. What if we had an accident? What if we had to move? What if they didn't get to go to the party? The list of unknown and frightening what ifs can be endless. I spent time talking with the children about God and His watch care over our family. God's Word assures us that He will give us the grace to bear up under any circumstance that comes into our lives; however, He doesn't promise us the grace to bear up under the worrisome "what ifs" that we grasp onto by ourselves. Until a perceived worry is an actual reality, we don't need God's grace to bear up under it. Instead, the Word of God commands us to: "Take every thought captive" (2 Corinthians 10:5), and to "be anxious for nothing" (Philippians 4:6). Memorizing scriptures like these can be a great tool to help our children control their worrisome thoughts. Speak daily and naturally about God's loving care and protection over your family. As our children begin to recognize how deeply God loves and protects them, they will begin to cast off fear and trust Him more fully. The same is true for worried adults. Allow the Word of God to transform your understanding of God, and then abandon your fears and embrace trust and faith in your faithful God.

The Week in Review

Take some time to gather as a family and discuss the character qualities that you learned this week. Here are some questions to get the conversation started.

- **List the character qualities we studied this week.**

- **Which character quality was the hardest for you to practice this week?**

- **Did you see a family member consistently practicing one of this week's character qualities? Which family member?**

Use your imagination and add questions of your own. After your time of discussion, spend some time praying together, thanking the Lord and sharing one another's burdens. Pray ahead of time for teachable hearts to incorporate and put into practice the character qualities your family will learn in the upcoming week.

A Slow Talker

W ords can certainly get us in trouble, can't they? It isn't just what we say but how we say it, when we say it, or to whom we say it that can cause a world of hurt for ourselves and others. Today's verse reminds us of the need to be circumspect when it comes to our speech. Often the character quality of circumspection seems to be limited to actions, but learning to be careful and consider- ate of our speech and manner of speaking is just as important. This is an area where we all need to self-evaluate. Consider yourself carefully. Do you spend more time talking or listening? Do your words build up or tear down? Do you just talk too much? Ask the Lord to help you become a wise and careful speaker and avoid the trap of sinning with your words.

Proverbs 10:19

Parenting Point

Today's verse is one of the most often-repeated memory verses in our home. It is absolutely true that when any of us - child or adult - speaks too much, transgression is unavoidable. We must teach our children to listen more than they speak. There is no shortage of unnecessary words in our homes. Foolish jesting, critical speech, and unwholesome communica- tion of all kinds brings no glory to God. Have your children memorize this verse! When they are headed down the road of too many words, ask them to recite their memory verse back to you. Allow God's Word to soften and change their hearts. Sometimes, for children that just weren't incorporat- ing the lesson of "less talking," I would take away their freedom to speak for a period of time. Having to go speech-less caused them to stop and think more carefully when they regained the right to talk. Don't underes- timate the damage that careless words can bring into your home. Work hard to develop a home atmosphere of sweet, careful speaking that builds up and never tears down. Believe me, this is HARD WORK but don't give up! The sweet fruit you'll experience makes the effort worthwhile and will strengthen your family's testimony to others.

Integrity

Preserving Integrity

What possible personal benefit is there for us when we act with integrity? Beyond personal satisfaction and building a good reputation, there doesn't seem to be much benefit for us personally when it comes to integrity; however, according to Psalm 25:21 integrity actually preserves us. Integrity protects us from harm. A person who acts with integrity, regardless of the situation, will develop a reputation for courage, honesty, trustworthiness, and honor. It is not we who preserve integrity; it is in fact, integrity that preserves us.

Psalm 25:21

Parenting Point

Too often, we wrongly approach character as a means to an end, rather than a moral and God-pleasing end in itself! Integrity must be what characterizes our every thought and action. If we only tell the truth when it benefits us, or if we are only trustworthy when there is something in it for us, we cannot be considered to have integrity. Read Psalm 25:21 out loud to your children and ask them what it means to be "preserved" by integrity? Next, ask them what their lies and half-truths do to preserve or damage that protection? What do lies and half-truths do to preserve or damage God's glory? Take the time to have a family discussion. Give each family member a piece of paper, and have him or her record areas of strong family integrity. Next, have them write down any areas of lack in the family testimony of integrity. Discuss both written observations. Praise the family for the positive integrity that has been recorded. Spend some time discussing the areas that have emerged as areas that lack integrity. Help your family to avoid finger pointing, blame assessing, and defensiveness by asking good dialog questions. Perhaps, what has been seen is a misunderstanding or a judgment of motives; however, if there is an area in your family that truly is lacking in integrity, take the necessary steps to seek forgiveness from the Lord and one another. Then, develop a plan to address that area. Covenant, as a family, to work together to implement positive, pro-active change that will strengthen your family's testimony of integrity and that will bring glory to God.

Peaceful or Pugnacious?

How would you define peace? I think most of us would agree that the character quality of peace, or peacefulness, is one that we long to have in our lives. The dictionary definition of peace is this: an agreement or a treaty to end hostilities, freedom from quarrels and disagreement, harmonious relations. In Galatians 5:22 peace is listed as a part of the "whole" of the Fruit of the Spirit. What a wonderful goal for our homes! However, peace simply for the sake of peace should never be the goal of a Christian. Our peace cannot come at the expense of the Word of God or at the expense of the convictions the Lord has laid on our hearts. Romans 12:18 reminds us that peace is not a given. While we must do our part to pursue peace, faithfulness to the Lord and His Word may not allow for immediate peace. Check your heart and your motives when you sense a lack of peace, and then, "If possible, so far as it depends on you, be at peace with all men."

Romans 12:18

Parenting Point

What is the opposite of a peaceful person? I would say that the opposite is a pugnacious or quarrelsome person. If you have more than one child in your family, I would venture a guess that when there is strife, there is one child who always seems to be involved in the conflict. These children, who seem to always "stir the pot," need concentrated times of instruction on what it means to bring peace, not strife, to a situation. The heart of quarreling is found in James 4:1-3, and this is a great memory verse for quarrelsome, pugnacious children. These children are not peaceful or happy, and eventually, they will begin to drive away friends and family members. Don't allow them to remain in such a state, help them to put off quarreling and put on others-oriented peace. Help them to seek forgiveness, as necessary, and to learn to enjoy peaceful and pleasant relationships. Even if it seems as though their personalities are just bent toward trouble, help them to refine their personalities to honor God and to elevate peace and joy.

Punctuality

P unctuality is defined as the habit or quality of adhering to an appointed time. Punctuality, or a lack of punctuality, can be a defining quality of our testimony for Christ. How are you doing? As a character quality, punctuality highlights our respect and concern for others. Everyone has the same 24 hours in each day. When we disregard punctuality, we are stealing some of the time allotted to another person's day. Time is not a renewable resource; once it is gone, it can never be replaced. We show our love toward our neighbor as we carefully respect their time. With a little forethought and pre-planning, our testimony will be enhanced as we faithfully practice punctuality.

Ephesians 5:15-16

Parenting Point

What is your family's testimony? Are you known for being on time or is your testimony one of habitual tardiness? Punctuality with children can be difficult. Trust me, with eight children of my own I have great sympathy for you! However, punctuality with children is NOT an unattainable goal. Look at your routines and determine what you need to change to make punctuality a consistent and regular habit for your family. Without a consistent practice of punctuality, we will find ourselves late, flustered, and ill-prepared for what we need to accomplish. In my experience, when this happens, my mouth tends to get out of control; then, besides being late, we arrive with feelings wounded and ruffled emotions. Perhaps, you need to prepare the night ahead for success the next day. Punctuality will not just naturally occur; it takes hard work! Take heart, the more diligent you are to practice punctuality, the easier the habit will become, and you will be training your children to be careful of others' time and their own testimony.

Joy

Initiating Enthusiasm

Whether you're a businessman, part-time cashier, stay at home mom, or student, the end of summer signals the beginning of a new season in all of our lives. Even more than January 1st, the return to "normal" days of work and school require new routines, schedules, and priorities. While I think most of us work hard to prepare ourselves for these new paradigms, just how enthusiastic are we in the process? As we step into autumn and new opportunities, are we enthusiastic about what the Lord will bring our way or simply resigned to the end of summer? As believers, every new day and every new season bring with it a multitude of opportunities to minister, serve, and bless others. Dawson Trotman, the founder of Young Life, used to say that he could transform a high school with just two excited sophomore girls. How much more could the Lord do with multiple excited believers? Embrace what's coming next and let your enthusiasm shine!

Colossians 3:23

Parenting Point

For many children, change is a difficult concept. The beginning of a new school year with different books, different requirements, and different routines, can cause our children to worry and become anxious. We can help them make the transition easier by making them part of the planning process. Encourage your children to make a list of the exciting new opportunities they will have this coming year. Help them to organize their routines and possessions to make the change from the more relaxed days of summer to the more scheduled days of autumn a smooth transition. Most importantly, spend time praying with your children about the new friends and service opportunities that the Lord will bring them this year. Preparing ahead and cultivating enthusiasm for what is coming will take the fear out of the inevitable change.

Faithfulness • Leadership • Resolve

A Trustworthy Leader

Read today's verse. What kind of leader are you? Do you encourage others to walk faithfully with God? Anytime we mock or tease another believer for the convictions they hold, we are acting as a negative leader in their life. Whether we agree with another believer's convictions or not, we are responsible as brothers and sisters in Christ to encourage them to live up to what the Lord has shown them. Instead of trying to draw them away, perhaps the right response is to seek the Lord and discern whether their conviction should be ours as well.

Proverbs 28:10

Parenting Point

Sometimes it is hard to stand up for our convictions when others disagree; however, each family must answer to God for what He has shown them personally. If we want others to honor our convictions, we must show them the same respect. While it is fine to set boundaries in our own homes, we do not have the right to tell others how they must live. Often, I was more comfortable with my children spending time with unbelievers than with Christian families with vastly different convictions than our own. It is easy to explain to children why families with no knowledge of Christ make ungodly decisions... They have no reason to make those decisions; however, when our children spend time with Christian families who don't hold to our convictions, or who, worse yet, mock our decisions, there is great opportunity for confusion. Be wise in the friendships that you allow. Make sure that your children understand the biblical basis for your decisions. Under no circumstances should you disparage another family's choices. The simple answer: "Others may; our family doesn't." is sometimes the best and only answer your children need to hear. Make sure your non-negotiable choices are based in Scripture and teach your children how to defend what they believe. If a child visiting your home is held to a stricter standard than what you allow, teach your children that the loving thing is to help that child uphold their own family's standard. That may mean curtailing certain entertainment choices or food choices, but friendship sometimes means sacrifice. When faced with a standard that is higher than your own, take time to pray and seek the Lord. Perhaps that higher standard is one you should adopt, but sometimes it is just another family's different choice. Asking the Lord to direct you will give you peace either way.

The Week in Review

Take some time to gather as a family and discuss the character qualities that you learned this week. Here are some questions to get the conversation started.

- List the character qualities we studied this week.
- Which character quality was the hardest for you to practice this week?
- Did you see a family member consistently practicing one of this week's character qualities? Which family member?

Use your imagination and add questions of your own. After your time of discussion, spend some time praying together, thanking the Lord and sharing one another's burdens. Pray ahead of time for teachable hearts to incorporate and put into practice the character qualities your family will learn in the upcoming week.

Magnifying God

One of my favorite praise songs is "O Magnify the Lord... For He is worthy to be praised!" This song has a catchy melody that will stay in your mind for a long time, but what is the reality behind the lyrics? Magnifying God is the same as glorifying God. When you magnify God, you make Him look bigger. Just like a magnifying glass makes an object appear bigger and more sharply focused, so our character-healthy testimony makes our God appear bigger and more sharply focused to those around us who are watching. So, how will you magnify God this week? Will you magnify Him with kind words, responsible actions, and respectful behavior? Or, will He look small because of your harsh words, broken promises, and critical behavior? If He is worthy of your praise, He is worthy to be magnified.

Psalm 34:3

Parenting Point

Help your children to make the connection between their words and magnifying God. Ask them if they feel bigger when someone puts them down with unkind words. Next, ask them if they feel bigger when someone encourages them with kind words. Finally, make a plan for how the family will speak more kindly to each other and remember to always bring it back to the (magnifying) glory of God. To help your children incorporate the practice of using magnifying words, take some time to role-play various situations with your kids. Have them enact scenes at home, on the playground, in school, with adults, and with other children. Practicing magnifying communication within the safe confines of their home will build confidence in our children to practice that same magnifying conversation outside of the family circle. Remember, your example will either provide positive reinforcement of your teaching, or it will tear down and negate what you are trying to impart to your kids.

Sanctification • Faithfulness

Children are Arrows

Much has been said over the years about the number of children you should or should not have. Many have taken Psalm 127:4-5 and made it say something that God did not intend. The point of this verse is to remind us of the importance of character development in our children. Our children are like arrows in a hunter's quiver. They are the extension of our lives and at the cutting edge of our testimony. We are truly blessed when we have children who are responsible, respectful, loving, compassionate, courageous, and bold for the Lord. Happy hunting!

Psalm 127:4-5

Parenting Point

Regardless of how many children you have, are those children sharp? I'm not speaking of academics; I'm speaking of character. This Psalm equates children to arrows, and arrows must be sharp and straight to be effective. Our children must demonstrate godly character to be considered sharp and straight. The character-health of your children is important to God; how important is it to you? Is it important enough to say "NO" and mean it? How often do your children see you make character-healthy choices? Character is the whetstone that keeps our kids sharp! As you persistently and consistently take the time to inject character into their days and daily choices, the language of character-healthy living will become second nature for your family. Your children will internalize the God-honoring character that you take the time to teach them. Conversely, if character training is missing from your home environment, your children will internalize the character-less training this world has to offer. Teaching character takes time to sink in and become habitual.

Alertness

To be alert means to be watchful and ready to deal with whatever happens to come our way. Character healthy believers are to be clear headed and responsive to God's direction in their lives. If you are having trouble discerning the will of God, perhaps it is because of the influences that you are allowing in your life; influences that have dulled your alertness to God's leading. Take some time to self-evaluate the input you are receiving. If necessary, discard those activities and associations that keep you from being alert and prepared.

2 Timothy 4:2-5

Parenting Point

As parents, make a list (on paper) of the influences that you are allowing into your family that may be dulling your spiritual senses, for example, carnal movies, raunchy music on your IPod, questionable music on your children's IPods, inappropriate T.V., Internet sites, magazines, or books. Even a small amount of ungodly or inappropriate content can cause great damage in our homes. A lack of parental knowledge regarding what children are seeing, hearing, or exposed to is no excuse. Wise parents take the time to evaluate the influences that are infiltrating their home. In our home any IPod is actually a "MyPod," and we take the time to periodically check the contents of our children's mobile devices. The same concept must hold true with reading material and television shows. Spend some time looking at what your children are viewing. Is it clean? Is it edifying? Is it appropriate? If not, what fruit will it produce in your children's lives? After you have evaluated the influences that are affecting your family, call a family conference. Read today's scripture together. Talk about the importance of being alert, and the equally important task of evaluating influences to be sure that nothing is robbing your family of their ability to be alert. Ask your children to share any areas that they believe are robbing your family of its necessary alertness or dulling your family's senses. When they have shared their observations, share the areas that you have listed as well. As a family, make a plan to raise the standard in your home and to hold one another accountable to enact appropriate change. Finish your time together by praying with and for one another. Make sure that you hold yourself to the same standard of godliness that you are enforcing for your children. Allow your pro-active example to be an encouragement to growth and change in your family.

A Character of Praise

Although God doesn't require the sacrifice of burnt offerings any longer, there is a sacrifice that is a sweet savor to our Lord: the sacrifice of praise. Read today's verse. Praise isn't simply songs or prayers, but praise is found as the fruit of lips that give thanks to His name. Obviously, in order for our lips to give thanks to God's name, our heart must be overflowing with thanksgiving as well. Spend some time today meditating on God's goodness to you and fill your heart with the fruit of thanksgiving.

Hebrews 13:15

Parenting Point

Is your family characterized as a family that continually offers up praise to God? I know a few families I would say that about, and we are always delighted when we have the opportunity to spend time with them. What makes those families different? I believe it is a family commitment to thankfulness. These folks are the people who continually remind me of God's faithfulness and bountiful goodness. Such a testimony shouldn't be limited to a select few. As followers of Christ, we all have the ability to bring that kind of sacrifice of praise to God. Read today's verse aloud with your family. Spend some time discussing God's faithfulness as shown to your family, and then join together in prayer and praise to your faithful God.

Regarding Respect

I think we would all agree that respect is an absolutely essential character quality; however, the word respect, all by itself, is a nebulous term. For whom or what are we to have respect? Perhaps we have no problem respecting our parents or our employers, but do we respect our spouse, or our pastor, or the law? Take some time today and ask God to search your heart regarding your overall attitudes of respect. We must avoid hypocrisy by practicing the character quality of respect everywhere that it is required, not just in the areas that are easiest for us.

Romans 14:11

Parenting Point

Although today's scripture passage does not use the word "respect", this verse shows us clearly what it means to respect God. This respect shows itself in awe and deference. Our children will never develop an awe or deference toward God if they do not see that attitude exemplified by us, their parents. How do you refer to the Lord? If we only convey the attitude that God is our friend (which He is) and never the truth that God is Holy and righteous, we are doing our children a disservice. Spend time, as a family, worshiping God by using terms of adoration, respect, and awe. You will be surprised by how easy it is for your children to show respect and reverence to their Holy Father and Friend. Holding God in reverential awe will in no way lessen our children's love for their Heavenly Father; rather, they will build strong bonds of security and trust in the One who alone is worthy.

Love Believes

What does it mean to believe all things? Does it mean that we are gullible and naive? No, for the believer in Christ, to believe all things is to trust that God will work every situation out for our good and His glory. Time in the Word will build the spiritual muscle necessary to believe God when our circumstances seem unbelievable. The more we know God, the more we will eagerly believe that He has a plan for our lives!

I Corinthians 13:7

Parenting Point

Our children, because they are young and trusting, often do fall into a trap of believing things that are not true. How do we teach them to discern biblical truth from worldly or societal beliefs? I think the first place we should turn is to the Word of God. Our children need to become students of God's Word so that they will have the ability to discern good from evil. The more time they spend reading, studying, and meditating on the Word, the more they will be able to differentiate true wisdom from the false wisdom of the world. How intentional are you about incorporating the Bible into your family's daily life? There are countless resources available to help you guide and direct your children as they learn about God. Your example of daily time spent in the Word can be a catalyst to spark your children's own commitment to personal study and application. Don't expect the church or Sunday School to fill this need! The responsibility is ours, and if we take our responsibility seriously, we will soon see a new generation of biblically literate and wise decision makers.

The Week in Review

Take some time to gather as a family and discuss the character qualities that you learned this week. Here are some questions to get the conversation started.

- List the character qualities we studied this week.
- Which character quality was the hardest for you to practice this week?
- Did you see a family member consistently practicing one of this week's character qualities? Which family member?

Use your imagination and add questions of your own. After your time of discussion, spend some time praying together, thanking the Lord and sharing one another's burdens. Pray ahead of time for teachable hearts to incorporate and put into practice the character qualities your family will learn in the upcoming week.

Obedience

Do You Have an Obedient Ear?

O bedience...it isn't just for children! Read today's verse and consider the consequence that God sets for those who will not listen to His voice. Remember, the goal here is not simply "hearing" what the Lord instructs, but listening with a heart already attuned to obedience. I've counseled with too many young people who began their rationalization for poor behavior with, "I'm ___ years old. I guess I can make my own decisions!" Really? I can't find anywhere in scripture where we are told that we reach an age where submission and obedience are no longer required. Check your heart. Are you an obedient listener or a haphazard hearer?

I Samuel 12:15

Parenting Point

The very first verse we had our children commit to memory was Ephesians 6:1. As they memorized this key verse, we often referred back to it as we were instructing them and correcting them concerning their disobedience. It was easy for our little children to understand that when they disobeyed, they were choosing to not do what was right according to Ephesians 6. That understanding of disobedience and the memory of consequences enacted for disobedience, laid the groundwork for them to understand their need for a Savior. From the earliest days, we helped them to understand that disobedience and sin are one and the same thing. Yes, it is essential for our children to know, without a doubt, that God loves them; however, it is just as important for them to realize that they are sinners in need of a Savior. Don't skip one part of this important equation by allowing disobedience without consequence and by failing to call disobedience what it really is: sin.

Honesty

To Tell the Truth

Honesty is defined as the quality, condition, or characteristic of being fair, just, truthful, and morally upright. Wow! There is so much encompassed in that definition. Too often, we simply think of honesty or dishonesty, as the words we say. According to the definition, honesty is a necessary component of every aspect of our lives. So, the question is this: In your speech, your actions, and even your thought life, how important is honesty to you?

Ephesians 4:25

Parenting Point

How important is honesty in your home? When we allow "little" untruths, we are building an atmosphere where dishonesty can blossom. Soon the "little" untruths will lead to habitual lies. Don't wait for those habits to take root. Begin today to look for and correct any lack of truthfulness. Imagination is a wonderful thing, but as with anything else in our lives, imagination has its appropriate place. Teach your children to be totally truthful in what they say, infer, and even more importantly, leave unsaid. If you have a sense that something just doesn't seem right, take the time to dig a little deeper. Don't leave your children to carry the burden of unconfessed lies! At times, it may seem like you are overwhelmed by the dishonesty you see in your children's words and actions. Don't give up! This is a battle that must be won when they are young to avoid great pain when they become young adults. Parents, pray daily that God would give you eyes to see and hear what is really going on and the courage to deal with those circumstances appropriately. Remember, when God answers that prayer and reveals hidden sins within our homes, our response should be one of thankfulness. Uncovering dishonesty never comes at a convenient time! However, we can still be thankful that God loves us, and our children, enough to bring dishonesty to light and to then equip us with His Word to appropriately deal with the dishonesty that has been uncovered.

Proactive Leadership

Proactivity, increased responsibility, and leadership all have one character quality in common... INITIATIVE. Those who lead most effectively are those who take proactive initiative. In fact, those who show initiative are most often the same people who are offered promotions, receive bonuses, and garner praise from those with whom they come in contact.

Isaiah 6:8

Parenting Point

Initiative means taking action even if no one else sees the need. After reading Isaiah 6:8, ask your children why God called on Isaiah. Hint: God usually calls on those He knows will take the initiative to follow Him in faithful obedience. As parents, we often get frustrated by our children's lack of initiative yet, we too, often lack the motivation to attend a marriage retreat, come to a parenting conference, or simply put the DVDs we already own into the machine. Although we can try to define initiative simply by using our words, it is our example of proactive initiative that will make the biggest impression on our children. When they see us actively engaged in helping one another or taking on tasks with no prompting, they will learn that initiative is the accepted standard in our home. To help your children incorporate initiative as part of their normal lexicon, use the word often and in context. For example, "I saw you pick up the trash in the front yard. Thank you for showing such great initiative!" Showing initiative is a great reason to celebrate with a special dessert or by bestowing the "You did great!" plate. One area in which it is important to teach our children the character quality of initiative is in the area of prayer. Teach your children to initiate prayer with each other and their friends. When someone is sick, struggling, or discouraged, the quickly initiated prayer of another believer can provide comfort and encouragement. Make it a point to initiate prayer for your children when they are in need, and soon they will effortlessly and naturally pick up your practice of prayer.

Appropriateness • Respect

Glorifying God

You may not think of glorifying God as a character quality, but it is the essence of being a Christian. Everything God does is designed to bring glory to Himself. His desire for us is the same; that is why it is a sin to diminish the glory of the Lord. Our poor character makes our God look small in the eyes of those watching. When we diminish God we demonstrate our poor character. Dishonesty, irresponsibility, and disrespectful behavior all make God look a little smaller... and that is sin. Our greatest good is to magnify our Lord. Take some time to consider the following verse.

1 Corinthians 10:31

Parenting Point

1 Corinthians 10:31 encompasses our mandate to bring glory to God. Notice how Paul picked two of the most mundane things in life to demonstrate how we are to bring glory to God: eating and drinking. Mealtime is a very important time and should be done decently and in order. Here are some helpful tips for using mealtime to magnify God. Designate one child each meal to be the runner for seconds (not Mom). Next, make sure no one eats until Mom is seated at the table; this displays respect and self-control. Have the male children stand behind their seats until Mom is seated, then they may sit. Again, this shows respect toward Mom. Finally, have one of the boys hold Mom's seat for her each meal. Make sure that the children sit during the remainder of the meal. Mom will love it, and you will be training young men who understand how to respect and affirm women. As well, your daughters will begin to recognize the type of respectful behavior they should expect and demand from the young men who desire to build a relationship with them.

Faithfulness • Resolve

Easily Enticed

The dictionary defines entice this way: to lead on by exciting hope or desire, to allure, to inveigle. Being easily enticed stands in direct opposition to steadfast faithfulness. In what ways are you easily enticed by sinners? Whether we are allured by friends to engage in sinful activities or tempted by the Internet to indulge our flesh, being characterized as one who is easily enticed will destroy our testimony and weaken our walk with the Lord. Dare to be different! Rather than be easily enticed, become a believer whose steadfast faithfulness draws others to Christ.

Proverbs 1:10-16

Parenting Point

A child who has never been instructed and trained to love virtue and biblical character is a child who will have no strength to say "No" to the crowd. We should be continually stocking our children's moral warehouse, filling it to the brim with godly character qualities such as honesty, respect, courage, commitment, faithfulness, etc. In the moment of temptation, this well-stocked moral warehouse will provide the courage our children need to choose wisely and to avoid the trap of sin. Observe your children carefully. Enticement comes in a variety of forms. Although our children's actions may be acceptable, are they enticed to grumble and complain along with their friends? When someone posts a negative or unwholesome status on Facebook, do our children refuse to be drawn into the conversation, or do they heedlessly follow the crowd, posting comments that they would be ashamed to speak out loud? Help your children recognize the friendships and activities that tend to entice them. Then, help them make proactive decisions about how to handle those temptations. Ask them this simple question: "What types of things entice you, and what can I do to help you stand firm against those temptations?" Knowing that you are on their team will be a relief, and by asking questions rather than asserting accusations, you will open lines of communication. Share some areas of enticement that you battle (if appropriate) and spend time praying for one another. We are all enticed. The enticement itself isn't necessarily the problem, but our response to it can either strengthen our faith or damage our testimony. Stand firm and steadfast; refuse to be inveigled (isn't that a great word?) by sin.

Preaching and Patience

One area in which we need to show especial patience is in our handling of the Word of God. In fact, as we communicate the Word of God to our unsaved friends and relatives, we are to do so in season, and out of season, and with great patience. Earning the right to be heard with co-workers, friends, and family, requires patient prayer, patient communication, and patient preaching. Don't grow weary of patiently proclaiming the Gospel!

2 Timothy 4:2

Parenting Point

How long will it take for our children to finally "get it?" To incorporate the Biblical truths we work so hard to sow into their lives? It depends. The answer is different for every child, and that is why patience is so imperative in our parenting. Too often, Scripture becomes a club we use to ensure our children obey us and follow our directions. Instead, we must patiently lead our children to and with the Word of God; gently building a love for God's directions and a heart's desire to show their love for God through their obedience to Him. Join your children in memorizing Scripture and incorporate that Scripture into your conversations with your children throughout the day. Sharing the Word isn't just about planned family devotions and assigned memory work, though. As we spend time conversing naturally about the Lord throughout the day and recognizing and thanking Him for His work in our lives, our children will begin to easily incorporate Biblical truths into their own lives. God's Word assures us that the Scripture we sow will bear godly fruit in our children's lives; we just need to be patient!

The Week in Review

Take some time to gather as a family and discuss the character qualities that you learned this week. Here are some questions to get the conversation started.

- List the character qualities we studied this week.

- Which character quality was the hardest for you to practice this week?

- Did you see a family member consistently practicing one of this week's character qualities? Which family member?

Use your imagination and add questions of your own. After your time of discussion, spend some time praying together, thanking the Lord and sharing one another's burdens. Pray ahead of time for teachable hearts to incorporate and put into practice the character qualities your family will learn in the upcoming week.

Kindness • Compassion • Generosity

Generous Kindness

Kindness and generosity go hand in hand. When you meet a generous person, you are inevitably meeting a kind person. It is virtually impossible to extend generosity in our actions, words, and attitudes, if we are not committed to kindness at the same time. The opposite of kindness and generosity is self-centeredness. When we are more concerned with making sure that our needs are taken care of, rather than showing consideration for the needs of others, kindness will slip away. What are you characterized by? Is your testimony one of kindness and generosity? Not sure? Ask a trusted friend, parent, or teacher for their input regarding your level of kindness. Finally, examine the following passage regarding generous kindness and write down any insights you gain from the example of Tabitha (Dorcas).

Acts 9:36-43

Parenting Point

We've all seen the bumper stickers advocating the need to "Practice Random Acts of Kindness." Yes, I would love my children to randomly see needs they can fill, and then fill those needs because their hearts overflow with kindness. However, I strongly believe that unless our children are encouraged and taught to perform INTENTIONAL acts of kindness, they will never "randomly" act out in kindness. Kindness goes against our human (sinful) nature. We must find ways to help our children learn to make the choice to act kindly. As our children make those choices consistently, they will build strong habits of others-oriented kindness. Pick one day a week and have your children choose a family member to encourage that day through words and actions of kindness. Make it a family affair and surprise a child or spouse with your especially kind and generous actions toward them. Kindness can be shown through acts of service, words of encouragement, or sometimes, just a listening ear. Encourage family members to be creative as they lavish others with kindness, and you'll soon see a new family characterization. Kindness, practiced habitually, makes our God look great!

Sanctification • Encouragement

Living as a New Creation

I t's a simple paradigm, really. If any man is in Christ, the Scriptures tell us, he is a new creature. Old things have passed away and all things are new. Easy to say, but how is this paradigm working itself out in our lives? When we cling to old ways of living, we are clinging to those old paradigms that God's Word tells us must "pass away." Only you can examine and evaluate what things need to pass away in your own life. Take some time today to determine what old things are cluttering your life and take steps to discard those old, tired out paradigms and replace them with new, God-directed, character-healthy practices.

II Corinthians 5:17

Parenting Point

As adults, we must evaluate our own lives and examine our own paradigms; however, in the lives of our children, we fill a unique role. As their parents, it is our privilege and responsibility, to help them clearly evaluate their lives. For children who have accepted Christ as their Savior, encourage them to memorize this verse. When you are dealing with areas of sin that are continual and repeated, allow God's Word, through this verse, to speak to your children. Help them to determine concrete ways to recognize old behaviors that need to pass away and new behaviors that will proactively replace their old paradigms. For children who have not accepted Christ as their Savior, using this verse will help them to understand why they cannot seem to stop old behaviors; it is because they are not "in Christ," and, therefore, they are stuck in their old ways. When you see your children making proactive and biblical changes in their lives, affirm their actions. Make sure they know that you are noticing the positive steps they are taking to honor God.

Courageous Confrontation

Courage is truly a defining character quality. It takes courage to stand against injustice. It takes courage to tell the truth. It takes courage to walk away, when everyone else is participating. It takes courage to say "NO." And, it takes courage to confront others when necessary. Although we are called to be peacemakers, there are times in the life of a Christian when loyalty to our God requires confrontation. I would rather eat tree bark than confront another person! Pray that God would give you the courage to disregard yourself and confront when He makes it clear that confrontation is your duty and responsibility.

Esther 8:4-7

Parenting Point

If you want your children to have the courage of an Esther or a Daniel, take the time to read the stories of the great heroes of the faith found throughout the Bible. As well, fill your bookshelves with wonderful biographies of men and women who were willing to give their all to stand for what was good and right. Our children need heroes to look up to, but be careful whom you are extolling to them. Major League baseball player Kevin Youkilis, recently said, "Sports stars aren't heroes, we just play a game. The real heroes give their lives for others." Well said and an important lesson for our children. Athletic prowess is nice; courage and character are priceless. Help your children to recognize the difference. The wise parent takes the time necessary to evaluate the activities in which their children are involved. If, upon evaluation, you realize that your children's activities are building worldly and earthly prowess but inhibiting spiritual growth, make the changes necessary to bring about the spiritual maturity that is so necessary in your children's lives. Who knows, perhaps one day your child will be the subject of the newest Christian biography extolling a life of honor, courage, and commitment!

Decisiveness

A typical day may force us into hundreds of decisions. A decisive believer is a proactive believer. When we are decisive, we demonstrate the ability to make decisions quickly, firmly, and clearly. Arguably, not every decision should be made quickly but most of our daily decisions are to be made in a timely manner. Total immersion in God's Word on a daily basis will help to prevent indecisiveness. Many of the choices we are called to make have already been made for us in the Bible. Joshua 24:15 spells out the most fundamental and important decision that we can make... The decision to serve God or not to serve God! What is it for you and your family? Are you God-servers? Read and study the following text.

Joshua 24:15

Parenting Point

Help your children be decisive by being decisive yourself. Force them to choose and stick with their choice. You are not doing them any favors by letting them ponder endlessly. James says, "Let your yes be yes, and your no be no." Mean what you say and say what you mean, and you will raise self-confident, God-fearing, decisive adults. To assist your slower thinking (and acting) children, make use of some "pre-activity" instructions. In our home, we have several Thinker children. To help these children learn to process in a timely manner, I would say to them, "I'm about to ask you a question. This question demands a quick answer. Prepare your heart to answer me quickly." Just this little reminder was very helpful in training those children to formulate their decisions quickly. Although it isn't always necessary for our children to make decisions quickly, there are times that an immediate decision can help them to forgo devastating consequences. If we don't take the time necessary to teach them how to process quickly in the decision making model, we are setting them up for failure. When your Thinker children respond in an appropriately decisive manner, make sure that you take the time to praise them and encourage them to even more success. Remember, these same children are the children that will employ stall tactics in their obedience. Teaching them to act decisively and in a timely manner will produce fruit in the area of first time obedience as well.

Taking Up Your Cross

At the heart of taking up our cross and following Christ is self-denial. In an age of overindulgence, it seems strange to be talking about self-denial, yet for the Christian self-denial is an essential character quality. When was the last time you truly denied your flesh of some gratification that you could have supplied but did not for the sake of taking up your cross? Success, that is *true success*, is not found in wealth, accomplishment, or prestige. Rather, it is found in sacrifice, suffering, and self-denial. Don't believe me? Just look at the most successful man in all history, Jesus, who took up His cross and paid sin's penalty for us. Praise God!

Luke 9:23

Parenting Point

Take your children to this passage and read it out loud. Ask them what it looks like to take up your cross. Next, ask them to tell you what it looks like to practice self-denial. Finally, be prepared as a family to participate in some areas of self-denial such as voluntarily giving up a privilege or a right, in order to prefer a younger brother or sister. Mom and Dad, how can you take up your cross for your kids? Think about it. Do they see that you are willing to practice sacrificial service for them in the same way that you extend service to others? Too often, we save our best for those outside the family and expect our spouse and children to simply understand. Instead, we should practice giving our best at home in order to build the habit of extending excellence to everyone. When you see your children practicing voluntary acts of service, with no prior prompting, take the time to praise and affirm their efforts. The praise you bestow on them will help to build courage in their hearts to show even more sacrificial service to others.

Shh! Shh!

S ometimes, it isn't *what* we say or *how* we say something but just the sheer *volume* of our speaking that gets us into trouble! I don't know about you, but some days I just talk way too much. Read today's verse and consider what God shares about the consequences for careless words. Being known as a "talker" isn't really a compliment, and too many words will simply get us into hot water.

Matthew 12:36

Parenting Point

When I was little, my mother used to tell people that I had been vaccinated with a phonograph needle. (Does anyone even know what that is anymore?) In other words, I was a blabbermouth! While that sounded funny and all of my mom's friends would laugh at her analogy, my big mouth got me in trouble more often than I care to remember. It's my guess that we all have some children in our homes that talk more than they should. Instead of just assuming that they were born talkative or hoping that they will outgrow their blabbering ways, we must diligently teach them to be careful about their quantity of speech. Although I would never have intentionally hurt someone with my words, it was those times that I was careless and undisciplined with my words that I caused others pain. There have been times that one or another of my children have been told that they lost the freedom to speak. Usually, it wasn't because what they were saying was wrong, but they were just too busy talking and sharing their opinions heedlessly. I would take away their right to speak for one hour. For gabby children, an hour without speaking is like torture! When the hour was over, I would spend time talking with that child about the importance of choosing their words carefully and the danger of talking heedlessly. For some, this lesson had to be reenacted over and over. For other children in our home, losing their voice just twice was lesson enough. Help your children break the over-talking habit while they are young. When their over abundance of speaking does cause damage, teach them how to humbly seek forgiveness from whomever they have offended. There are times that silence really is golden!

The Week in Review

Take some time to gather as a family and discuss the character qualities that you learned this week. Here are some questions to get the conversation started.

- List the character qualities we studied this week.

- Which character quality was the hardest for you to practice this week?

- Did you see a family member consistently practicing one of this week's character qualities? Which family member?

Use your imagination and add questions of your own. After your time of discussion, spend some time praying together, thanking the Lord and sharing one another's burdens. Pray ahead of time for teachable hearts to incorporate and put into practice the character qualities your family will learn in the upcoming week.

Resourcefulness

Would you consider yourself a resourceful person? In a materialistic, you-need-to-own-it-all culture, it is easy to relegate the character quality of resourcefulness to a by-gone era; however, learning to make do with what we have or to use what is already at hand to meet a need, will equip us to be ready and useable when the Lord calls. Resourcefulness will develop our imaginations and creativity. Especially in a tight economy, the character quality of resourcefulness will allow us to steward well the resources that God has graciously provided for us.

Luke 16:10

Parenting Point

There is an old depression era saying that goes like this:
> Use it up,
> Wear it out,
> Make it do,
> Or do without.

This sentiment is at the heart of resourcefulness. Even when it is possible to provide our children with all of their wants and desires, we do so at the expense of their character. When our children don't have to earn what they get or they don't have to care for what they already have, we are teaching them to be materialistic consumers rather than faithful stewards of what God has provided. Too many possessions can cause the same type of consumer mentality. Perhaps, now is a good time to call a family conference and discuss your children's possessions. If they are faithful stewards of what you have provided, PRAISE them! If you see attitudes of entitlement, encourage them to give some of what they have to bless another child. Resourcefulness is not punishment. Our children will grow and flourish as they are forced to use their imaginations to create their own fun!

Resolve

In 2002, I had the opportunity to return to my old high school and give a speech on the first anniversary of September 11th. The topic that day was "Resolve." On the eve of the war with Iraq, I encouraged the student body to look beyond the next few years and peer into the eyes of the next generation. America's military might is not in doubt but her resolve is! Now, many years after the tragic events of 9/11, we face a crisis of resolve. The once (albeit temporary) cooperation among lawmakers has turned into an all out assault. Resolve defined, means to come to a firm decision about something; to find a solution to a problem. At the heart of resolve is patience, diligence, and delayed gratification. Take a moment to think about our "on demand" culture in light of our lack of resolve.

2 Timothy 4:7

Parenting Point

Do your children grow frustrated easily? Do they act out in bursts of temper? If so, they lack age appropriate resolve. One of the best ways to help your children develop resolve is to ensure that they learn delayed gratification. Today's guilt ridden parent often overindulges their child to ease their own conscience, at the expense of delayed gratification and ultimately resolve. Most things that are important in life require resolve (i.e., marriages, parenting, success at work, the war on terror, etc.). Make it your purpose to hold off indulging your children until they have earned the reward. Never reward bad behavior. Sit down with your kids and plan out a long-term goal. Then, work the plan over time to achieve that goal. You will find that resolve is a pleasant character quality, but it can't be bought overnight. Make sure your children observe you practicing the character quality of delayed gratification as well. If all they observe is their parents quickly and recklessly purchasing all of their perceived "wants," they will have no reason to build resolve and goal-oriented patience in their own lives.

Appointed As Ambassador

When we appoint an ambassador from our country to live in another country, what is their job? Much like a steward carefully cares for and maintains another man's possessions, an ambassador is responsible to care for and maintain someone else's reputation. An ambassador must accurately represent the country or person by whom they were appointed. Read today's verses. Paul saw himself as an ambassador for Christ, and as such, he endeavored to present Christ and the gospel with the same clarity that God, Himself would utilize. Like Paul, we too are ambassadors for Christ. Are you carefully maintaining His testimony and reputation?

II Corinthians 5:20 and Ephesians 6:20

Parenting Point

In the same way that we are to be ambassadors for Christ, our children are the ambassadors for our family name and reputation. When they are among others, they are presenting a picture to the world regarding our family's beliefs, standards, and allegiance. Although we never told our children to simply do what was right so that we wouldn't be embarrassed, we did exhort our children to do right because they were "Scheibners." We explained clearly to our children that because they were Scheibners, they needed to be a clear representation of what we believed and practiced in our home. The reason for this careful ambassadorship wasn't so that others would think well of us; but instead, was so that the name of our God would not come into disrepute. In our times of family devotions and discussion, we talked about the various convictions that were the basis of our family's beliefs. Sometimes, as we searched the Scripture, it became clear that our choice in a certain area was simply a preference and not a biblical conviction. In fact, after discussing some of those preferences, we occasionally changed our mind regarding certain choices we had made. When that happened, we shared our new decision with the children to make sure that they understood the reason for our change of direction. Be certain that the standard you are setting for your family is biblical. Perhaps, you should officially appoint your children as family ambassadors. Remind them that they are powerful representatives not only for your family but also for the God of the Universe! Being an ambassador is easy when the One we represent is so completely worthy of our praise and adoration.

275

Appropriateness • Others-Oriented

Family as a Blessing

In Genesis we see that at the same time God is announcing his promises to Abram, He presents Abram and his family with a tremendous task as well. This task was to be a blessing to others. From the earliest times God's intention has been to use His people to bring blessings into the lives of others. It has never been about us. As God's people bless others, they magnify their God and earn the opportunity to proclaim the greatness of their Lord.

Genesis 12:2

Parenting Point

How intentional are you in teaching your children to be a blessing to others? Left to themselves, our children won't naturally seek to be others-oriented; however, with just a little coaching from you, they can learn to love blessing others. Call a family conference and discuss ways that your family can bless others. Your example will be the greatest teaching tool in your parenting arsenal. Share ways that you are working to bless others. Perhaps, you will need to share what you WILL be doing, if blessing others hasn't been a priority activity in your life. Ask your children to make a list of what the whole family can do practically to reach out to and bless others. Once you have the list, get out your calendar and schedule times to put your ideas into action! Take the time to build a family legacy of blessing. Serving as a family should be the backbone of your children's favorite family memories. When our grown children visit home they often recall with fondness the many family ministries we participated in and enjoyed together.

Loyalty

The dictionary defines loyalty this way: faithfulness, or faithful adherence, to a person, government, or cause. Who or what holds your loyalty? In our hearts, we may know what we are loyal to, but is that loyalty evident to others? Perhaps everyone know that you are loyal to your special football or baseball team, but is your loyalty to the Lord Jesus Christ as obvious? When it comes to the Lord, it is great to wear your loyalty on your sleeve!

I Corinthians 1:9

Parenting Point

It is important for our children to learn to be loyal and faithful, but it is imperative that our children understand how loyal and faithful the Lord is toward them. Take time throughout your day to emphasize to your children the loyalty God shows toward them as He protects them, provides for them, and lavishes His blessings upon them.

Budding Responsibilities

Budding responsibilities are those responsibilities, which are primarily focused on self. While it is easy to understand the budding responsibilities of a child: make your bed, brush your teeth, change your clothes, etc., what are the budding responsibilities of an adult? Adult budding responsibilities are those activities that build the foundation for more and greater responsibilities. Responsibilities such as preparing a job resume, setting up student loan payments, establishing a budget, and caring for a home are all responsibilities that are focused on caring for self. In the spiritual realm, budding responsibilities would include the self-control and discipline necessary to pray, read the scriptures daily, and faithfully attend church. These budding responsibilities are the stepping-stones necessary to build a firm foundation on which to construct the primary responsibilities. Although these responsibilities may seem tedious and humdrum, without them, the structure of future responsibilities will be unable to stand firm.

Isaiah 28:10

Parenting Point

It isn't hard to train your children to embrace their budding responsibilities! Honestly, sometimes we, the parents, are the biggest hindrance to learning these necessary responsibilities. Moms, especially, seem to find it difficult to allow their children to perform tasks that they, the mother, can do so much better. Yes, a bed made by a three year old will not look perfect, but when you step in and perform this chore for your children, or worse yet, redo the bed after they have completed the task, you are robbing your children of an important developmental life-lesson. Instead, help them to succeed! In a few years, you will remember with fondness the crooked comforter and bumpy bedspread. Make a list of budding responsibilities for each of your children and begin to systematically train them to be responsible members of your family. As today's scripture reminds us, our children will learn "Line on line, line on line; a little here, a little there."

The Week in Review

Take some time to gather as a family and discuss the character qualities that you learned this week. Here are some questions to get the conversation started.

- List the character qualities we studied this week.
- Which character quality was the hardest for you to practice this week?
- Did you see a family member consistently practicing one of this week's character qualities? Which family member?

Use your imagination and add questions of your own. After your time of discussion, spend some time praying together, thanking the Lord and sharing one another's burdens. Pray ahead of time for teachable hearts to incorporate and put into practice the character qualities your family will learn in the upcoming week.

Patience Takes Practice

I wish I could just hurry up and gain patience; this whole "working to develop patience" makes me impatient! Ever feel like that? Patience is defined as: the bearing of provocation, annoyance, misfortune, or pain, without complaint. Ouch! It's that last part that seems to cause me the most difficulty. Learning to wait patiently, without grumbling or complaining, is a character quality that certainly doesn't come naturally. What are you waiting for today? Ask God to help you bear up under the waiting and to demonstrate a peaceful and non-complaining attitude, as God works to perfect His patience in you.

Philippians 2:14

Parenting Point

Are your children impatient? I know mine are! Honestly, I don't think many children have a natural propensity towards patience; therefore, as their parents, it becomes our job to (patiently) instill this character quality. Too many times, we give in to our children's desires simply because we don't want them to whine or be unhappy. Delayed gratification holds a wellspring of valuable lessons for our children. As they learn to wait patiently for whatever it is that they desire, they are learning self-control, thwarting a covetous spirit, and building anticipation and gratitude for the time that they finally acquire the hoped for possession, privilege, or activity. Don't rob them of this lesson. Even if you can afford what is wanted immediately, sometimes, the lesson of waiting is more beneficial than the fulfillment of wishes; however, don't simply withhold the desire object or activity. Instead, take the time to teach into the waiting process. Talk about the positive character qualities that you are trying to help your children develop. Waiting becomes easier when our children know that sometimes we have to practice patience and wait for things as well. Share some instances with your children of things you prayed for that the Lord's answer was simply, "Wait." Let them know what you did to help with the development of patience and self-control. Remind them that you haven't arrived, but just like them, you are enrolled in God's school of patience training!

Your Character = Your Testimony

How important is your testimony to you? As you go about your day, is the integrity of your testimony in the forefront of your mind? When we simply give lip service to the importance of our testimony and do not spend time carefully scrutinizing our actions to make sure that they align with what we say we believe, we run the risk of damaging our testimony, and we are living the life of a hypocrite. Read today's verse. If even a child is known by his actions, how much more so will we, as adults, be recognized by what we do and not simply by what we say? Inward character prompts outward actions, and those outward actions will either build or destroy our testimony for Christ.

Proverbs 20:11

Parenting Point

It's never too early to begin teaching your children to recognize that their outward actions will either build or destroy their reputation and testimony. As today's Scripture makes clear, even a child will be recognized by their actions. The New American Standard goes on to say that a child will be distinguished if their deeds are pure and right. The only way that our children can learn what constitutes "good and right" is through our diligent training. Although it is easy to disregard poor behavior in our children and to assume that eventually they will outgrow that behavior, we are setting our children up for failure when we do not intervene and enforce change in their actions. It is a heavy burden for a teenager to have to reestablish a good testimony simply because they were allowed to behave poorly as a child. Remind your children that their personal testimony should be their most precious possession. When our children choose to live lives of great character, they will have the ability to influence other children and even the adults with whom they interact. There is no magic age when a testimony finally matters. Your child's testimony is just as important and impactful as your own. Sharing stories of your child's mistakes and sinful choices with others will only damage their testimony and reputation. Share positives about your children, both when you're alone with others and when your children are there to hear your encouraging report. Positively praising good behavior in our children will always be an impetus to more good behavior. Guard your own testimony carefully, and teach your children to guard theirs as well.

Give Up Your Rights

Have you ever thought of preferring one another as a way to show love? Actually, preferring someone else may be the most self-sacrificing way we are afforded to show that we love one another. When we choose to prefer someone else over ourselves, we are always forced to relinquish something that we think we have a "right" to possess. Preferring forces our importance to take backseat, while others are esteemed as more important than us.

Romans 12:10

Parenting Point

Teaching your children to prefer one another may be one of your most difficult parenting tasks. It is simply in our sinful natures to want what we want, and even more, what we think we deserve. Learning to sacrificially give up these perceived rights will produce children with the most others-oriented character. Look for practical moments throughout the day to teach this important character quality. For example, in our home the oldest child was entitled to the front seat in the car. Giving up that right was almost impossible for some of our children; they just didn't want to surrender what they felt they deserved in order to bless a younger brother or sister. What an important lesson to learn. Other teaching opportunities will arise over the last cookie, who gets to pick the DVD, including younger siblings when friends are over, etc. Don't miss these opportunities to teach into the character producing quality of preferring others. To help your children learn how to incorporate preferring behavior into their lives, spend some time role-playing various circumstances. Act out situations of preferring and situations of looking out for self. Have your children explain the difference between the two situations. Ask them what fruit is produced when we only look out for our own interests. Then, ask them what fruit will be produced as we prefer one another. When you see your children proactively preferring each other, take the time to praise them and encourage their Biblical character.

Ready or Not

The military spends time, money, and assets, on developing the readiness of their troops. This readiness is what will bring victory and safety when the unexpected happens. No soldier can foresee every eventuality on the battlefield, but the time spent developing the actions and an attitude of readiness will equip each soldier to respond appropriately when surprises come. It seems like the character quality of readiness is just as important in the life of a soldier of Christ. As believers, we cannot foresee the people, situations, and difficulties that the Lord will send our way. As we work hard to equip ourselves through Bible reading, prayer, fellowship, scripture memorization, and service, we will be building spiritual readiness that will prepare us to minister on a moment's notice.

2 Timothy 4:2

Parenting Point

Are your children ready for whatever spiritual eventuality comes their way? In the midst of our busy days running our children to sports, music, and a multitude of other activities, we must be careful to spend an appropriate amount of time building their readiness to serve the Lord. Consider your child's day. Do they spend a disproportionate amount of time on worldly activities, only to find themselves exhausted and unable to spend the time they need to grow in the Lord? You need to be the guardian of their time and day. Do whatever it takes to arm your children for spiritual readiness in the spirit of Ephesians 6:13-18.

Just Do It!

How many of you read the title of today's character quality and immediately knew what product was associated with this saying? As this catchy phrase reminds us, there are times that we need to "Just do it!" the Word of God reminds us of this same dynamic in James 1:22, where we are exhorted to be doers of the Word. Obviously, hearing the Word is essential, but sometimes it is too easy to just listen and walk away. All of us need the occasional reminder to not simply sit back and rest in our spiritual lives, but to "do" the things we have been learning. How is your doing...doing?

James 1:22

Parenting Point

Fill in the blank for this statement: "Delayed obedience is _____." As parents, we all know the answer is disobedience, but are we teaching that concept to our children? It is of utmost importance to teach our children the important character quality of being a doer. Without this firmly in place, they will easily be lured into delaying their obedience, not just with us but also in their relationship with the Lord. Take some time this week to evaluate how your children are doing in their first-time obedience and make adjustments as necessary. If, after evaluation, you recognize that your children are slow to obey, or worse yet, refusing to obey, teach into this negative character quality. Clearly communicate your standards of obedience and have your children repeat those standards back to you. Then, role-play some different "obedience" situations. Reward your children for their good decisions and commitment to obedience. As necessary, bring correction into the lives of any children who choose to disobey or delay in their obedience. As your children incorporate the need to obey their parents, they are building the habits necessary to learn to obey the Lord.

Appropriateness

The Home Priority

How important is your family? While it is important to be characterized as a servant in your church and community, that characterization will lose its power if you do not have the same testimony of care concerning your own family. Home is the place to learn how to serve unconditionally and sacrificially. Although the praise may not be as exuberant and public, showing "piety" at home first will only serve to build your witness and testimony outside your home as well.

I Timothy 5:4

Parenting Point

Is your family a top priority? Is it a priority for your children? In our busy days and with a myriad of activities to choose from, it is easy to overlook our families and the importance of a strong family dynamic. Many teach their children the simple JOY acronym (Jesus, Others, Yourself). I would encourage you to change up the acronym a bit. Instead, teach your children to consider JOY this way: Jesus, Our family, Your other friends. Don't worry, your children will find plenty of time to consider the missing "Yourself" part! With this different perspective, however, your children will be encouraged to consider their own family and the importance of that priority. Remind them that even when you are old and gone, they will always have one another. In light of this fact, building strong family relationships and serving one another at home should be of utmost importance. This is an area where what you model will speak louder than any words you say. What does your model look like today?

The Week in Review

Take some time to gather as a family and discuss the character qualities that you learned this week. Here are some questions to get the conversation started.

- **List the character qualities we studied this week.**

- **Which character quality was the hardest for you to practice this week?**

- **Did you see a family member consistently practicing one of this week's character qualities? Which family member?**

Use your imagination and add questions of your own. After your time of discussion, spend some time praying together, thanking the Lord and sharing one another's burdens. Pray ahead of time for teachable hearts to incorporate and put into practice the character qualities your family will learn in the upcoming week.

A Critical Thinker or Just Critical?

Although it is absolutely true that our world is in need of more critical thinkers, I'm afraid all that we're developing is a generation of critical spirits. Wisdom shows itself in the lives of people who can carefully and consistently evaluate the situations and circumstances of our world and then make deliberate decisions and choices. The fool, however, simply criticizes or complains about what is happening in their world. They have no shortage of negative opinions, but a real lack of problem-solving skills. Consider yourself today. If you fall into that "critical" category, what must you put off in order to replace a critical spirit with a oritically thinking mind?

Ephesians 4:29-32

Parenting Point

Wow! It is easy to slip into the habit of having a critical spirit! Whether our soup is too cold, our sleep is too short, or our neighbors are too noisy, when we are characterized by complaints and criticism, nothing seems to go right. It should come as no surprise then, that children who live in a critical home, surrounded by critical comments and facial expressions, will become small critical imitations of their parents. What a terrible family testimony but one that can easily be remedied. Take some time to evaluate your family's characterization. Listen to the comments and conversations engaged in by family members. If you recognize a preponderance of critical or negative comments, the time to take action is NOW. Write down some of the common critical comments overheard in your home. Then, call a family conference table to discuss your findings. First, as parents and the leaders in the home, own up to your responsibility in setting a critical tone in your home. Humbly seek your children's forgiveness for allowing and perpetuating a critical tempo in your home. Share some of your written observations and ask your children to tell you whether those statements were positive and uplifting or negative and hurtful. Have your children share "replacement" statements that would be more God-honoring. Read Ephesians 4:29-32 with your family. Brainstorm together what types of communications would be edifying, kind, and tenderhearted. Close your time in prayer, committing together as a family to put-off critical spirits and to instead develop a heart of wisdom and edification.

Christ Lives in Me

Today's character quality is closely linked with the paradigm of becoming a new creation. In our own power, we can never successfully put away our old paradigms and find everything to be "new" in Christ. Today, we learn how to replace these paradigms successfully; it is by living our life in faith. Because Christ loved us and delivered Himself up for us, we can trust Him to live in us and to help us crucify our flesh and those old, tired paradigms. As we, in our flesh, are daily crucified, Christ can more fully live in us.

Galatians 2:20

Parenting Point

What does it mean to crucify our flesh? Even as adults, this is a difficult concept with which to wrestle. How much more so for our children! Often, the battles we fight against our flesh are fought privately, simply between the Lord and us. When it is appropriate, I would encourage you to share your battles with your children. As they see you daily crucifying your own flesh, they will have a clearer idea how to do battle in their own lives. Most importantly, share clearly with your children how it is Christ living in you who helps you to have victory and to live by faith. As they see Christ's loving hand working to bring change in your life, they will build spiritual muscle to trust His work in their lives as well. Be careful to share with your children that change doesn't simply come about by trying harder or making changes in our own strength; rather, it is as we walk closely and obediently with Christ that He will empower us to make lasting and biblical change.

Spiritual Hunger • Diligence • Perseverance

Go For the Gold

Every four years we witness athletes who have spent hours developing and honing their particular skills. In order to compete in the Olympic games, they are willing to forgo social opportunities and lazy days in favor of practice time and extra workouts. Their total commitment should raise some questions in our minds. Are we as committed to training our thoughts and hearts to obey the Lord as they are to training their muscles to obey their direction? Are we willing to sacrifice fun for the sake of spiritual growth? Only you can answer those questions for yourself, but as today's verses remind us, those who discipline themselves for the sake of godliness will not be disqualified for the prize of the crown that lasts forever.

I Corinthians 9:25-27

Parenting Point

As parents, we must be careful to teach our children the importance of sacrifice and discipline when it comes to developing their spiritual muscles. Too often, we abandon spiritual growth at the first hint of difficulty. We send our children to soccer with a cold, but at the first sniffle we skip church. We allow them to stay up late watching a favorite movie, but we keep them home from Bible study because they will miss their bedtime. Don't think for a moment that our children don't notice this double standard. What we are unwittingly teaching them is that spiritual growth is optional, it will always be there when you get around to it so there is no urgency or necessity. Instead, we must train our children to put spiritual growth first in their lives. In order to do this, they must see how important the Lord is in our own lives. One simple tool we have used with our family is the "No Bible, No Breakfast" rule. We don't always have this rule in place, but when we sense that we, or the children, are slipping in our commitment to time in the Word, we announce that without individual Bible time no one eats breakfast. This is a great accountability for me, since often I want to get busy with my "to do" list first thing in the morning. If time in the Word isn't on the list, I run the risk of skipping it for the day. Consider your own family dynamic. What routines could you put in place to emphasize the importance of spiritual discipline?

Honor in Action

Honor, courage, and commitment are the U.S. Navy's core values. During my 28 years of service, I had many opportunities to put those values into action. What does honor look like in your life? The Bible tells us to honor our parents. We are told that our pastors are worthy of double honor; yet we know that Jesus was afforded no honor from those in His own country (John 4:44). Although honor is something that is earned, it is also granted based on position. Parents, pastors, and the police should be granted honor due to their positions of authority. We honor those in authority by treating them with respect. Our words, tone, posture, and eyes communicate our level of honor. So, what does honor look like in your life, and how can you raise your standard of honor toward those in your circle of influence?

Ephesians 6:1-2, 1 Timothy 5:17

Parenting Point

How do you show honor toward your parents? Do your children hear you verbally disparage Grandma and Grandpa? Do your tone, posture, and demeanor communicate respect? Remember, respect is different than obedience. We can still respect those with whom we may have to lovingly disagree. Showing respect for age, position, and authority communicates the importance we place on honor. When was the last time you thanked the policeman for pulling you over when you were speeding? His job is difficult, and showing him disrespect when we are in the wrong makes his job even harder. It also communicates a terrible message to our children, who are intently watching from the back seat. To help your children understand the somewhat nebulous term "honor," spend some time teaching into the term. Call a family conference table and role-play different scenarios in which you or your children could show honor to others. By example, show them what honoring communication looks like by speaking respectfully and kindly to one another. When you hear your children speaking in a tone, or with words, that are dishonoring, take the time to stop and bring correction. Don't simply tell them, "Don't talk that way!" Instead, use the Biblical term "honor" and help them to understand how the way they were communicating was not honorable, but rather, dishonorable and, therefore, displeasing to the Lord.

Single-minded Focus

Deuteronomy 6:5 states, "And you shall love the Lord your God with all your heart and with all your soul and with all your might." Heart, soul, might. Those three words sum up the areas that are to be focused on the Lord; however, perhaps the most important word in this verse is a simple three-lettered word: ALL. To embrace the character quality of single-minded focus, ALL of our heart, ALL of our soul, and ALL of our mind must be directed toward the Lord. Although these words come easily off our tongues, it takes individual and introspective examination to determine how carefully we are living out this imperative from the Lord. Take some time today to examine the areas of your life that threaten to take priority over the ALL for God.

Deuteronomy 6:5

Parenting Point

Today's parenting point is for our hearts more than our children's hearts. How are you doing, parent, in loving God more than you love your children? It is easy to say that God is our priority, but our children, simply by virtue of their presence and immediate needs, can usurp that #1 position that should only be filled by God. It is not enough to tell our children that God is the most important relationship in our life; they need to see that importance acted upon in daily choices. Telling our children "NO" in order to make a priority choice for the Lord, will do wonderful things for their hearts and security. They may not show their appreciation for your choices right away, but you will be helping them to see what single-minded focus looks like in practice. As you love God with ALL your heart, and ALL your soul, and ALL your might, you can trust that He will bless your efforts, and your children will be the recipients of that blessing as well. Ask the Lord to give you eyes to see who truly fills the #1 priority position in your life. Spouses, help one another to recognize when the children have usurped God's position.

A Character of Full Provision

Read today's verse. According to Philippians 4:19, every true need we experience will be met by God through the riches of Christ Jesus. God's Word is true, but does our character show that we believe this truth? Do we live as those who have been blessed to have every true need met by the Lord? It is easy to look at what we don't have or what we wish we had, but have we spent time meditating and praising God for what we already have? Living a life that demonstrates full provision as provided by God, will be a winsome testimony to our friends and family. As we share the fullness of God's provision in our lives, they will be encouraged to recognize His provision to them as well. What a light fully provided for Christians can shine in a never satisfied world! Take some time today to make a list of the bountiful blessings that God has provided for you.

Philippians 4:19

Parenting Point

Are your children satisfied with what has been provided for them? Friends, television, magazines, and social media all conspire to convince our children that they are in need. Without the latest gizmo how can they ever be happy? Don't be fooled. The more time our children spend filling their minds and eyes with the "I gotta haves!" the more difficult they will find it to be thankful and content with what the Lord's provision has already provided for them. Even when we are financially able to provide whatever the latest item is, to do so is often at the detriment of our children's character. If your children seem to always desire something more, take some time to teach into gratitude, contentment, and thankfulness. Call a family conference and together with your children read today's verse. Then, encourage your children to look around the room you are in and make a list of 10 things for which they are thankful. After they share their lists, recite some of the many ways that you, as parents, have seen God provide for your family. Spend time praying and thanking God for His bountiful provision. Whenever you sense your children becoming dissatisfied or demanding, repeat the above exercise. The more time they spend recognizing God's blessings, the more they will be thankful rather than continually desiring more. When you see God fill a need, make sure to point it out to your children. Thankfulness will change a family from always needing more to gratefully sharing what God has provided.

The Week in Review

Take some time to gather as a family and discuss the character qualities that you learned this week. Here are some questions to get the conversation started.

- **List the character qualities we studied this week.**
- **Which character quality was the hardest for you to practice this week?**
- **Did you see a family member consistently practicing one of this week's character qualities? Which family member?**

Use your imagination and add questions of your own. After your time of discussion, spend some time praying together, thanking the Lord and sharing one another's burdens. Pray ahead of time for teachable hearts to incorporate and put into practice the character qualities your family will learn in the upcoming week.

Characterized by Faithfulness

Faithfulness is not a now and then attribute. It is an oxymoron to say, "I was faithful for a while." Much like "Jumbo Shrimp," "Accidentally on Purpose," or "Original Copies," periodic faithfulness just doesn't make any sense. Read today's scripture and consider the contrast between faithfulness and unrighteousness. For the follower of Christ the choice is clear: There are no part-time positions available; our only option is full-time faithfulness!

Luke 16:10

Parenting Point

Are your children characterized by faithfulness? Every day we are either training our children to live lives of faithfulness, or we are allowing them to build negative habits of unfaithfulness. Really, the difference lies with us. We, ourselves, must make the choice to be either faithful in diligently training our children, or lazily allowing half-completed work and lowered standards. We train our children to be faithful when we insist that they complete their work 100% and when we hold them to a high standard of obedience and responsibility. If our children can count on us to check their work and to consistently correct poor attitudes and communication, they will be well on their way to learning how to be faithful; however, if our children know that we will overlook the standard on days we are tired, or days we have company, or when we're out of the home, you can be sure that they will take advantage of that fact. Our faithfulness is the example they will model. This is not to say that we can never *choose* to make an exception, but an exception must be just that, a deviation from the norm. Although it is hard work some days to get up and deal with our children's irresponsibility or unpleasant attitudes, diligently carrying out their training will reap the sweet and long-term benefits of a character marked by faithfulness.

The Heart of a Killer

I s it possible that God would ever call us to have the heart of a killer? When it comes to our own sinful appetites and attitudes, the answer is a resounding yes! When God confronts us with areas of sin that we are holding onto, our only response should be total annihilation. No half-measures, no prisoners of war, when it comes to sin we are to be ruthless killers. Who's winning the war in your heart today?

Ecclesiastes 3:3

Parenting Point

Are there areas of sin in your children's lives that you hesitate to address? Whether we tolerate certain sins because we are unsure of how our children will respond or whether we tolerate them because they seem "cute," sin is serious in God's eyes and needs to be dealt with seriously. Sometimes parents will allow disrespectful or disobedient attitudes and actions from young children because they think it is endearing in a young child. If something is sinful for an older child, it is sinful for a young child as well! When you allow precocious behavior, you are setting your children up to build habits that will be difficult, if not impossible to break when they are older. Teach your children to view sin the way God views sin. He hates it! It is because of our sin that Christ went to the cross, and we should never forget that fact. Radical amputation of whatever is causing our children to sin is the only answer to sinful appetites and attitudes. As always, our children need to see evidence in our lives that we treat our own sin with the seriousness that we treat theirs. Don't cut yourself a break in this area. When God reveals a sinful pocket of rebellion, kill it!

The Honor Exercise

One who is honorable is one who is not disposed to cheat or defraud; not deceptive or fraudulent. Such a person is honest, genuine, ingenuous, sincere, square, straight, true, trustable, and trustworthy. Could you be described as honorable? Honor, like integrity, is something we ought to be characterized by, not just something we do on occasion. Rendering honor where it is due and acting honorably ought to be the earmarks of the character healthy follower of Christ. Read the following verse and note the role our thought-life plays in being honorable.

Philippians 4:8

Parenting Point

Do an honor exercise with your children. Pick a suitable video or movie that has a strong contrast between good and evil in the story line. Next, watch the movie together as a family and plan to stop the movie at certain points to ask your children to explain whether the character(s) in question acted with honor or dishonor. Be mindful of "good" characters, which act dishonorably to achieve some greater good. Hollywood is tricky that way! Remember, it is never acceptable to God for us to do what is wrong in order to accomplish good... Never! Our culture may try to redefine honor, but for the follower of Christ, the Bible is our standard of measurement and must always be our final authority in defining this important character quality. Don't hesitate to challenge your older children on their definition of honor. When they share quotes from dishonorable television shows or Internet clips, take the time to ask them good dialogue questions. Ask them questions such as: "Does that show encourage you to show respect for others?" "How do you feel about how those characters speak to one another?" "Does that show support a Biblical worldview?" When our young adults can make their own discoveries regarding the choices they are making, the necessary changes will be much easier to implement. Resist the urge to simply say, "That show is horrible! Stop watching it!" Such communication will simply cause division and will be counter-productive in our children's lives. Present a consistent example of honor and respect, both in front of your children and toward your children, and trust God to bring about the Biblical change in their lives.

Faithfulness

What's the 411?

What's the 411, the scoop, the lowdown, on your life? If someone were to ask your family, pastor, or co-workers, to describe and characterize your life, what would the result be? Your testimony is the most noticeable character quality in your life. Proverbs 20:11 reminds us that even a child will be known by his character. How much more so an adult? Perhaps, today would be an opportune time to ask a trusted friend to honestly evaluate your 411!

Proverbs 20:11

Parenting Point

Do your children realize that even today, they are building a testimony and a characterization of their lives? I believe that many young people persist in making ungodly or unwise choices because they think that their actions and attitudes won't count for, or against them, until they are older. Read today's Scripture together. Ask your children to define what actions would be characterized as pure and right. Help them to self-evaluate what type of testimony they think others would share about them. Encourage and exhort them, as necessary, to build a distinguishing, character-healthy testimony. Remind them that in the same way that you evaluate their friends based on the character of their actions, your children will also face that same type of judgment themselves. Too often, we judge ourselves on our motives and others on their actions. Help your children to recognize that it is their actions that will be observed by others, and that they will ultimately build and enhance or tear down and destroy their own testimony.

A Return to Respect

Have you ever spent time asking the Lord to reveal any areas of disrespect in your life? May we encourage you to take any conviction that God brings to mind and develop an action plan for success? Too often, we discover a truth about a change needed in our lives and then stop short of taking action. As you work to obey God and His direction, your testimony of change will be an encouragement to others. God is aching to bless our obedience, give Him the opportunity to bless you today!

Ephesians 4:22

Parenting Point

Help your children consider the other people and situations in their lives that require them to show respect. Write down the list with your children including people such as their parents, pastors, teachers, etc. and such situations as respecting other's possessions, obeying the law, esteeming the elderly, etc. Your family will come up with more ideas, I am sure. Along with compiling the list, help your children to determine practical ways to show respect in each relationship or circumstance. Pick one area, as a family, and spend time helping one another to develop more respectful attitudes in that one area. When you see positive and proactive change occurring in your children's lives, take the time to encourage them with words and actions. Insist that all family members treat one another with respect, and you will begin to build a strong foundation of respectful behavior towards all.

An Others-Orientation

Today's Scripture reminds us that as followers of Christ, along with loving the Lord, we must be oriented to the needs of others. This others-orientation is demonstrated as we love our neighbor as ourselves. Many of the character qualities that seem less important, or perhaps more optional, are character qualities that are oriented toward showing respect and care to others. Although they may seem less important, remember, for our character to possess integrity or wholeness, all areas of character must be working together, in a unified and harmonious way. No area of character is optional. The scripture, in Matthew, shows us God's heart considering the importance of others.

Matthew 22:36-39

Parenting Point

It does not come naturally for our children to put others first. Honestly, it doesn't come naturally for us to put others first either. Spend some time reading today's Scripture together and discussing how each family member can "love their neighbor as themselves." Ask your children who makes up the category of "their neighbor." Although there are some people that are easier to love, we don't have the freedom to pick and choose whom we will love as ourselves. Begin praying, as a family, that you will love both God and others in a wholehearted way. Get your children excited about the lesser recognized, but equally important, character qualities related to honoring and respecting others. Challenge them to choose someone to honor each day. At the dinner table, allow them to share the honoring actions that they have initiated. Encourage great character, and you will see your children strive to show even greater character!

The Week in Review

Take some time to gather as a family and discuss the character qualities that you learned this week. Here are some questions to get the conversation started.

- **List the character qualities we studied this week.**

- **Which character quality was the hardest for you to practice this week?**

- **Did you see a family member consistently practicing one of this week's character qualities? Which family member?**

Use your imagination and add questions of your own. After your time of discussion, spend some time praying together, thanking the Lord and sharing one another's burdens. Pray ahead of time for teachable hearts to incorporate and put into practice the character qualities your family will learn in the upcoming week.

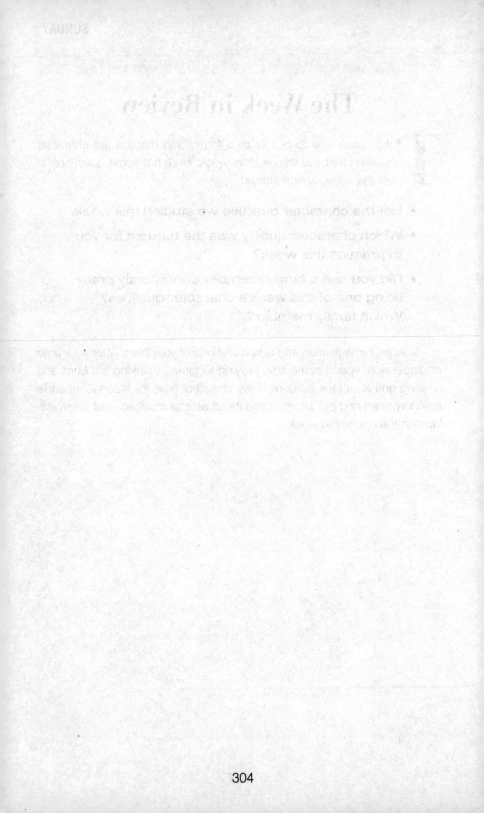

Courage

Courage is the glue that keeps our moral integrity intact. Real courage shows up in the daily decision-making process. It takes courage to elevate virtues above feelings. It takes courage to hand back the extra change when the cashier gives you too much. It takes courage to change the channel on the TV when the subject matter is not appropriate. It takes courage to say no to worldly pursuits, especially when "everybody else" is doing it. In short, it takes courage to do what's right. How steep is your courage curve? Would you consider yourself courageous or cowardly when it comes to elevating virtues above feelings?

Esther 8:4-7

Parenting Point

The overindulgent parenting culture of 21st century America squeezes us into the mold of being a friend and a buddy with our children. If we act more like a peer than a parent, what our children lose is the protection of an adult who wisely and firmly says "No" to overindulgence and "Yes" to self-discipline and delayed gratification. Your children need a mom and dad who have the courage to lovingly lead. Your courage will be the glue that helps keep their moral house in order. Yes, they will test your resolve on a daily basis, yet their hearts truly hope that you will mean what you say and say what you mean. When we are capricious in our standards and inconsistent in our discipline, we build insecurity into the hearts of our children. Because they cannot be sure that we will enforce the standards we have verbalized, they will become natural gamblers, weighing the cost of doing business with us against the potential for any consequences. Often, parents are shocked when their disobedient children obey and perform for a demanding athletic coach. Really, this is no surprise. Those coaches demand certain standards, and they are willing to enact discipline for those athletes who choose to ignore their standards. For kids, this firm stand equals security. They know what is required; they also know the consequences if they fail and the reward for disciplined behavior. Friendship with our children is a laudable goal; however, it cannot be achieved at the expense of their character. If we do the necessary hard work of consistent parenting when our children are young, friendship will become the achievable and natural outcome of our parenting.

Rejoice!!

Do you ever wonder about God's will for your life? Today's verse makes clear one area of God's will for His children...We are to rejoice! What do your circumstances look like today? Are you facing trials and difficulties? God's will is for you to rejoice. Are you blessed and content? God's will is for you to rejoice. This rejoicing isn't a Pollyanna type of putting on a happy face, but rather comes from a deep and settled relationship with the Lord and a clear understanding of His graciousness towards us, His children. If you are struggling to rejoice today, begin to list the many acts of kindness that the Lord has shown you. Gratitude and thanksgiving promote rejoicing and a rejoicing Christian finds peace, regardless of the circumstances.

Philippians 4:4

Parenting Point

Is your home characterized by an atmosphere of rejoicing? If not, why not? There is no shortage of the problems our homes face and grumbling certainly comes naturally. It takes a concerted effort on our part to keep our homes a place of joy and rejoicing. Take time each day to rehearse the goodness of God with one another and with your children. I would suggest keeping a notebook handy to write down the blessings that God brings to your family each day. Without a commitment to recognizing those blessings, it is easy to focus on the negative and never notice how God is protecting and providing for your family. Teach your children to look for "God Sightings," those times that God unexpectedly brings blessing into your home. Make it a game, and you'll see your children begin to actively watch for God's intervention on their behalf. Whenever I'm having a particularly trying time, Steve will ask me to list three things I am encouraged about that day. The exercise of finding encouragement always reminds me just how much I have to be thankful for and thankfulness increases my ability to rejoice, regardless of my circumstances. A home characterized by rejoicing becomes a sanctuary for our families, friends, and those who need to see the goodness of God in action. What's God's will for our families? Rejoicing!

Wayward Wisdom

The dictionary defines wisdom this way: the ability to discern or judge what is true, right, or lasting; insight. Godly wisdom will protect us from harm, assist us in making wise decisions, and direct us onto the paths that we should follow; however, being wise in our own eyes is a different story altogether. This type of self-centered "wisdom," will only lead us to think of ourselves more highly than we ought, and then to trust in our own discernment rather than seeking godly discernment. True wisdom comes from an intimate walk with the Lord. Whose wisdom are you following today?

Proverbs 3:7

Parenting Point

Children, who are wise in their own eyes, will make some terrible decisions. As small children, their decisions may not have long-term consequences, yet as they grow older and have more freedom, those "wise in their own eyes" decisions can have devastating and life-long consequences. Begin when your children are young to teach them how to seek the Lord for wisdom. When you hear pronouncements about situations and other people that are ill-suited coming from a child, don't laugh! Instead, remind them that they are lacking wisdom and shouldn't be asserting opinions about things they do not yet understand. When young children interject themselves into adult conversations as though they are a peer, they are acting in a rude and disrespectful manner. Teach into those poor character qualities and help your children to replace rudeness with consideration and respect. Help them to put-off precociousness and put-on appropriateness. When we laugh at our children's precocious behavior, we are simply encouraging more precocious behavior. Then, when our children become teens and their behavior isn't "cute" anymore, we will suddenly see them as obnoxious rather than entertaining. We do our children a disservice when we set them up for failure in this way. Teach them how to develop true wisdom by encouraging them to spend time in the Word and time learning from those who are older and wiser.

Contentment

Ontentment is an action that results in a feeling of calm and satisfaction. Contentment is often found in simple things. Being content means that our conversation should be free from covetousness. The things that we lust after that are outside of God's will are those things that cause hate and discontent in our lives. Read and study the following text on contentment. What role does the love of money play?

Hebrews 13:5

Parenting Point

Ask your kids to define coveting. Write down their answers and read them back. Ask how coveting leads to discontentment. Tune your ears to recognize expressions of coveting and point them out. Coveting is an insidious and easy habit to slip into. In fact, in many ways we can become almost deaf to the habitual coveting that our children display. Commit some time to carefully listen to your children's conversation as you go about your day. When you walk through a store, do your children continually ask you to buy them something new? When you give something to another sibling, are certain children characterized by immediately asking what you have for them? As you watch television or listen to the radio, do your children request whatever is being advertised? Covetous children can so completely pepper their conversation with requests and demands that we inadvertently begin to tune them out. Ignoring their covetous behavior is not a solution to the problem. Instead, we must call their continual requests by the biblical name "coveting," and we must help them understand that their covetous nature is sin. Every time that we hear our children begin a sentence with, "I want..." or "Can I have..." we must quickly and consistently bring their coveting to their attention. For the children that are strongly characterized by coveting, it is important to help them swing the pendulum completely in the opposite direction. For a couple of our children, we had to implement a time of allowing absolutely NO requests. Because of their addiction to covetous behavior, even if a request was reasonable, those children needed to learn to be content with what they had and to wait for us to bless them rather than demanding to be blessed. We all covet; however, for some it is the predominant sin appetite. Don't allow coveting to go unchecked. Work diligently to help your children recognize their coveting behavior. Be careful not to be a poor example of coveting yourself, and watch your family's level of contentment soar.

Honor is no Little Thing

Honor ought to show up in the little things of life. We can honor our spouses by speaking kindly, lovingly, and respectfully to them. As well, we can honor our spouses by how we speak of them to others. We can honor our commitments by being on time for work, church, and appointments. We gain honor when we esteem others higher than ourselves and when we consistently elevate virtues above feelings. Honor doesn't happen by accident, it takes persistent and consistent action.

Matthew 6:33

Parenting Point

Teach your children the value of honor this week by celebrating the little ways they demonstrate honor to you and to the family. For instance, when they arrive on time, tell them you are honored by their punctuality. When they clean their room to your satisfaction, tell them you are honored by their commitment to cleanliness. When they speak kindly to you and others in the family, tell them you are honored by their considerate words. We can show honor, or dishonor, in almost everything we do. As your children hear your encouraging words regarding their honorable actions, you will be strengthening their heart's desire to find more ways of show-ing honor. Challenge the entire family to recognize one another's acts of honor. To cement the importance of honor in your home, spend some time celebrating the recognized acts of honor. Perhaps, you could initi-ate an "Honor Party" and use that time to share what honorable actions have been noticed within the home. Prepare some simple award ribbons and present the ribbons for different forms of honor, which have been extended to one another. Be the example for your children as you clap and celebrate one another's successes. Find a way to make the evening fun for every member of the family, and your children will be clamoring to practice more honor and to celebrate those honoring practices frequently.

Transformed Living

G od's mercies to us are rich and new every day. In light of those mercies, He wants us to live transformed lives. The Christian testimony is to be distinct, separate, and winsome to others. By resisting conformity to this world, we allow God's mercies to be demonstrated to us and through us. Transformed living is not a character quality for a select group of elite believers; rather, it is the mandate for us all.

Romans 12:1-2

Parenting Point

Today, make a list of areas in your family's life that need to be transformed. Think first of the ways in which you have conformed to the world. Next, create a plan to put-off those things and put-on the higher standard of God's Word. Your list might include such things as T.V. viewing choices, movie choices, Internet usage, etc. As you consider the changes that need to be made, you may need to seek your children's forgiveness. Often, we brought in the unbiblical activities and possessions that have invaded our home. Ouch! Humbly confess your poor choices to your children and seek their forgiveness. God has so graciously equipped our children to forgive their parents. Then, take the time to carefully consider the choices you make in the future. Proverbs makes it clear that the wise man sees the danger ahead and carefully avoids it. As parents, we must become those wise men. When we are deliberate and careful in our choices, we avoid becoming involved in a tug-of-war with our children as they try to hold on to those damaging activities and possessions that we first allowed in their lives.

The Week in Review

Take some time to gather as a family and discuss the character qualities that you learned this week. Here are some questions to get the conversation started.

- List the character qualities we studied this week.

- Which character quality was the hardest for you to practice this week?

- Did you see a family member consistently practicing one of this week's character qualities? Which family member?

Use your imagination and add questions of your own. After your time of discussion, spend some time praying together, thanking the Lord and sharing one another's burdens. Pray ahead of time for teachable hearts to incorporate and put into practice the character qualities your family will learn in the upcoming week.

Successful Like the Savior

How do you define success? The dictionary has two definitions for the word success, the first is this: the attainment of popularity or profit. To the world, this definition would probably make sense. Many folks, Christians included, spend their time, efforts, and ambitions, to gain popularity or profit. A lack of these attributes can make some people feel as though they are failures. Consider, however, the second definition of success: the accomplishment of an aim or purpose. Would Christ Jesus have been considered a success according to the first definition? He never owned property. He was reviled and spat upon. He was a suffering servant. He was not esteemed. Hardly consistent with one who has attained popularity or profit! But, when we consider definition number two... There was no other man who was as successful as our Lord. He completely attained His aim and purpose through His death, burial, and resurrection from the dead. Which definition are you seeking to fulfill? Perhaps, as faithful followers of Christ, we need to change our definition of success!

Isaiah 53

Parenting Point

It is easy to get caught in the success trap. We all want our children to excel and succeed, but we must be careful to teach them the true definition of success. Our goal for ourselves and for our children should be complete attainment of the aim and purpose of being well-pleasing to God. Take time today to read Isaiah 53 aloud with your children. Ask them to define success. As you read through the scripture, ask them to share the words used to describe Christ (i.e., smitten, despised, forsaken, a man of sorrows, etc.). Ask them if these words seem to describe a successful man. Lead them to understand what true success looks like from God's point of view. Pray together that as a family you would seek to be successful FIRST in the Lord's eyes and then to trust Him for whatever worldly success He deems right for your family.

The Heart That Uproots

As much as we hate to let anything go, there are times that all of us are called to have the heart and character of an "uprooter." If we want to be faithful followers of Christ, we must be willing to allow Him to point out areas of weeds and unfruitful growth in our lives. When we see those areas, it is time to pull them out by the roots. Don't avoid the Gardener. Ask the Lord to show you any areas of your life that need a good weeding!

Ecclesiastes 3:2

Parenting Point

When our children are young, we are the primary "fruit inspectors" in their lives. When we see areas that need to be weeded and uprooted, we can encourage, exhort, and assist our children in making the necessary changes; however, as soon as possible, we need to help our children learn to receive their instruction from the Master Gardener, the Lord Jesus. Often, the Lord has convicted my children about necessary areas of change in their lives without me even being involved. How much easier change comes when the children are dealing directly with God, through the Holy Spirit, without the intervention of Mom or Dad! Too often, we become the issue and they are able to ignore what God is trying to point out in their lives. So, while your children are young, certainly you have the responsibility to point out their weedy areas, but as soon as they have a growing relationship with the Lord, begin to teach them how to seek His counsel, through prayer, study of the Word, and the counsel of other godly Christians. Be transparent with your children and share how God calls you to uproot unfruitful areas of your own life. Allow your children see you as a fellow struggler rather than an "already arrived" saint. Together you and your children can clear out the weeds from your individual garden patches.

Talent and the Multiplication Principle

Take a moment to consider how the Lord has gifted you with certain talents and abilities. Are you using those talents and abilities for Him? When we cling to our talents and claim them as our own possessions, our talents become limited and useless; however, when we recognize that our talents are on loan to us from God and He is the rightful owner, we can then use those talents for His glory, and He is delighted to multiply our talents.

Matthew 25:15-18

Parenting Point

Isn't it fun to see your children's developing talents? We have delighted to see our children become musicians, vocalists, athletes, filmmakers, culinary experts, and more. Although it is fun to watch our children's burgeoning talents grow, it is important to remind them that their special talents are a gift from God. As such, we must help them develop practical ways to use those talents for His honor and glory. We had one child who played an instrument beautifully but would refuse to play for the enjoyment and blessing of others. We carefully instructed her about using her gifts for God and helped her to realize that simply clinging to her talent for her own personal enrichment was robbing others of seeing God through her playing. Now, she happily plays for others and points to God as the source of her talent. With our athletes, we consistently encourage them to use their testimony of obedience to God for the edification of the whole team. It has been a blessing to hear from coaches who are thankful for our children's leadership on the team and "coachable" spirits. There is nothing particularly special about our kids; they are just learning to expend their talents for the kingdom of God. Help your children to realize that their talents are one of their greatest witnessing tools and should be viewed as just that: a tool for the Master's glory.

The Excellency of Etiquette

Consider this definition of etiquette, as shared by Naomi Polson, the founding director of The Etiquette Company. She states, "Etiquette has to do with good manners. It's not so much our own good manners, but making other people feel comfortable by the way we behave. So it's more or less thinking of others and how others perceive us." Sounds like the definition of an others-oriented Christian, doesn't it? Our society has discarded much that is considered good etiquette for the cause of expediency; however, that should not be the case with Christians. In a world that is becoming more and more self-centered and careless of others, our excellent manners will shine as a beacon for Christ. Simple statements such as "Please" and "Thank you" along with small actions, like thank you cards and handwritten notes will make Christians stand out as a careful people who are busy thinking of others. Regardless of what anyone else is doing, good etiquette is a simple way to exhibit loving your neighbor in a practical way.

Philippians 2:3-4

Parenting Point

Good etiquette begins at home! Spend some time today listening to how family members speak to one another. Are your children polite in their interactions with you and with their siblings? If they aren't polite at home, chances are good that they won't be polite outside your home, either. Take whatever steps are necessary to build an environment of good etiquette in your home. Take the initiative in training your children to write thank you notes. Of course, they should write thank you notes for gifts, but there are so many other opportunities to show thankfulness to others. Perhaps, they could write to their pastor or Sunday School teacher. We often took time, as a family, to sit around the table and write thank you notes to quiet servants in the church, people who might be overlooked for their service. As your children see you practicing this good etiquette, they will begin to emulate your model of caring for others. Moms and dads, when you see your children quietly serving others without seeking to gain recognition, take the time to write them a heartfelt thank you note. I guarantee that those little notes, written by a thankful mom or dad, will become important and treasured keepsakes for your children.

Honor and Trust

How long does it take to regain a bond of trust once it has been broken? Honor and trust are two different sides of the same coin. You cannot have one without the other. Take a few minutes today and think about the most respectable and trustworthy person that you know. Next, think about what it is they possess that makes them respectable and trustworthy. Compare their positive character qualities with your own life. What do you need to change to become characterized by honor and trust?

Proverbs 3:5-6

Parenting Point

Before bonds of trust are broken between you and your family, take a few minutes to write down those character areas where you need to grow, change, and conform to the image of Christ. Next, lead your family in completing the same exercise. Finally, pick an accountability partner within the family and exchange lists, committing to pray for each other. Periodically, check up on one another's progress. This exercise is especially fruitful when children who don't get along are assigned to be accountability partners with one another. It is very hard to have hurtful and bitter feelings toward someone you are uplifting in prayer. Remind your children often that God chose them to be members of the same family and that He makes no mistakes! When a bond of trust has been broken between family members, take the time to help the offending parties to seek forgiveness and to practice the restoration process. Broken bonds, left to fester and grow, will cause division, hurt, and bitterness in a family. When any members of the family are at odds with one another, the entire family's testimony is weakened. Time is not the answer to broken bonds of trust. Time will only mask the hurt and provide a temporary respite from a deeper problem. Mom and Dad, take the lead in showing how to restore broken bonds of trust. Be quick to ask your children's forgiveness when you have failed to follow through on a promise or when you have disappointed them with your words or actions. As they see you be willing to humble yourself in order to restore unity, they will be learning important lessons of humility and trust building behavior.

Obedience:
It Really is the Best Way
to Show What You Believe

J ust as God's Word lays out consequences for those who would refuse to listen to and obey God, the same Word promises blessings
for those with an obedient ear and heart. Why is it so hard to obey?
Pride and "self" keep us from joyfully obeying God. In an autonomous
society allowing anyone to tell us what to do is difficult, and that difficulty
extends to our relationship with God; however, as today's scripture reminds us, with obedience comes blessing. Don't rob yourself of the ability
to receive God's blessing because of stubborn and prideful disobedience.

Deuteronomy 11:26-28

Parenting Point

One of the greatest benefits of a relationship with Jesus Christ is the
great blessing He brings into our lives as we submit ourselves to His authority. God is not a harsh taskmaster requiring our obedience and dealing with us in a hard and confrontational manner. Instead, the Lord gently
woos our hearts. He makes obedience attractive as He lavishes His love,
grace, and forgiveness upon us. God is our example. In the same way
that He makes obedience attractive, we, too, can make obedience attractive to our children. They will be much more prone to obey our desires as
they grow close to us in a loving and compassionate relationship. Harsh
and demanding parents make obedience unattractive. Loving, gentle, and
encouraging parents draw their children along kindly, making obedience
a desirable outcome rather than a forced submission. Ask the Lord to
reveal your character to you. Are you winsome in your approach to your
children? If not, ask the Lord for direction and courage to make the necessary changes in your character.

The Week in Review

Take some time to gather as a family and discuss the character qualities that you learned this week. Here are some questions to get the conversation started.

- List the character qualities we studied this week.

- Which character quality was the hardest for you to practice this week?

- Did you see a family member consistently practicing one of this week's character qualities? Which family member?

Use your imagination and add questions of your own. After your time of discussion, spend some time praying together, thanking the Lord and sharing one another's burdens. Pray ahead of time for teachable hearts to incorporate and put into practice the character qualities your family will learn in the upcoming week.

Bringing Joy to the Watchman

Read today's verse. How can we bring joy to those who watch over us or exercise authority on our behalf? It is easy to think of ways that we can cause them grief. Sour attitudes, complaining, or belligerence toward their oversight can wound the hearts of those over us; however, when we exhibit thankfulness for their watch-care, we can lighten their load and bring joy to the hard work of oversight. Notice, it is not only our leaders who suffer when we bring grief to their job, this scripture makes it clear that such behavior is unprofitable for us as well.

Hebrews 13:17

Parenting Point

Have you ever thanked a police officer when he handed you a ticket? Were your children watching? You can be sure that a lesson was delivered to your children by your actions at the same time the policeman was delivering a ticket through the window to you. Spend some time talking with your children about how you, as a family, could bring joy to the heart of those who are your leaders. Perhaps you could write notes of encouragement or surprise them with a gift certificate for ice cream cones. Talk to your children about how to receive instruction, or even correction, from someone who is their authority. Learning to receive instruction with a sweet and thankful heart will ease the burden from the heart of the one delivering the instruction. Don't speak negatively about leaders. Whether your children can hear you or not, such negative attitudes do nothing to further the Kingdom of God, and they often tear down and wound those in leadership. Pray for those in leadership and purposefully seek ways to bless their hearts.

Learning to Cast

What does it mean to cast your cares upon God? The dictionary defines cast this way: to throw something forcefully in a specified direction. What a wonderful picture of what we must do with our worries. We are to take those worries and troubling circumstances and throw them forcefully to God. Scripture makes it clear that the only place to cast our cares is on God, and the more quickly and forcefully we throw them into His hands, and out of ours, the more quickly He can take care of our worries. Why can you throw your cares to God? Today's scripture gives us a beautiful and simple reminder...He cares for you!

I Peter 5:7

Parenting Point

Teaching our children to cast their cares on God begins with teaching them to cast their cares on us, as God's representatives in their young lives. As our children become proficient at allowing us to carry their heart-hurts and burdens, they will learn easily how to transfer that casting off of cares to God. Use a simple object lesson to teach your children how to cast off their cares. Take a soft ball and have them throw it to you. After you catch the ball, roll it back to them and have them throw it again, more quickly this time. Each time roll the ball back to them. Explain to them that you, with the help of God, are equipped to carry their problems and God has given you that responsibility as their parent. They, however, are not equipped to carry your problems, so you won't throw your problems back at them. Encourage your child to throw the ball more quickly each time and help them understand that God doesn't want them to hold onto their worries for even a millisecond. Rather, as soon as a worry surfaces, He wants them to forcefully pass the concern off to Him. Make sure they understand that the reason God carries their burden is because He loves them so much and cares deeply for the worries and concerns they face. Good news! He cares just as much for your parental worries, so your whole family can rest secure, nestled in the loving care of our Heavenly Father.

Love Remembers No Wrongs

I don't know about you, but if I had my choice the people whom I have wronged would have their memories wiped clean. Life would be so much simpler if once forgiveness and restoration had been completed, it was as though the unfortunate incidents in my life had never happened. According to today's verse, that wish can be a reality. We can choose to live as if the wrongs that come into our lives had never happened. What wrongs are you clinging to today? Make the choice to wipe the record clean and free yourself to love others with the forgiving love of Christ.

I Corinthians 13:5

Parenting Point

Is it hard for you to let parenting disappointments go? Sometimes, the hurt that our children bring into our homes and families through their bad choices, seem like it will never lessen let alone be forgotten. When we cling to those wrongs, when we keep a record of disappointments and failures, we handicap ourselves and handcuff our children. It is important as parents to teach our children how to seek our forgiveness and how to restore broken bonds of trust. They need the cleansing power of forgiveness, as found in I John 1:9, to move on from their failures; however, it is just as important for us to allow them to move on. God desires all of us to change and grow. When we keep our children locked into their failures by our recordkeeping of their wrongdoings, we are interfering with the cleansing power of the Holy Spirit. Aren't you glad that God forgives us and allows us to change? We must be daily committed to extending the same love and grace to our erring children, not blindly accepting their sinful choices but graciously allowing them to move on from the past. What records do you need to wipe clean today?

The Hospitable Heart

Would your friends say that you are characterized by hospitality? Today's scripture makes it clear that hospitality isn't limited to a select few but is to be practiced and extended by all believers. Consider your resources and decide what you must do to become a practitioner of hospitality. It doesn't have to be big or elegant. Simply open your home, apartment, or room and allow God to minister through you.

Romans 12:13

Parenting Point

Our homes should be places where hospitality is a habitual practice not an occasional event. Too often, we limit our hospitality because we are nervous about the resources we have to offer to other folks. No worries! True hospitality isn't about impressing; it's about blessing. Simply opening your home for coffee and games can provide much needed fellowship for a lonely heart. Don't wait for your children to be older to practice hospitality. Young children can get involved by helping to straighten the living room, folding napkins, and even taking drink requests. Some of our most wonderful memories revolve around the friends and acquaintances, who would quickly become friends, who stayed in our home. Help your children practice their own hospitality. Arrange times for them to invite friends over and help them plan what activities will go on, what food they can serve, and whom they will invite. Don't limit hospitality to those with whom you already have relationships; invite folks you don't know over as well. Teach your children how to welcome guests, listen attentively, and ask good questions. Practicing hospitality doesn't need to be intimidating. A few simple preparations ahead of time will make opening your home a blast for you and a blessing to others.

Consideration

To be considerate means to exercise careful thought or deliberation. It is thoughtful concern for, or sensitivity toward, the feelings of others. When you are considerate, you demonstrate high regard and esteem for someone else. Generally speaking, we have no problem showing consideration for ourselves! Philippians 2:3 instructs us to consider others more highly than ourselves. Friends, family, and acquaintances shouldn't have to earn our consideration; because of our relationship with Christ, we should always show them the utmost care and consideration.

Ephesians 4:29-32

Parenting Point

Are you more considerate of strangers than you are of your own family? Read and study the following scripture on consideration and make a list of the other character qualities that accompany consideration. Pay close attention to the role words play in being considerate. Ask your kids to define consideration. Write down their answers, and then read those answers back to them. Ask them what role their words play in being considerate toward each other. Finally, start from oldest to youngest and have them finish this sentence: "I would like others to be more considerate of my_____." You might be surprised at what your children share with you. In our home, we are quick with our tongues, often to the detriment of one another. Although the things we say are good for a quick laugh, many of our children shared that they wished others would be more considerate of their feelings. While it is important that our children learn to laugh at themselves, that lesson shouldn't be taught at the expense of their personal dignity. For our family, words are too often inconsiderate! If a certain area of inconsiderate behavior becomes apparent during your family discussion, take the time to help your children walk through the forgiveness process. Don't allow bitterness to grow in any child's life because they have been hurt by continually inconsiderate behavior. Perhaps, it is you that needs to seek forgiveness from one of your children or even from your spouse. Don't allow pride to keep you from being an example of repentance and restoration. It is important for our families to realize that they are incredibly important to us and are a precious gift from God. Don't mar their trust by being considerate to those outside your home, while allowing inconsiderate words, attitudes, and behaviors to be your characterization at home.

Appropriateness • Service

A Life Without Lines

Today's character quality is hard to pin down and assign a specific title to, but perhaps the best description is the character quality of a willing servant. A willing servant is a person who refuses to draw a line in the sand concerning where they will go, what they will do, and whom they will serve. Servants without lines are the most useable and dependable servants for the Lord. When we draw lines in the sand, we make life difficult for everyone else. Living a "specialist" lifestyle causes problems for those in leadership when they need someone to fill an immediate need. Are you willing to do whatever, whenever, for whomever? Let the Lord wipe away your lines and bless others with your willingness to serve.

Galatians 5:13-14

Parenting Point

How willing are your children to do something outside of their comfort zone? It is important to train our children to be willing to try new things, eat new foods, and meet new people. Although it is easy to give in to our children's reticence to be adventurous, resist the urge! When we allow them to refuse to try new things, we are handicapping them for later in life. When our children go to someone's home and refuse to eat what is served, the honest explanation is rudeness. When our children are unwilling to reach out to visitors, the honest explanation is rudeness. I Corinthians 13 reminds us that "Love is not rude." Kindly, but firmly, insist that your children move beyond what is comfortable and easy. We do not know what God has in store for them in the future. Help them to prepare to be willing servants by beginning the process of learning to sacrifice their rights now. Whether it's a simple sacrifice such as giving up the last muffin at dinner or a bigger sacrifice like sharing their possessions with children who are less fortunate, learning to be a sacrificial servant will prepare our children for productive and fruitful service for the Lord.

The Week in Review

Take some time to gather as a family and discuss the character qualities that you learned this week. Here are some questions to get the conversation started.

- **List the character qualities we studied this week.**

- **Which character quality was the hardest for you to practice this week?**

- **Did you see a family member consistently practicing one of this week's character qualities? Which family member?**

Use your imagination and add questions of your own. After your time of discussion, spend some time praying together, thanking the Lord and sharing one another's burdens. Pray ahead of time for teachable hearts to incorporate and put into practice the character qualities your family will learn in the upcoming week.

Eternal Compassion

Would you characterize yourself as a compassionate person? Compassion is defined this way: sympathetic consciousness of others' distress together with a desire to alleviate it. Naturally, when we think of showing compassion, we think of meeting physical and emotional needs. Read today's verses. Peter showed compassion by meeting the deepest need in his listener's lives. By sharing the gospel and showing them how to be in a right relationship with God, Peter provided them with compassion that would eternally change their lives. Don't be afraid to share the good news of Christ... It is the most compassionate care you can give to someone in need!

Acts 2:38-40

Parenting Point

Is there someone in your family who needs to hear the compassionate truth of the gospel of Christ? I know in our immediate family, we had many who did not know the Lord as their personal Savior. At times, my children would boldly share Christ to the very family members with whom I was so hesitant to initiate a spiritual conversation. Sometimes, I cringed at their boldness. Shame on me! Often, through their innocence, our children can share truths that we would be unable to communicate. As a family, we always spent time praying for other family members who did not have a personal relationship with Christ. Not surprisingly, my children took those prayers seriously and consciously looked for opportunities to share their testimonies or to let their beloved family members know how much they wanted to see them in heaven. My own mother heard the gospel from my children and shortly before her death told me that she had done what my children did and asked Jesus into her heart. Don't stop your children from sharing the Lord! Teach them how to be gracious and how to stop when the conversation becomes unwelcome, but certainly encourage their loving attempts to win others to Christ.

Practice Makes Perfect

Do you realize that righteousness doesn't just happen? Although, at salvation we are justified by faith, our righteousness must be an ongoing and imperative part of our life in Christ. People who are characterized as righteous are the same people that have worked hard to develop the practice of righteousness in their lives. Our righteousness should be an ever-growing and dynamic pattern of change on a consistent basis. God is aching to come alongside of us and help us to achieve that righteous change, as evidenced by Philippians 1:6.

I John 3:7

Parenting Point

Take some time today to read the above Scripture aloud as a family. Ask your children what they think it looks like to "practice righteousness." After they have shared their thoughts with you, spend some time encouraging them with the areas of righteous living you observe in their daily choices, actions, and attitudes. This is not the time for correction or scolding; let today's family gathering be a time for building up and recognizing positive change and growth. Remember, as you consistently encourage them, you infuse them with the needed courage to live even more righteously. Encourage your children to share the positive fruit they observe in one another's lives as well. Often, it is easy for our children to recognize the annoying or obnoxious behavior of their siblings. Today's exercise will help them to recognize and verbally acknowledge the positive fruit that is evident in the lives of their brothers and sisters.

Characterized by Spiritual Motives

What is the motivating force behind your actions and thoughts? Are you motivated by a desire to bring glory to God in all that you do or are your motives mixed: sometimes God-centered and sometimes self-serving? Today's verse reminds us that in whatever we do, our motivation must be to bring glory to our God. Eating and drinking are two of the most mundane activities we can participate in, but even in the mundane, our responsibility remains the same. Others only see your outward behavior; ask God to help you recognize your inward motives.

I Corinthians 10:31

Parenting Point

Even though we are our children's parents, we are not to judge their motives; however, we certainly can be "Fruit Inspectors" carefully examining their actions and attitudes while helping them to recognize the motivation behind those behaviors and thoughts. Being a fruit inspector requires diligent training by the Word of God and consistent prayer to see our children's choices through spiritual eyes. Without this training and prayer, it is too easy to simply judge our children according to outward actions. Some children can easily put-on the outward trappings of spiritual behavior when there are other adults around to observe their behavior. While these hypocritical children never fool other children, sometimes we allow ourselves to just assume our children are spiritually minded because they look so good in public. Just because a child can recite verses or sit still in church, doesn't mean that they have a heart for the Lord. Be careful to observe what goes on behind the scenes with your children. We are certainly not looking for perfection, everyone fails, but rather we are looking for children with soft hearts and a desire to please the Lord through their actions. If you have a child who is characterized by simply putting it on in public, take the time to discuss their motivation with them. Perhaps they have never surrendered to the Lord, and so they are simply imitating what they see Christians doing without a heart that has been saved. Take the time to ask them good questions. If they have begun a relationship with the Lord, teach into the necessity to do all, whether noticed or unnoticed, to the glory of God. Encourage their good choices, but help them to recognize any hypocritical behaviors as well.

Diligent Resolve

O h, how quickly we fade. It seems that character qualities such as commitment, patience, and discipline are relics of some by-gone day. Today, we want our problems resolved in 30 minutes or less, plus or minus a few commercial breaks. We live in a disposable world where we expect our products to be downloaded in seconds and our demands to be met without resistance. Instant gratification is not part of Gods plan, whereas, delayed gratification is. God wants us to build character that is diligent and resolved. Such character is the stuff of great-ness. Nothing, that is nothing *significant* in this world, ever happened apart from diligent resolve.

James 1:22-25

Parenting Point

Help your children set some long-term goals, goals that will require diligent resolve. If you have an athlete, help them set realistic physical goals. Perhaps, shaving some time off of their current interval or more consistently fielding the ball. If you have a musician, perhaps they should set out to memorize a challenging piece of music. Set some spiritual goals also. Resolve to memorize an entire chapter such as Philippians 4, James 1, or Romans 8. If you are looking for something less ambitious, try mem-orizing Psalm 101 or Proverbs 3. Be creative, stick with it, and you will teach your children the importance of diligent resolve. For fun, you could encourage another family to set some Scripture memorization goals as well. Once the goals have been met, plan a time of fellowship and have each family recite their chosen Scripture. Provide some yummy desserts and enjoy the satisfaction of goals successfully accomplished!

Coveting Consumes Contentment

Coveting is a nasty little character quality. All of the sudden, out of the blue, we can find ourselves no longer content with what God has provided simply because we are coveting something we see, hear about, or know someone else possesses. For a believer, a heart characterized by coveting is an affront to our God. Coveting is a decision to regard what the Lord has given us as inadequate, unacceptable, and incomplete. We must replace coveting with contentment. Take your thoughts of coveting captive, confess them as ingratitude to the Lord, and begin to recall the many blessings that God has bestowed on you. Then, like Paul, you can say that you are content in all circumstances.

Philippians 4:11-12

Parenting Point

Are your children thankful? The first step to developing a contented heart is learning to be thankful for what has already been provided. Take some time to observe your children's level of thankfulness. Do they naturally and spontaneously thank you and others for what is provided or must they always be reminded and prodded? Teaching your children to be thankful will go far in teaching them to be content. Content children will be eager to be generous instead of being envious and coveting what others possess.

Humility

H umility is simply defined as being modest or respectful. Although the definition is simple, learning to humble ourselves and to esteem others as more important than ourselves, is a difficult and life-long process. The most humble people are the folks who are the most others-oriented. Instead of worrying about their own reputations, desires, and "stuff," these people invest their time and energy in building up and encouraging other people. The easiest way to "put-off" pride and to "put-on" humility is by serving others and entrusting your needs to the Lord.

James 4:6

Parenting Point

As James 4:6 reminds us, God is opposed to the proud. Pride is the opposite of humility and is the basis for all of the sin in our lives. I don't know about you, but I certainly don't want God to oppose me. As well, I don't want to see my children in the position of being opposed by God. We can help our children by assisting them in recognizing the pride in their lives and by helping them to see how God opposes them. Too often, we give credit for hard times to "bad luck" or circumstances; I believe that, often, our children and we are thwarted in our desires by the opposing hand of our loving Lord. Humble people are a joy to spend time with and act as a winsome magnet to draw others to the Lord. Proud people cannot admit that they are wrong. Model humility to your children by your eagerness to admit when you are wrong, seek forgiveness, and restore what has been broken, whether it's relationships, trust, or physical property. The only thing keeping us from humbling ourselves and seeking relationship-restoring forgiveness is our stiff-necked pride. When we are willing to humble ourselves, others will be encouraged to act in humility as well. God opposes the proud, yes...but thankfully, He gives grace to the humble. Will you join me in killing our pride and in seeking to please God with a humble, thankful heart?

The Week in Review

Take some time to gather as a family and discuss the character qualities that you learned this week. Here are some questions to get the conversation started.

- **List the character qualities we studied this week.**

- **Which character quality was the hardest for you to practice this week?**

- **Did you see a family member consistently practicing one of this week's character qualities? Which family member?**

Use your imagination and add questions of your own. After your time of discussion, spend some time praying together, thanking the Lord and sharing one another's burdens. Pray ahead of time for teachable hearts to incorporate and put into practice the character qualities your family will learn in the upcoming week.

Commitment

Have you committed your plans, hopes, and dreams to the Lord? As today's Scripture reminds us, if we want our plans to be established, we must first commit them to the Lord. Too often, we plan and scheme before we ever seek the Lord's face regarding our direction. As you spend time in the Word of God allowing His conviction and exhortation to transform your life, it will be easier and easier to commit your works to Him. The life transformed to emulate Christ will be the life that desires the same things that Christ would desire. The simple children's song reminds us of how to make this transformation in our lives: Read your Bible; pray every day; and, you'll grow, grow, grow.

Proverbs 16:3

Parenting Point

Have you handed the ownership of your children over to the Lord? I am surprised by how many Christian parents live as though their children belong to them, and only to them. Not only does God love our children more than we could ever imagine, He alone knows the absolute perfect path for their lives. Although it is hard to remember that we are simply temporary guardians of the Lord's children, it is important to recommit your children to the Lord frequently. You can trust Him, for He cares for them abundantly! When we allow ourselves to become indispensable to our children, we will set them up for fear and insecurity. Their overdependence on us will become a detriment to their growth and maturity in their relationship with the Lord. Affirm your love and commitment to your children, but then make sure they realize that they belong first and foremost to the Lord, and that He is more than capable of caring for them. We all love our kids; however, our earthly love pales in comparison to God's deep and abiding love for them.

Gentleness • Self-Control • Forgiveness

Gentleness

Gentleness is defined as having a mild and kind nature or manner; or, to have a gracious and honorable manner. Although gentleness may not be easy or natural, we can all learn to be gentle. Gentleness is not "wimpyness" but rather, strength under control. Although Jesus was God in human flesh, he didn't balk at displaying gentleness, and it was that very gentleness that made Him winsome and compelling.

Matthew 5:5

Parenting Point

When it comes to gentleness, more is caught than taught. We can teach our children over and over the need to respond gently; however, if our responses are harsh, the lesson will be lost in the translation. Children will receive our instruction much easier when it is communicated gently and lovingly. Proverbs 16:21 states that "Sweetness of speech increases persuasiveness." Begin today to teach your children to speak to others with a gentle tone. Pay special attention to how your children respond to little children and the elderly. Role-playing appropriate words and tones will go far in training our children (and ourselves) to think before we speak and to incorporate a gentle tone and attitude. For me, personally, I know there are certain triggers that tempt me to abandon gentleness in favor of a harsh or aggressive tone. When I am late and rushing to get somewhere, my tone too often becomes harsh, and I say things in haste that ought never to be uttered. A majority of the time, the reason I'm running late is my own lack of planning; my children and husband shouldn't reap the negative fruit of my bad decisions. Truthfully, we will all blow it and speak harshly. At those times, it is imperative we stop and seek forgiveness from those whom we have wronged. It's tempting to just try to speak more kindly or to crack a joke but neither of these options fit Biblical parameters. The more quickly we seek forgiveness and restoration, the more quickly our lack of gentleness will be resolved. If you're characterized by a harsh tone, learning to speak gently will take hard work and self-discipline. Don't give up! The fruit of your gentle spirit will bless your family and friends.

No Partiality, Please

Many character qualities are oriented toward the care and blessing of others; however, all of those same character qualities have the potential to tempt us to show partiality. Today's Scripture reminds us that the wisdom from above has no hypocrisy and no partiality. We must be careful, as we diligently implement these character qualities, so that we don't choose to exhibit them to some and not to others. Are we as punctual to church as we are to work? Are we as polite at home as we are outside the home? Are we as willing to serve when it will be noticed as when no one will know? It takes work to be consistent and evenhanded, but your testimony for Christ is worth it!

James 3:17

Parenting Point

Remember, as you are modeling character qualities for your children that more is caught than taught. We can tell our children over and over that they need to treat everyone with the same care and concern, but if they see partiality and hypocrisy in our lives, then that is the lesson they will learn. Sometimes, it is our children that suffer from our partiality toward others. I know that I have been guilty of blessing others with my time, or a meal, or some other sacrifice, while giving my children the sloppy seconds. Ask the Lord to reveal any areas of partiality in your life, and, if necessary, seek your children's forgiveness for your poor model. Children are always generous in their forgiveness and you can move on, as a family, to practice others-oriented character with a liberal and impartial hand. When you see your children serving and reaching out to those whom society would deem as less than desirable, encourage and praise them for their Christ-like attitude.

Honesty

Honesty is a character quality that by its definition leaves very little wiggle room. Either you are known to be honest or you are not. Either you can be trusted to tell the truth, both in words and action, or you cannot. A reputation for being dishonest is not easily changed or overcome. Do you agree or disagree with the following quote?

"Honesty is the cornerstone of all success, without which confidence and ability to perform shall cease to exist." —Mary Kay Ash

Read the following verse to see how God defines honesty.

Proverbs 12:17

Parenting Point

The seemingly easier decision to ignore lying, or digging for the truth, will always lead to hard consequences in the end. We do our children no favors when we allow them to continue in the sin of deceit. Be diligent to fulfill your responsibility as parents and help your children catch the little lies that will cause permanent damage to their lives and testimonies. Too often, our children learn the habit of telling half-truths and leaving out pertinent information from their careful observation of our lives. Moms, do you tell your husband all the details of your shopping excursions? Dads, do you underestimate the amount of time you spend on the computer? If our children see us "bending" the truth in order to divert attention from our actions or to avoid uncomfortable exposure, they will learn that hedging the truth is an acceptable alternative to honesty. We should never instruct our children with the words "Don't tell your father." or "Don't tell your mother." As we are training them to withhold information, we are making them vulnerable to others who would instruct them that, "This is our little secret!" All of our training is training for the future, so be careful to train your children appropriately. Covering up another's deceit will only cause them trouble and heartache. Teach your children to speak the truth in love, and you will have prepared them to successfully navigate the relationships and situations they will encounter as young adults.

Problem Finder
or Problem Solver?

O ur days have no shortage of problems, do they? When it comes to daily problems, there are two types of people: those who point out problems and those who find solutions to problems. The disciples had no difficulty pointing out the many problems they encountered. They came to Jesus to solve the problem of what to serve for dinner (Matthew 14:17), how to pay their taxes (Matthew 17:24), and how to develop a pecking order of importance (Luke 22:24-26). Yes, the disciples found no shortage of problems! However, the Lord's example to us is of a problem-solver. He went beyond discovering problems and took the important step of finding solutions. Anyone can find problems, but if we want to be like our Lord, we must develop the character of a problem solver. The next time you are tempted to hand someone else a potential problem to solve, instead take the time to seek the Lord's help to find a problem-solving solution yourself.

Matthew 14:15-21

Parenting Point

When our children bring us their problems, it is so easy to want to solve those problems for them. In fact, it seems like the most loving thing for us to do; however, when we quickly solve all of our children's problems for them, we are robbing them of the important discipline of becoming problem solvers themselves. Instead of solving your children's problems, ask them dialogue questions to help them come to the needed solution on their own. Questions such as: "What do you think you should do?" or "How can we make this work?" will help your children think through problems and develop their own workable answers. Although their solution may not be exactly what you would do, allow them the freedom to develop their own solution, and if necessary, let them deal with the consequences of less than perfect decisions. Help them evaluate, guide them as appropriate, but **don't** solve all of their problems for them. They'll be learning to problem solve, and as parents, we'll be learning self-control... a win-win situation!

Wise Character

How is it possible to become biblically wise? Read today's verse to find the answer. As we listen to counsel and accept discipline, we will develop wisdom, which will serve us well for all of our lives. There's only one problem... It's hard to listen to counsel and accept discipline! Our pride pops up and too often our response is very much like the toddler's: "You're not the boss of me!" Ask the Lord to show you any areas of pride that are keeping you from receiving counsel and discipline. Don't let pride keep you from developing godly wisdom!

Proverbs 19:20

Parenting Point

Are your children teachable and willing to be instructed? Or, do you have to battle each and every instruction you share with your children? Teach-ability is one of the most important character qualities that our children must develop. We, as their parents, play a huge role in modeling what it means to be teachable. If our children hear us complain every time the boss corrects us or someone says we're wrong, they will quickly learn to be proud and unteachable. Conversely, if they see us humbly receive instruction and make the necessary changes in our lives, they will learn to be teachable and to receive discipline. Don't think for a second that your children don't notice your attitude toward instruction, and your actions will always speak more loudly than your words. It is a mistake to laugh at small children, who, with hands on hips, declare their autonomy and unwillingness to be instructed. Our laughter will encourage a habit that will take root and cause destruction later in their lives. Instead, firmly but kindly tell them that their attitude is unacceptable and that they must say "Yes, Mommy." or "Yes, Daddy." when they are being instructed or disciplined. Call pride by its rightful name and help your children understand just how unacceptable their self-willed pride is and the damage it can cause to relationships and to their testimony.

The Week in Review

Take some time to gather as a family and discuss the character qualities that you learned this week. Here are some questions to get the conversation started.

- List the character qualities we studied this week.
- Which character quality was the hardest for you to practice this week?
- Did you see a family member consistently practicing one of this week's character qualities? Which family member?

Use your imagination and add questions of your own. After your time of discussion, spend some time praying together, thanking the Lord and sharing one another's burdens. Pray ahead of time for teachable hearts to incorporate and put into practice the character qualities your family will learn in the upcoming week.

As Stubborn as a Mule

Read today's verse. King Saul was a stubborn man, and he refused to subordinate himself to anyone, including God. The Word of God tells us that the Lord considered King Saul's insubordination to be sin and idolatry. Eventually, because of his stubborn insistence on doing things "his way," Saul lost the kingship and ultimately his life. The idol at the center of stubbornness is self. When we demand our way, our rights, and our autonomy, we begin down a road of self-destruction. Today is the day to root out any stubborn areas in your life and to purposefully submit them to the authority of God.

I Samuel 15:23

Parenting Point

Do you catch yourself telling others that your child is "just stubborn?" Beware! Little ears are listening, and unless you deal with stubbornness firmly, those little ears will hear their stubbornness is strength rather than a debilitating weakness. With my children that had a tendency toward stubbornness and self-centeredness, I spent extra time beseeching the Lord on their behalf. I prayed diligently that their stubbornness would be transformed into a firm resolve and conviction regarding the things of the Lord. Whenever stubbornness reared its ugly head, I stopped and took the time to point out the damage that one child's stubborn attitude could cause for the whole family. Your children won't outgrow stubbornness; instead it is a weedy character flaw that will grow and flourish. Take the time necessary to address and teach into the need to abandon stubbornness and embrace submission and humility.

The Character of Nonconformity

Have you ever thought of nonconformity as a character quality? For the believer to live out the truth of Romans 12:2, we must develop this important quality. Nonconformity just for the sake of being different is of no spiritual value; however, nonconformity to the world in order to be transformed to be more like Christ is a goal of eternal value. Spend some time today asking the Lord to reveal any areas of worldly conformity in your life that need to be changed to Christ-like nonconformity.

Romans 12:2

Parenting Point

Are we teaching our children that it is okay to be a nonconformist? I'm not speaking of training up children who are misfits, awkward, and unable to be used for the Kingdom of God. Instead, we need to be raising children who are well-equipped to minister to others, while not feeling the need to look like, act like, and emulate the non-Christian world around them. Their security in your family identity will give them the strength and boldness to stand out from the crowd. The more closely related and linked they feel to their own family, the less effective peer pressure will be in forcing them to fit the conformist mold. How is your family dynamic doing? Unless we are busy spending time intentionally building our family testimony and unity, we can be sure that our children will be wooed by the world and all that it seems to offer. Spend some time considering ways to strengthen your family bonds. Perhaps you will accomplish this through service to others, through hospitality as a family, or through prayer and time in the Word; whatever you decide to do, make it a regular part of your family dynamic. Children, who delight in their family identity, will have the courage and conviction to disregard the lure of the world and to stand strong for the Christian faith.

Love is Kind

Accoring to the dictionary, to be kind means to show a friendly, generous, and considerate nature. I'm surprised by how much easier it is sometimes to show those attributes to total strangers or acquaintances than it is to exhibit friendliness, generosity, and consideration to my own family members. I Corinthians chapter 13, the Love Chapter, reminds us that part of showing love to others is extending kindness. Has your love been shown through kindness today? Those we love the most deserve our kindest care and compassion.

I Corinthians 13:4

Parenting Point

Your example of kindness will be the strongest influencer of kind character in the lives of your children. Would your family members agree that you are friendly, generous, and considerate? We stand without excuse when we are characterized by showing this type of concern for co-workers, neighbors, and store clerks, while allowing ourselves to be short-tempered, irritable, and harsh with our own families. Honestly, everyone deserves our kindness, but those in our home deserve it the most. Gather your family around the table today and discuss the level of kindness or unkindness that you show to one another. Spend time praying as a family and together set a high standard of kind and compassionate care for one another. Help your children to brainstorm practical ways that they can exhibit generosity to one another. Your whole family will benefit by a kind home environment, and habits of kindness will overflow easily to those outside your home as well.

Spur Them On!

B esides showing the Christ-like character quality of love through giving and serving, we have many opportunities throughout the day to show love through edifying one another. Simply stated, edifying is accomplished when we verbally encourage another person with the desire to spur them on to even higher or better accomplishments. Edifying is not just complimenting someone's looks or position; instead, it is the recognition and affirmation of the positive character we observe in their lives.

I Corinthians 8:1

Parenting Point

Spend time today taking careful note of the words that are exchanged in your home. Whether it is conversation between adults or children, are the words used encouraging and edifying? Or, are they words that are sarcastic, belittling, or meant to get a cheap laugh? As always, we must first examine our own words, then, we will be able to discern, and if necessary, correct the communication in our homes. It costs us nothing to edify one another, except a small amount of time and a commitment to look for the good in others, rather than concentrating on our own accomplishments. An edifying home is a delightful home and a place where all family members feel secure. If you have more than one child, make sure that no child becomes the brunt of careless words. It's easy for children to gang up on one another, and that paradigm should never be present in our homes. If necessary, bring corrective discipline into the lives of those who continue with unprofitable communication. Don't allow ungodly communication to continue in your home! Take whatever steps are necessary to change a negative atmosphere. You'll be thrilled with the positive results! If it is your words that have promoted a negative attitude in your home, quickly seek your family's forgiveness and take the necessary steps to promote change and restoration in your home.

Fearful No More

The dictionary defines fear as an unpleasant emotion caused by the belief that someone or something is dangerous, likely to cause pain, or a threat. For some of us, that "unpleasant emotion" can be absolutely paralyzing, but for the Christian there is a clear biblical answer: seek the Lord. Today's verse reminds us that we have the freedom to seek the Lord, and that His response will be to deliver us from all of our fears. Notice: not "some" of our fears but ALL. As God delivers us from fear over and over again, we will begin to lose our fearful character and will instead develop a character marked by confidence and courage. Don't wait! Seek the Lord today.

Psalm 34:4

Parenting Point

All of our children at some point or another deal with fears. Sometimes their fears are legitimate, but sometimes their fears are unfounded. Regardless, as their parents we need to give them the weapons necessary to fight off the fears they face. First and foremost, we must teach them to run to the Lord with their fears. Too often we are tempted to run to our friends, our churches, or seek knowledge from the Internet to help resolve our fears. While all of these venues may be helpful, the Lord is the only source of deliverance from our fears. The Bible is full of verses that address fear and handing that fear over to the Lord. Teach your youngest children one or two simple verses to recite when they are fearful. For your older children, help them use a concordance to make a list of "fear" verses. After they have compiled their list, have them choose which verses they will memorize. Having God's Word hidden in their heart will be a safeguard against fear when they are away from your presence. Share with them your own journey of seeking God when you are fearful and model what it looks like to run to a faithful God. There is no need for a Christian to live a life characterized by fear; God has given us the tools we need to forsake fear and develop courage.

A Character Overcome by Anger

Read today's verse. Proverbs 25:28 paints a clear picture of the overwhelming and overcoming nature of anger. People who have allowed the character of anger to take root in their lives will too often find themselves overwhelmed by feelings they can no longer control. It is a frightening thing to find yourself in a relationship with an angry person. Don't allow this negative character quality to reign in your heart! Seek the Lord's forgiveness for your inappropriate anger and replace anger with the peace that comes from a steadfast and trusting relationship with Christ.

Proverbs 25:28

Parenting Point

Do you have children who are characterized by angry outbursts or angry actions? Sometimes anger seems like a one-size-fits-all emotion for some children. We must diligently teach our children that their angry outbursts are always an inappropriate response to life's challenges. Do not allow them to vent or to simply go to another room to work out their anger without an audience. Either of these short-term solutions does nothing to address the inner heart issue and instead makes anger an acceptable alternative as long as no one else is physically hurt. Scripture is full of verses regarding the danger surrounding anger. In a time of non-conflict, help your children who are prone to respond angrily to make a list of verses and references addressing anger. Hang that list in a spot where they can find it for easy reference. When you see them headed down the road of anger, encourage them to go to the list and spend time replacing their angry thoughts with the Word of God. As well, pick one or two key verses for them to commit to memory as a safeguard against anger when they cannot get to their list. Make the memorization fun, but require them to complete each verse completely and accurately. It is hard work, but remain diligent in catching each episode of anger. Every time they slip by with angry reactions and no comment or training from us, their anger becomes a more deeply ingrained habit and will be much harder to break.

The Week in Review

Take some time to gather as a family and discuss the character qualities that you learned this week. Here are some questions to get the conversation started.

- **List the character qualities we studied this week.**

- **Which character quality was the hardest for you to practice this week?**

- **Did you see a family member consistently practicing one of this week's character qualities? Which family member?**

Use your imagination and add questions of your own. After your time of discussion, spend some time praying together, thanking the Lord and sharing one another's burdens. Pray ahead of time for teachable hearts to incorporate and put into practice the character qualities your family will learn in the upcoming week.

A Prayerful Character

In the same way that we can have a loving, or kind, or punctual character, we can be known for having a character marked by prayer. Everyone needs prayer, and when our family, friends, and acquaintances know that we will faithfully pray for them, we will become a safe haven where they can bring their fears and concerns. Even those who don't know the Lord will often seek out someone with whom to share their needs, and your prayers on their behalf can provide an opportunity to share the gospel of Christ. There's no special training or equipment required, just a sensitive heart that is willing and ready to seek the Lord on the behalf of others.

James 5:16

Parenting Point

As soon as our children can sit upright on our laps, we can begin to include them in times of prayer. Although in the beginning their prayers will most likely be a repetition of what they hear us pray, this early practice will prepare them for the day that they themselves can come to Him in prayer for others. For years, we kept two jars with our family devotional materials. In one jar were tabs (file markers) with the names of people for whom we were praying. Each day we would pass out a tab to each family member and pray for the name it held. Then, we would put the tabs into the other jar. When one jar was empty, we would celebrate with ice cream sundaes or some other treat, and then we would start all over with the tabs. I always try to pray immediately when someone shares a request. Whether it is over the phone or in person, praying with our friends builds their faith, strengthens our prayer resolve, and keeps us from forgetting to pray. Remind your children that they should keep their friends' prayer requests private with the exception being to share those requests with you. Teach your children what type of requests they need to share with you (i.e., anything harmful, such as drugs, deceit, or suicidal thoughts). While they should pray for their friends' serious requests, they should not have to carry that burden alone. Children who have become consistent prayer warriors will become adults who are consistent prayer warriors. What a difference they could have in our churches and communities. You are the key! Make prayer a normal and consistent part of your life and your children's lives, and prayer will become your family's characterization.

One Foot in Front of the Other

How do we develop the character quality of faithfulness? Faithfulness is developed as we practice obedience every day, every month, every year, etc. Take some time to read today's Scripture. I John reminds us that to have fellowship with one another and to live a life cleansed from sin, we must faithfully walk in the light, one foot after the other, a daily walk with the Lord. It is easy to allow busyness, distractions, and crisis situations to deter us from that daily walk, but faithfully walking step-by-step and mile-by-mile with the Lord will develop proven character and strength for the future.

I John 1:7

Parenting Point

Today is simply a fun parenting activity. Take some time to get out of the house and walk with your children; however, instead of just walking and talking, use your time to initiate a prayer walk. As you walk along, begin praying for whatever comes to mind. After a time, stop and encourage a child to pick up the thread of prayer. When they stop, encourage another child to continue on in prayer. At some point, you can begin to pray again, and on and on. You will be amazed at the different prayer needs your children remember and bring to your attention. Start with a short walk but plan to add these "prayer walks" to your family's spiritual calendar. If an individual child seems particularly needy or discouraged, a prayer walk is a great way to initiate further conversation and show yourself trustworthy and available for counsel. Husbands and wives, prayer walks build sweet intimacy in a marriage as well. Make the Lord an integral part of your relationships and watch how He blesses those relationships.

That Green-eyed Monster

Interestingly, the color green was historically associated with illness and the sickly color a person's skin became while they were ill. The expression, "Jealousy is a green-eyed monster." was used to emphasize the illness and death that jealousy could bring to a person's heart. This is just as true today! The negative and destructive character quality of jealousy will destroy relationships and cause bitterness and sickness of heart. As believers, we must put-off jealousy and learn to be happy for others.

Galatians 5:26

Parenting Point

Have you ever tried to comfort your child with the words, "They're just jealous of you?" Although there are times that as parents we can see the harm and ill-effects that another child's jealousy are causing, such a statement brings little comfort or relief to our child. In fact, in the long run, telling our children that others are jealous of them could cause them to think more highly of themselves than they should! Instead, use those hurtful moments to help your child think about how they should treat others. When they are wounded by hurtful words, gossip, or exclusion, encourage them to think how they respond when they have the opportunity to be unkind. Ask them what they could say to help someone who has been hurt in the way that they are hurting. Empathize with them, but quickly help them to take the focus off of their own hurt by concentrating on how they could be a blessing to others. Unfortunately, there will always be children who are prone to jealousy and who act out in hurtful ways, but our children can learn to be healers, gentle spirits who ease the pain of others and are careful not to inflict pain themselves.

Gently, Gently

Does gentleness seem like a weak or womanly character quality? Consider this quote from Ralph Sockman, the Senior Pastor of the Christ Church of New York in the 1900's: "Nothing is so strong as gentleness, nothing so gentle as real strength." Gentleness, in its truest manifestation, is strength under control. Our Lord Jesus was gentle, but He also had the strength that carried Him to the cross. Gentleness, backed by strength, will enhance our testimony for Christ. Gentleness does not show weakness, but rather, a willingness to control one's strength to woo and win others over for the cause of Christ. Christians, through their gentleness, can show a watching world what true strength looks like in action but, yet, under control.

Matthew 5:5

Parenting Point

Gentleness does not come naturally to our children. It is much easier for children to be rough and self-centered rather than gentle and others-oriented. Begin teaching your children, as early as possible, how to speak, touch, and nurture gently. Provide your little girls with baby dolls and encourage them to treat them kindly and gently. Let your model of gentleness set the example for their imitation. Teach your sons to speak to their mother and sisters in a gentle and considerate way. This early training will pay huge dividends when they are grown and ready to begin their own families. What a blessing to see brothers and sisters who treat each other kindly and gently. Work hard to make this the testimony of your family. When ungentle or unkind attitudes rear their ugly heads, don't ignore them or hope that they will just disappear. Instead, call a family conference, address what has been happening, and set a new path toward gentleness and an others-orientation.

Forgetful Hearer or Reliable Rememberer?

hat is the character quality involved in choosing to remember and continuing to live up to what we already know to be true? Perhaps, it is integrity, or faithfulness, or diligence, but regardless of the title, we are all called to be good "rememberers" of what the Lord has already revealed to us. Sometimes, it is helpful to keep a written record of the areas in which the Lord has worked to change our lives. When we are tempted to feel discouraged, this written record can be a great encouragement to us as we look back and see how the Lord has grown and changed us. In contrast, when we look back through the written record and realize there are lessons we had already learned and are no longer being faithful to, we can make the necessary changes to once again remember what we forgot.

James 1:25

Parenting Point

Are your children characterized by forgetting? Listen closely in your interactions with your children and see how often they use the excuse of forgetfulness as a legitimate rationale for a lack of obedience. Often, this excuse is simply a dishonest rationalization for the willful choice they made to disregard our instructions. Do not allow them to continue with this type of disobedience and dishonesty. When our children said, "I forgot," and we knew this wasn't the truth, we always used the same phrase: "You didn't forget; you chose not to remember." It is important to remind our children that it was their choice to disobey, not a circumstance into which they were forced. As you are diligent to catch them in their "forgetfulness," you will begin to see them taking on ownership for their own choices of obedience or disobedience. Always look toward the future in your child training. Their future spouse will thank you for the effort you expended to train your children in careful obedience.

The Big Put-On

Change in the life of a follower of Christ is a two-step process. This process, as found in Ephesians 4:22-25, involves putting off our old ways, those things that are not glorifying to God, and putting on new, Christ-honoring ways. Sounds easy, doesn't it? Although the concept sounds easy, the practice of putting on and putting off can be difficult and sometimes, painful. Too often, we try to put on a new behavior or practice without first discarding the old, harmful habit. This is like putting a band aid on an oozing wound without first cleaning and sterilizing the injury. Underneath the band aid, the wound continues to fester and the ensuing infection is often worse than the original injury. Take time to seek the Lord and get His direction for the areas of change needed in your life. Then, painstakingly put off the old and replace it with God-honoring new practices and paradigms.

Ephesians 4:22-25

Parenting Point

Help your children to learn the put-on and put-off principle. Do some family role-playing to bring the process to life. Have your children come downstairs in the morning wearing their pajamas. Read aloud the scripture above. Without discussing the scripture, have them put on their play clothes, over top of their pajamas. Ask them what is wrong with what they just did. Use their answers to bring to light the truths found in Ephesians 4:22-25. We must help our children learn to discard, or put-off, ungodly practices and the earlier they learn this important lesson the better.

This week we will consider some areas of put-off that may not be very obvious. As well, we will look at the corresponding put-on that acts as a replacement for the wrong practice.

The Week in Review

Take some time to gather as a family and discuss the character qualities that you learned this week. Here are some questions to get the conversation started.

- List the character qualities we studied this week.
- Which character quality was the hardest for you to practice this week?
- Did you see a family member consistently practicing one of this week's character qualities? Which family member?

Use your imagination and add questions of your own. After your time of discussion, spend some time praying together, thanking the Lord and sharing one another's burdens. Pray ahead of time for teachable hearts to incorporate and put into practice the character qualities your family will learn in the upcoming week.

An Eternal Focus

More important than focusing on our priorities and refusing to have a faulty focus, is the developing of an eternal focus. Remembering that we are but sojourners on this earth and our eternal home is in heaven with the Lord, will help us to keep all of our other areas in order. As urgent and important as circumstances here appear, nothing is more urgent or important than developing and maintaining our relationship with the Lord. An eternal focus is a security and safeguard from the pull of the world. How's your eternal focus today?

John 14:2-3

Parenting Point

Sometimes, it is difficult for us to maintain an eternal focus. So, if it's hard for us, how do we teach our children to have an eternal focus for themselves? The more we teach our children about Heaven and about the Lord, who will welcome them there, the more our children will develop an eternal focus. The Bible has so much to say about Heaven. Use your concordance and look up all of the verses you can find that deal with our heavenly home. Take time to share and discuss those verses with your children. When things on earth seem huge or overwhelming, remind them that someday they will be with the Lord for an eternity!

Putting On Love

Take the time to read today's verse. Does this seem like an impossible command to obey all the time? What about those who are unlovely or unlovable? While it may not always be easy to love others, the Lord makes it clear that it is His desire that His followers show their obedience to Him by loving others. At its core, love is not a feeling but an action. Although we may not always be experiencing the warm fuzzy feeling of love, as faithful disciples of the Lord Jesus Christ, we must always subordinate our lack of feelings at the moment to the higher call of carrying out the actions of love. Love shows itself in a variety of ways: through compassion, through tenderness, and sometimes through confrontation. Who needs to receive your acts of love today?

John 15:12

Parenting Point

It is so easy to love our children late at night, when their eyes are closed, and we gaze on their dear little sleeping faces; but, how about at 2:00 in the afternoon after a long day of training, correcting, and refereeing? It is at those times that we have the wonderful opportunity to show our children what it looks like to perform the acts of love when the feeling is waning. Disciplining ourselves to maintain a calm and kind tone of voice will go far in teaching our children how to respond when they are feeling less than loving toward a sibling or friend. Sometimes I have told my children that I was struggling to feel very loving because we had been experiencing a difficult day, but that I was committed to always showing love to them because God always shows love to me. If needed, take a few minutes alone to pray and ask the Lord to strengthen you to behave lovingly. Whenever I have sought the Lord's help to exhibit love, He has graciously shown me many reminders of all that I do love about my children. Those reminders have helped to dictate and control my actions. Remember, little eyes are watching, and little hearts will record your actions of love.

Dependable Dependability

The dictionary definition of dependability is to be trustworthy or reliable. How's your dependability quotient? Sometimes, it is easy to be dependable at our jobs, in our ministries, or in our outside relationships, but are we as dependable at home? I don't believe we have any wiggle-room to squirm out of the need for dependability at home. In fact, our homes should be the proving ground for the truth of our testimony of trustworthiness and reliability outside the home. Ask your spouse or children, "How dependable is my dependability?" See if your perspective and their perspective are the same. If not, it's time to make some changes!

Psalm 19:7-11

Parenting Point

Whenever possible, we should use the Word of God to teach character qualities to our children. Take some time today to read Psalm 19 aloud with your family. Discuss, as a family, what it means when the Scripture defines itself as trustworthy. Ask your children to think of areas in your family where their dependability or trustworthiness is absolutely essential. As you see areas of positive character surface in the discussion, take the time to praise your children and encourage them to an even higher level of trustworthy dependability; however, if you recognize areas of faithlessness instead of faithfulness, take the time to address those areas. Ask your children to help you understand why they are inconsistent or untrustworthy in those areas. Do they understand what is required of them? Do they have the tools necessary to complete their requirements? If not, help them to understand your standard and then equip them to carry out their responsibilities faithfully. Don't allow extra privileges until responsibilities are faithfully and consistently carried through to completion.

Thankfulness

Thankfulness is a character quality that is hard to describe to another person. We can recognize thankfulness when we see it and sense its importance when it is missing, but true thankfulness is difficult to describe with mere words. Thankfulness is not just saying "please" and "thank-you" it is an attitude of gratitude that makes up our innermost person. Why aren't we more thankful? Is it because we consider ourselves entitled to whatever comes our way? Romans 6:23 reminds us that we are only entitled to eternal separation from God because of our sin. Thankfully, the gift of God is eternal life in Christ Jesus our Lord. I need to remember to be thankful for Jesus... How about you?

Romans 6:23

Parenting Point

On a practical note, one of the best things I ever did was to make a list of the 5 things I was thankful for on a 3x5 card. After I wrote them down, I put the card in my Bible so that I would look at it every time I opened the Scriptures. After 20 years the "Thankful" list is still fresh and has been a constant reminder of the goodness of God. Take a few minutes today to get together with friends or family and write out individual "Thankful Cards" on 3x5 card stock and place them in your Bibles. I hope this exercise will produce many thankful returns.

Appropriateness

Everything in life has a distinct context. I was taught years ago that "Context is king," and "The rule of context is: context rules." Ecclesiastes chapter 3 speaks to the importance of context in everyday life. When we disregard the clear context of a situation, we risk behaving in an inappropriate manner. The KJV uses the word circumspect to describe one who behaves appropriately. The dictionary defines appropriateness as anything suitable for the occasion or circumstance. How appropriate is your behavior?

Ephesians 4:29-30

Parenting Point

Spend some time in careful family self-evaluation. Make a list of those inappropriate actions that you have allowed to continue unheeded and uncorrected in your family. For example, children standing on chairs in a restaurant are behaving inappropriately. Children who don't respond to adults when spoken to are behaving inappropriately. Children who respond to your directions with the verbal response of "No" are behaving inappropriately. Inappropriate children will grow up to be lonely and isolated adults because inappropriate adults find themselves unwelcome in most social settings. Don't set your children up for failure by allowing them to develop well-formed habits of inappropriate behavior. The first step toward necessary change is for you to seek your child's forgiveness for neglecting to correct and direct their behavior in an appropriate manner. Then, share the observations you have made about your own family's unique areas of inappropriateness. Explain why those behaviors are wrong, and teach your children the correct behavior that is necessary to replace their wrong and inappropriate behaviors. For example: "It is rude to ignore an adult when they speak to you. You must be polite and answer their question." It's a simple matter of "put-on" and "put-off" behaviors. Spend time role-playing various situations with your children to help them discover for themselves what appropriate behaviors can replace their inappropriate behaviors. Praise them for positive change as you see them making a good effort. When necessary bring correction for repeated inappropriate actions, but always couple that correction with further training in appropriateness. Pray for eyes to recognize new areas of inappropriate behavior that crop up and for the courage to deal with those areas quickly before they become a new habit for your children.

Honor and Courage

Honor, courage, and commitment are the U.S. Navy's core values. Yet, honor, courage, and commitment are not just character qualities that fit the military mission, they are qualities that soldiers in God's army ought to possess, too. Honor, after all, is a byproduct of courage and commitment. To act honorably in today's world takes both commitment and courage. Owning up to our mistakes, seeking forgiveness when we've blown it, and surrendering our pride are all acts of committed courage that will help create an honorable reputation. How honorable is your reputation?

Judges 13-16

Parenting Point

Read the story of Sampson out loud to your children. Then, ask them where and when Sampson dishonored God? Next, ask them if there is anything in their life that dishonors God. Help them to recognize examples such as a messy room, moody disposition, or disobedience towards Mom and Dad. Share areas in your own life in which you struggle to show honor towards God. As you transparently share your own struggles (as appropriate) and also share the positive steps that you take to overcome those struggles, you will be encouraging your children to develop the moral muscle necessary to make God-honoring choices. Consider other examples in Scripture that you could share with your children. If you have older children (eleven or older), assign them to look up various characters in the Bible and share what type of character those Biblical people possessed. Assign both positive and negative characters for your children to investigate. Plan a family evening to share their findings. Make the evening a fun family time. After everyone reports on the Biblical character, spend some time discussing areas in which your family could raise their standard of honor. Brainstorm practical ways to incorporate those changes in your family. Close your family time with prayer with and for one another. Ice cream sundaes can make a sweet close to a special family time. When you see your children showing honor to one another, don't just smile inwardly! Take the time to infuse them with the courage to show even more honor by recognizing their positive character and by praising their honorable acts. Remember, it takes courage and commitment to act with honor, so praise your children for their courageous character.

The Week in Review

Take some time to gather as a family and discuss the character qualities that you learned this week. Here are some questions to get the conversation started.

- List the character qualities we studied this week.

- Which character quality was the hardest for you to practice this week?

- Did you see a family member consistently practicing one of this week's character qualities? Which family member?

Use your imagination and add questions of your own. After your time of discussion, spend some time praying together, thanking the Lord and sharing one another's burdens. Pray ahead of time for teachable hearts to incorporate and put into practice the character qualities your family will learn in the upcoming week.

Considering Kindness

To whom do you extend your most gracious acts of kindness? It is usually easy to show kindness to our friends or to those who are kind to us; however, how do we respond to strangers, or perhaps of even more difficulty, to those who have wounded or offended us? It is only through developing a heart of obedience and submission to God that we can make our kindness a consistent act of character. God is kind to us! Even when we were lost and undeserving, He graciously showed us the kindness of His character. Pray for a heart that extends kindness in a manner like your Lord's.

Colossians 3:12-14

Parenting Point

Are your children as kind to those at home as they are to their friends? If not, why not? Nothing saddens my heart more than seeing my children act sweetly and kindly toward their friends, while behaving harshly and un-kindly toward their siblings. If this is the paradigm in your home, it is time to address the inappropriate heart attitude that is producing such poor be-havior. When I teach into this issue with our children, I use the ugly, but biblical word "hypocrisy" to define their behavior. According to the diction-ary, a hypocrite is one who feigns some desirable or publicly approved at-titude, especially one whose private life, opinions, or statements belie his or her public statements. Yuck! What a horrible characterization to own. The Pharisees were hypocrites, and they earned some of Jesus' harshest criti-cisms. Ask your children to help you to understand their actions toward their siblings. When they are forced to define and defend their own behavior, the lesson will take much deeper root in their hearts. If we simply tell them, "You must be kind to your brothers and sisters." we may get outward assent, but inwardly there may be no heart transformation. Occasionally, we have had to limit outside influences in order to rebuild sibling relationships. We did this not as a punishment but as a tool to solidify family ties. From their youngest days we reminded our children that God had chosen them to be a family, and when we are gone, they will still have each other. How sad to see families splintered and broken because kindness toward one another was disregarded. Insist on kindness in your home. As well, make sure that your children clearly see that you treat them with the same kindness you extend toward friends, neighbors, and brothers and sisters in the church.

369

Forgiveness • Repentance

Undoing Unbelief

Often, when we think of unbelief, the first thing that comes to mind is someone who doesn't have a relationship with the Lord Jesus Christ. As today's verses remind us, however, unbelief can also occur in the life of a follower of Christ. To some extent, whenever we display a lack of faith, we are showing a heart of unbelief. But, more destructive, is the believer who, through the deceitfulness of sin, has hardened his heart and fallen away from the living God. If this describes you, the antidote is confession, repentance, and a change of direction; however, if this unbelief describes a loved one or friend, the Word of God exhorts us to continue to encourage them day after day. Our encouragement can be used by God to soften their hardened heart. Who needs your encouragement today?

Hebrews 3:12-13

Parenting Point

Sin destroys, and sin left unchecked can harden a heart and cause someone to turn his or her back on God. Our children are not immune to this hardening. Although it is tiring to deal on a daily basis with their sin, it is our responsibility to admonish our children and to encourage them to walk faithfully with God. Sin that is left to fester and grow will soon become a deeply ingrained pattern of life. Pray daily that God would help you to discern any hidden sins or sin patterns that are developing in the life of your children. God will be faithful to show you things that otherwise might go unnoticed. As God reveals those areas, prayerfully talk to your children and help them to seek forgiveness. Sometimes, I have been tempted to grumble when God has shown me those areas...I just didn't feel like dealing with them; however, the right response is thankfulness to a faithful God who loves my family enough to bring what is hidden to light. Today's verses remind us that sin is deceitful, that is why it is so important to be on the alert. Jeremiah 17:9 tells us that our hearts are desperately wicked and easily deceived. Sin takes advantage of our ability to be deceived and draws a net around our hearts. Don't allow your children to be ensnared! Pray for discernment and take whatever steps are necessary to keep them from "falling away from the living God." Continue to encourage them day by day. Your encouragement can help to infuse them with the courage they need to turn from their sin and embrace the Lord.

A Focus on Flexibility

One of my mother's favorite sayings was, "You can't teach an old dog new tricks!" Catchy saying but really untrue in the life of a follower of Christ. Part of being a teachable Christian involves being willing to yield our rights, those plans, desires, and expectations that we cling to so possessively. As the Spirit works in our lives, challenging us to change and conform to the image of Christ, we must be flexible and eager to change. Perhaps today is the day to give your flexibility muscles a stretch.

James 3:17

Parenting Point

It is so easy for our children to become creatures of habit. I'm sure you have experienced trying to change a routine or schedule and hearing your children say, "But we ALWAYS do it this way!" While routine and orderliness is important in our children's lives, an inflexible, demanding, "I have to have it my way!" child is not a child that makes their God look great. Work hard to teach your children to be willing to yield what they perceive to be their rights for the good of others. Others-oriented children will have a strong testimony for the Lord! These same children will handle the curve balls of life with greater ease because they have been trained to be flexible, not rigid, in their habits of life. One of the few things we can count on in life is the constancy of change. Help your children to embrace, not fear, the inevitable changes that will occur in your family. When change is God-initiated, it is an exciting thing and something to look forward to with anticipation.

Faithfulness Builds Fellowship

Faithfulness is defined as adhering firmly and devotedly, as to a person, cause, or idea; loyal. That certainly sounds like the definition of a believer in the Lord Jesus Christ, doesn't it? Faithfulness is not a once and done action but instead, encompasses a continual habit of making our actions, attitudes, thoughts, and associations, faithful to the Lord. Perhaps today is a good day to spend time seeking the Lord in prayer and asking Him to reveal any "little" areas of unfaithfulness in your life. A lack of faithfulness to the Lord will cause distance in your relationship with Him. Conversely, as you faithfully surrender to the Lord, in all areas of your life, your love for and fellowship with the Lord will grow by leaps and bounds!

Psalm 31:23-24

Parenting Point

As we daily insist that our children obey us, "Right Away, All the Way, the Happy Way," we are paving the way for them to learn how to live lives of faithfulness. As they grow in their faithfulness to your directions, you are laying the groundwork for them to understand what faithfulness to God really looks like. Keep an eternal perspective! Sometimes it seems like all we do as parents is remind our children over and over to obey us completely; however, that daily, consistent training will pay huge spiritual benefits when they are grown. You will delight as you watch them grow in fellowship with you and with God as a result of their well-trained faithfulness.

Determination

Doers, according to James 1:22, are determined people set on serving God. They are unlike the hearer, who is deluded in his/her lack of action. The Christian walk is not a spectator sport. God does not want us to sit on the sidelines and observe the game from the bleachers. God wants us to be determined doers of His Word, thus proving to a watching world what a great God He is. Have you got your "do" on today?

James 1:22-25

Parenting Point

When our children are determined to have something, they tend to be relentless about it. I remember, as a child, the many and varied ways in which I would wear down my mother's resolve until I got what I wanted. As responsible parents we must be as determined as they are, and then some. Capitulation to manipulation will be detrimental to their character maturation. J Don't be afraid to be the parent. Pray with determination that God will help you direct your child's self-willed stubbornness into Christ-focused determination for the Kingdom of God. Don't be surprised when they consistently push against the established walls of rules and standards you have set for them. Pushing against the walls is their natural bent; however, make sure that you are standing firm and refusing to be manipulated. Your firm determination will provide them with security and a strong sense of confidence in you.

Careful, Careful

A re you characterized by carefulness in your choices and decisions? Read today's Scripture and evaluate your life in light of what the Word says. Although some choices or decisions can absolutely *feel* like the right thing to do, if it is not within the parameters of God's Word and the boundaries of His will, it will never be appropriate. Conversely, some actions can seem like an awful or difficult task, but if it is "God's way" for you, the end will be life not death. Take the time to seek God, so that what seems right to you is also what is right in His eyes.

Proverbs 14:12

Parenting Point

Help your children learn how to seek counsel and godly input as they are making decisions. Observe your children. Do you have children who make their decisions based solely on how they "feel" about something? This is not a life-habit that will serve them well! Take time to discuss with them the deceitfulness of emotions. (Jeremiah 17:9) When they make poor decisions based solely on emotions, help them to evaluate what could have been done differently but don't necessarily free them from the consequences of those bad decisions. Praise them when you see them practicing godly decision making. Although they may not appreciate your input now, they will thank you for the good training in the future. Parents, how are you doing in this area? Decisions, based solely on how we feel about a situation, can cause long-term and harmful consequences for our whole family.

The Week in Review

Take some time to gather as a family and discuss the character qualities that you learned this week. Here are some questions to get the conversation started.

- **List the character qualities we studied this week.**

- **Which character quality was the hardest for you to practice this week?**

- **Did you see a family member consistently practicing one of this week's character qualities? Which family member?**

Use your imagination and add questions of your own. After your time of discussion, spend some time praying together, thanking the Lord and sharing one another's burdens. Pray ahead of time for teachable hearts to incorporate and put into practice the character qualities your family will learn in the upcoming week.

A Testimony of Trust

Read today's verses. By his actions and attitudes, King Hezekiah built a reputation for trust in God. In fact, the scriptures record that there was none like him again nor had there been anyone before him with such a trust in God. What a wonderful testimony for a young man to attain. Hezekiah didn't simply say that he trusted God, his actions of obedience showed that trust in both practical and radical ways. What do your actions say about your trust relationship with God?

II Kings 18:4-5

Parenting Point

How trusting are your children? I'm confident that we all want our children to grow into a personally trusting and obedient relationship with the Lord, but are we taking the necessary steps to point them in that direction? Our children learn to trust in their faithful God as they practice trusting their faithful parents. Something as simple as handing your baby to the nursery worker and assuring him/her that they can trust you to return is a foundational step in teaching our children to trust us. We encourage young mothers to allow trustworthy friends to hold their babies. Teaching our children that we will never hand them off to someone who is untrustworthy will help them grow in confidence and trust. Use statements like: "You must trust Daddy." "Mommy will be back; you must trust me." Fearful children are unhappy children and learning to trust their parents will help them abandon their fearfulness. As our children mature, it is imperative to speak often and naturally about the faithfulness of God and how we can trust Him to care for us. As they see you trusting God implicitly, they will begin to emulate your model of trust. Obviously, it is important to do our homework as well. Make sure that the people and situations you are entrusting your child to are, in fact, trustworthy. Unfortunately, there are people we trust that let us down; it's simply the reality of living in a sinful world. At those times, seek your children's forgiveness, pray for the people who have disappointed or wronged them, and move on as a family. The more willing our children are to trust us, the more easily they will learn to trust their Heavenly Father.

Kindness Defined

The word kind is defined as: having or showing a friendly, generous, and considerate nature. Like compassion, although we may or may not be naturally kind, we must choose to "put-on" a heart of kindness. Christians, who exhibit friendly and generous behavior, are a compelling witness for the Lord. As an added blessing, the very act of choosing to respond to others in a friendly manner often brings us more friends as well. Regardless of our circumstances, recognizing the kindness that God extends toward us can infuse us with the courage to extend kindness to others.

Colossians 3:12-14

Parenting Point

Over the years, people have shared many nice compliments about my children and their behavior; however, the compliment that I cherish the most is hearing that people notice that my children are kind to one another and to those outside our home. Nothing brings out the Mama Bear in me more than hearing other children speak unkindly to or about my children. Although I sometimes want to respond poorly to such words, the Word of God reminds me that I must be an example of kindness even in the wake of unkindness. When someone speaks unkindly to my children, I try to take a few moments to help them process and discard any hurt feelings. Often, we discuss how unhappy someone must be in order to speak in such a way to others. I always remind my children that we don't know what goes on in other people's homes; perhaps that child is spoken to harshly or unkindly, and they are just repeating the example they learned at home. I always encourage my children to stop and pray for those who have treated them unkindly. Praying for others is a safeguard against bitterness and hurt memories taking root in my own children's lives. It is never the right choice to respond to unkindness with more unkindness!

Whom Do You Follow: The Shepherd or the Sheep?

As a Christian, it is imperative to develop the strong character of a follower; however, we need to be careful to make sure that we are following Christ and Christ alone. While our friends, church, and other mentors can give us great encouragement, edification, and exhortation, unless their leading points us to Christ we are in danger of following the wrong voice. II Timothy 2:15 reminds us to be diligent in learning how to accurately handle the Word of God. Our diligence in this area is a safeguard to keep us from following anything or anyone other than Christ. The better we know Him and His Word, the less likely we are to be led astray. How accurate is your handle on Scripture?

I Corinthians 3:4-9

Parenting Point

In parenting, it is so easy to become what we refer to as a "sheep parent." Instead of basing our family decisions and convictions on the Word of God, we slip into the trap of doing what everyone else is doing. If the majority of the church home schools, we home school. If the majority of the church plays soccer, our children play soccer. The opportunities to follow the herd are endless. While these activities in and of themselves are fine, simply following the crowd in participation is a problem. Take the time to seek God, study the Scripture, and pray; only then can you make decisions that will be right for your family. God has made each family unique and special. What is appropriate or edifying for one family may be absolutely the wrong path for another family. Children who grow up in a home directed by sheep parents will be prone to fall prey to peer pressure. They will respond to the pressure to conform in just the same way they saw modeled by their parents. Resist the urge to follow the herd! Make sure you know the voice of the Shepherd and follow His direction to lead your family.

Appropriate or Proud

The dictionary defines appropriate as suitable for a particular person, condition, occasion, or place, fitting. There are some behaviors that are always appropriate for the believer. For instance, in Luke 17 Jesus tells us that it is always appropriate to forgive; even if we must forgive another person seven times a day. According to John 13, 1 Corinthians 13, and Matthew 22, it is always appropriate to love one another. The Psalms make it crystal clear that it is always appropriate to praise God. Conversely, it is inappropriate and sinful if we refuse to forgive, if we are lazy with our love, and if we are stingy with our praise of God and others. So, is there anyone in your life that you are refusing to forgive? Is there someone in your life that you should show love towards, but you just won't do it? If so, are you surprised that your praise of God feels flat and empty? Finally, what do an unforgiving spirit, an unloving attitude, and a lack of praise have in common? Pride; and, pride is never appropriate for the believer.

I Corinthians 13

Parenting Point

Sometimes it seems like all we do is point out our children's inappropriate behavior or correct them for disobedience. Today do something positive instead. Call a family meeting, and challenge each family member to think of five ways that other family members demonstrate "appropriateness." You can use the examples from above to get their juices flowing. After everyone has written down their five examples, go around the table and share what each person has written. Think of those areas of appropriateness that your children practice on a consistent basis and use this forum to thank them and to praise them for their good and conscientious choices in those areas. Every time we encourage our children we are literally infusing them with the courage they will need to produce even more and sweeter fruit for our Lord. Don't be stingy with your praise! Remember, this isn't the time to segue your discussion to areas that need improvement. There will be plenty of time to deal with character deficiencies tomorrow. Today, just rejoice in the good you see! Make this family time memorable with ice cream sundaes or another special treat. Enjoy some "appropriate" celebrating!

Faithfulness Builds Fellowship

Faithfulness is defined as adhering firmly and devotedly, as to a person, cause, or idea; loyal. That certainly sounds like the definition of a believer in the Lord Jesus Christ, doesn't it? Faithfulness is not a once and done action but instead, encompasses a continual habit of making our actions, attitudes, thoughts, and associations faithful to the Lord. Perhaps today is a good day to spend time seeking the Lord in prayer and asking Him to reveal any "little" areas of unfaithfulness in your life. A lack of faithfulness to the Lord will cause distance in your relationship with Him. Conversely, as you faithfully surrender to the Lord in all areas of your life, your love for and fellowship with the Lord will grow by leaps and bounds!

Psalm 31:23-24

Parenting Point

As we daily insist that our children obey us "Right Away, All the Way, the Happy Way," we are paving the way for them to learn how to live lives of faithfulness. As they grow in their faithfulness to your directions, you are laying the groundwork for them to understand what faithfulness to God really looks like. Keep an eternal perspective! Sometimes it seems like all we do as parents is remind our children over and over to obey us completely; however, that daily, consistent training will pay huge spiritual benefits when they are grown. You will delight as you watch them grow in fellowship with you and with God as a result of their well-trained faithfulness. Quick and complete faithfulness to God will provide a safeguard for our children keeping them from presumptuous sin and guarding their hearts and minds in Christ Jesus.

Humility

Putting Off Pride

There is no question: the opposite of humility is pride. Pride is the source of so many of our poor character choices. In our pride we refuse to admit fault, we refuse to change, and we refuse to humble ourselves in submission to anyone, including the Lord Jesus Christ. Read today's scripture. There is nothing ambiguous about God's feelings regarding pride. He sees it as an abomination. Again, time in the Word of God is the antidote to pride, and sadly, pride is the very thing that will keep us from the Word of God. To be well pleasing to the Lord, we must put-off pride!

Proverbs 16:18

Parenting Point

Listen to your children's everyday communication. What is the major topic of their conversation? If you continually hear them talking about themselves or bragging of their achievements and exploits, it is time to take action. Spend time together looking into the Word of God. Help them to compile a list of verses regarding pride and humility. After compiling the list, help them choose several verses that they will commit to memory. Pride is an ugly sin to conquer. Encourage them to seek the Lord's forgiveness for their pride, and then ask the Lord for help to hate their pride and to love humility instead. Remind them that often, when they are feeling like everyone and everything is going against them, it is actually God opposing their pride. Pray with and for them as they seek to put-off their pride and learn to live humbly.

The Week in Review

Take some time to gather as a family and discuss the character qualities that you learned this week. Here are some questions to get the conversation started.

- List the character qualities we studied this week.
- Which character quality was the hardest for you to practice this week?
- Did you see a family member consistently practicing one of this week's character qualities? Which family member?

Use your imagination and add questions of your own. After your time of discussion, spend some time praying together, thanking the Lord and sharing one another's burdens. Pray ahead of time for teachable hearts to incorporate and put into practice the character qualities your family will learn in the upcoming week.

Love

L ove is probably one of the most overused words in the English language! We love our children. We love God. We love chocolate cake. One simple word covers a lot of ground. Scripture teaches us that God's love is an unconditional, undeserved love shown by the sacrifice of His beloved Son on the cross of Calvary. How far short our human love falls with that *agape* love as our example! However, as we grow in our relationship with Christ, we can then extend more and more of the unconditional love exhibited by our teacher, Jesus.

I Corinthians 13

Parenting Point

I John 3:18 says:"Little children, let us not love with word or with tongue, but in deed and truth." Our children must learn to exhibit love to one another through their actions! Often, my children would verbally speak of loving one another, while their actions toward one another were anything but loving. Allowing them to speak what wasn't true in their hearts would have built a terrible pattern and habit into their character, so I found myself often correcting and redirecting their actions. Instead of always being on the defense, I would suggest taking an offensive position. Call a family conference and spend the time discussing practical and pro-active ways to show love in "deed and truth." Have one of the older children record the suggestions and post them on your refrigerator. When you see a child headed down the road of unloving actions or attitudes, direct them to the family-generated list and encourage them to pick one option for showing love and then demonstrate that loving action to a family member. Just as we can build a habit of unloving attitudes, consistent and persistent practice in exhibiting love will build strong habits of love. Families, characterized by sacrificial and compassionate love toward one another, will gain opportunities to share the love of Christ.

Kindness

All around us, we hear people talking about the need to become a "kinder" and gentler people, but what exactly does kindness embody?

The definition of kindness is the practice of being, or the capability to be, sympathetic and compassionate, or an act that shows consideration and caring. Kindness is all about being oriented to the needs of others and acting in their interests, rather than our own. Kindness cuts deep at the root of our own self-interests and self-centeredness. To be kind to others requires thinking what would bless and encourage another person, regardless of the gain or lack of gain to ourselves. Sadly, too often we are kind to strangers and acquaintances, while allowing ourselves the freedom to speak, act, or think unkindly of our own family members.

Galatians 5:22

Parenting Point

Included in the Fruits of the Spirit, a Christian cannot be mature and useable without the character quality of kindness. This includes children, as well as adults. Do not allow unkindness in your home! Let me repeat... DO NOT allow unkindness in your home. When we allow unkind attitudes and actions in our home, while insisting that our children be kind to others outside the home, we are training them to be hypocrites, and people who live two separate lives. The best training ground for the character quality of kindness is your own family. Sarcastic, cutting remarks should be recognized and addressed immediately. Also, watch for actions that wound. Too often, the unkind actions of our children go uncorrected, simply because we have not trained ourselves to be constantly aware of the actions going on around us. Don't be guilty of allowing an atmosphere of unkindness. Begin today to correct the problem, encouraging your children to seek forgiveness and to restore as necessary. Take time to help them put off unkindness and replace those actions or attitudes with kind behaviors that will bless their family and build great life-long character.

Commitment

C ommitment is devotion or dedication to a cause, person or relationship. Commitments take time and energy to fulfill. Postmodern Americans seem to take their commitments lightly. Divorce is rampant among Christians and our commitments to recognized obligations are easily discarded if something "better" or "more fun" comes along. Sadly, we are less likely to read our Bibles, join a church, tithe, or share the gospel than any previous generation in our nation's history. To what are you devoted? Your calendar and checkbook know the answer! Read and study the following scripture on commitment.

Matthew 8:18-22

Parenting Point

Without careful consideration we can easily become overcommitted to many worthwhile but time-consuming activities. Sometimes, that over commitment creeps up on us unaware. To gain a clear picture, call a family conference. Give each member of the family a blank sheet of paper and instruct them to list every activity to which they have made a commitment. Take your time with this activity and encourage everyone to carefully think through his or her own days, weeks, and months. Some commitments to remember might be: scouts, sports teams, classes, meetings, service activities, church, etc. After everyone has completed their lists, begin your family calendar project. On a blank calendar, and using different colored pens for each family member, write in each family member's monthly commitments. If a commitment happens once a week, write it down on each week. After every family member's list has been recorded on the calendar, take some time to evaluate your family's level of commitment to activities. Hopefully, you'll be thrilled to see that your family is using their time wisely; however, I'm afraid that many of us will view our calendars with horror. When it's all written down for everyone to see, it often becomes apparent that we are overcommitted and involved in far too many activities. If this is true of your family, spend some time in discussion and prayer. Determine which commitments must stay and which can be discontinued. If a commitment is nothing but filler or busy-time, consider gracefully disentangling yourselves from that commitment. It's important to honor commitments but make sure that the commitments you honor are of benefit to the peace, security, and spiritual growth of your family.

Continuous Contentment

Contentment can be an elusive character quality. Just when we're certain that we've settled into an attitude of contentment and thankfulness in our lives, something comes along to catch our attention and draw our hearts away. Why is that? I John 2:16 reminds us that the lusts of the flesh are not from the Father but from the world. A contented Christian just ruins Satan's day! The greatest antidote to discontent in our lives is a thankful heart. Count your blessings today; you'll display to the world the bounty and benefits of a living relationship with Christ.

Philippians 4:11

Parenting Point

Contentment does not come naturally to our children. Even when they are surrounded by beloved possessions and great family relationships, they naturally hunger and yearn for more. Help your children develop a heart of contentment by teaching them to be satisfied with what they already have. When your children want to "upgrade" to the next level of toy or replace what they are eating with something else just because they see another child enjoying something different, do not immediately give in to their desires. Continually replacing and upgrading what is perfectly acceptable will only serve to build greater discontentment in our children's hearts. Learning to be content with what they already have will benefit our children now and into the future. When you notice that your children are headed down the road of grumbling, coveting, and discontentment, take action. Point out the heart attitude of discontentment that is invading your family. Discontentment becomes the "put-off" characteristic that your children must discard. Then, ask them to explain to you what an appropriate "put-on" characteristic would be to replace that negative attitude. Let them think about the answer, but if they are truly stuck, share that the answer is "gratitude." Have them rehearse with you some of the things that they are grateful for and help them to recognize that those gifts come from God. Spend some time in the Word looking up applicable verses and discussing them together. Memorizing a verse, such as Hebrews 13:5, will provide a safeguard to keep us from sin. Verses memorized together, as a family, will provide a great jumping off point for discussion and encouragement. Grumbling and coveting can negatively affect an entire family. Don't allow a lack of thankfulness to hinder your family's positive testimony.

What Does Inappropriate Look Like?

In Ephesians 4:22-24, Paul details for us the need to reject inappropriate behavior and replace it with appropriate behavior. We are to put off the "old self" and replace it with the "new self." In other words, God wants us to abandon our old, sinful habits and desires and put on the new life that He has provided for us in Christ. Does your life in Christ bring glory to God at all times? Are you different on the Internet than you are in person? Do your Facebook friends know beyond a shadow of a doubt that you have a strong, unwavering commitment to Christ? How often do you quote Scripture, praise God, or encourage your friends to godly living through your chats and posts? It is inappropriate to live a double life. What life are you living?

James 1:5-8

Parenting Point

My paraphrase of Ephesians 4:22-24 goes like this: *"God wants me to be changing, to be more like His Son, by putting off the old man and putting on the new man, as a result of renewed thinking in the Spirit."* Parents, do you know what is going on daily on your teen's Facebook account? Or, in their Google chats? It is not invasive to check up on your children; it is your job as a concerned parent. It is important to gauge not only what your children are posting, but also, what is being posted to them. Take the time to check out the profiles of unknown friends on their friends list to make sure they will be appropriate influences. Don't flinch when your children complain because "no one else has parents that check up on them." Be the parent and encourage other parents to practice vigilance with their own children. The Internet, used correctly, can be a great tool for building relationships; however, used incorrectly, the Internet can tempt our children beyond what they are able to withstand. Talk to your children about their Internet communications. Take them to Philippians 4:8 and discuss the need to communicate in a manner that is true, lovely, pure, etc. Challenge them to raise their standard of communication and to use the Internet to encourage friends to become courageous and character healthy followers of Christ. Make sure that you are holding yourself to the same high standard of communication; your example will speak louder than your words.

Secondary Responsibilities

Today we get to discuss the fun stuff: secondary responsibilities. Secondary responsibilities reside at the very top of the responsibility continuum. These desirable responsibilities should only be put into place when we have proven ourselves faithful with the budding and primary responsibilities. Secondary responsibilities often look like privileges, but because there is an inherent element of trust necessary, they hold a greater importance than mere privileges. Secondary responsibilities are the "neat" things we crave: that promotion, a title at work or church, an invitation to join a committee. For our teens, secondary responsibilities would include a job, a driver's license, a personal computer, or IPhone. All of these responsibilities require care and integrity to be handled correctly. How are you doing in the budding and primary areas? Have you earned the secondary responsibilities that you enjoy?

II Timothy 2:15

Parenting Point

Take the time to read today's Scripture with your children. Ask them if they feel as though they are diligently completing their responsibilities in a way that makes them eligible to receive secondary responsibilities. With my own children, I helped each of them construct a responsibility tree with the trunk full of their budding responsibilities, the branches covered with their primary responsibilities, and then we made fruit that represented their desired secondary responsibilities. These trees hang on their bedroom doors and provide a visual reminder of what is expected of them and what they can hope to earn. Secondary responsibilities for children would include things such as: an IPod, overnights away from home, Facebook, team sports, etc. Be careful that you do not hand out secondary responsibilities before they are earned; you will only set a bad precedent for the future.

The Week in Review

Take some time to gather as a family and discuss the character qualities that you learned this week. Here are some questions to get the conversation started.

- **List the character qualities we studied this week.**

- **Which character quality was the hardest for you to practice this week?**

- **Did you see a family member consistently practicing one of this week's character qualities? Which family member?**

Use your imagination and add questions of your own. After your time of discussion, spend some time praying together, thanking the Lord and sharing one another's burdens. Pray ahead of time for teachable hearts to incorporate and put into practice the character qualities your family will learn in the upcoming week.

Forgiveness

Forgiving is defined as an ability to allow for, or cope well with, a degree of imprecision, lack of skill, or other imperfections. In other words, a forgiving person extends the same degree of mercy and grace to others that they assume for themselves. Forgiving others, and seeking forgiveness from those whom we have offended, protects our hearts from bitterness and keeps us humble. James 4:6 reminds us that God will give us grace as we exhibit the humility required to practice forgiveness.

Luke 17:1-10

Parenting Point

Offering and extending forgiveness are two of the most important lessons we can teach our children. As your children deal with daily offenses, help them to think beyond the offending actions to the underlying heart attitude that caused the problem. Teach them to seek forgiveness with the words, "I am sorry for _____. I was being (fill in the poor attitude or character quality). Will you please forgive me?" For example, "I am sorry for taking your toy. I was being selfish. Will you please forgive me?" Teach the offended child how to extend forgiveness. Remember, your example will be the best model. Don't be afraid to seek your children's forgiveness. They will be quick to forgive and restore, and you will be building great character into their lives. Seeking forgiveness and extending forgiveness are not optional, and they don't depend upon our feelings at the moment. As faithful followers of the Lord, our obedient actions regarding forgiveness will build our testimony of Christ-likeness. Conversely, if we are known to have a bitter and unforgiving spirit, we will dishonor the name of Christ. It's important to teach our children how to quickly seek forgiveness. Also, it's important to help them learn how to have a heart that is prepared to forgive. Even when another person is slow to seek our forgiveness, we must be humbly prepared to offer it, if they finally approach us. Holding on to an unforgiving spirit will cause harm in our own relationship with the Lord, and that harm will begin to spill over into our relationships with others. Be careful to model an appropriate and humble heart of forgiveness for your children to imitate.

A Single-Minded Servant

Every day, throughout the day, we face the choice whether to submit or rebel. Although the world would offer us a third choice, anything other than wholehearted submission to the will of God in our lives falls into the category of rebellion. It is work to develop the character quality of submission, but as we deliberately and habitually work to choose submission to God over acquiescence to self and the world, we will build strong spiritual muscles. Those strong muscles and the accompanying moral muscle memory will strengthen us to faithfully continue down the road of submission.

Joshua 24:14-15

Parenting Point

Do you realize that we can unwittingly train our children to choose rebellion over submission? Yes, all of us have a naturally rebellious heart because of sin, but we can actually strengthen that rebellious heart by our laziness or inattention to the actions and attitudes of our children. Every time that we instruct our children to do something and they give us less than complete obedience with no forthcoming consequence, we are teaching them that the road of rebellion is just as acceptable as the road of submission. Although this type of rebellion is subtle, it is rebellion nonetheless. There is no third choice and to allow our children to live as though they can disobey us, yet not be considered rebellious, is to do them a grave disservice. It is helpful for me to remember that the ultimate goal of teaching my children submission to my instructions is so that someday they will wholeheartedly submit to God. Children who are allowed to offer "sloppy" obedience and half-hearted attitudes to their parents, whom they can see, will struggle mightily to offer wholehearted obedience to a God, whom they cannot see. Insist on obedience while they are young, and you will be delighted to see them obey their God as adults.

Self-Control

S elf-control is defined as the ability to control your own behavior, especially in terms of reactions and impulses. Wow! Self-control, it seems, is a lost quality. When was the last time you went to the restaurant and saw a parent teaching their child to practice self-control? All too often, children are encouraged to roam the restaurant as they please, jump on the seats, and even sit on the table tops. Whatever happened to self-control? In fact, we live in a culture that rewards impulsive behavior and belittles thoughtful, deliberate, and patient behavior. MTV, VH1 and other similar T.V. channels glorify living by your hormones and never show the consequences of such actions. No wonder so many young people want to "live life in the fast lane." Oh wait, that was my generation! Anyway, you get my point... Self-control is good; impulsiveness is usually bad.

1 Corinthians 9:25-27

Parenting Point

What does self-control look like in your home? The best tool we ever came across for teaching self-control to the little ones was the folding of the hands exercise. Try this with your 2- to 6-year old crowd. Set up two chairs facing each other. You sit in one and junior sits in the other. Set a timer to go off in 30 seconds and challenge your child to join you in the "self-control" game by folding their hands with no talking for 30 seconds. If successful, reward the child with praise. Later that day try the same exercise for 45 seconds praising again when successful. Repeat the exercise each day until you reach 3 minutes. Once you and your child can sit still for 3 minutes, you have trained them to practice self-control. It is imperative that you play the game with them. Do not send them to a seat to try it on their own; it will backfire. Half the fun is having Mom or Dad practice self-control too. Next time you are in the car and things are getting out of control in the back seat, just look at them and say, "Self-control please." Then, gesture to fold the hands and watch how they respond. If you are successful with this exercise, you will hand your children an extremely valuable tool that will produce fruit for the rest of their lives. My adult children still fold their hands and take time out to pray when life is getting out of control. Good stuff. Give it a try.

A Merciful Heart

In a society that surrounds us with tabloids and reality shows that display celebrities' unrighteous choices for everyone to see, it is difficult to maintain a merciful heart; however, today's Scripture reminds us that not only are the merciful blessed, but they will also receive mercy themselves. We must be careful to extend mercy to others; often we know little of the true nature of the circumstances behind their decisions. God will take care of dealing with their bad choices; we have the opportunity to extend mercy and love when they feel most undeserving.

Matthew 5:7

Parenting Point

Take some time today to read Matthew 5:3-12. Discuss with your children what it looks like to extend mercy to one another. For children mercy can be an abstract term and hard to define. Until we make application of the actions of mercy, our children may not grasp what mercy looks like in day-to-day living. We often rationalize our own actions and attitudes, while at the same time we are judging another's actions and attitudes. Maintaining the character of mercy will keep us from judging others and then acting out on those judgments. Remind your children that they are not called to be the Holy Spirit in anyone else's life, but rather they are to be busy making sure that they are being obedient to whatever the Lord has shown them to do. Families who are characterized by being merciful will find themselves able to minister to many hurting and ostracized people. Knowing that they will not be judged but will instead receive mercy, enables folks to seek the help they need without fear of judgment. When we gain that testimony, we can act as the hands of Christ to comfort and meet many needs.

Resolved to be Resolute

The dictionary defines the character quality of being resolute this way: firm, or determined, unwavering. Let's consider how resolute we are to follow through in a determined and unwavering attitude. Jesus is our example of how to continue on, regardless of the pain or suffering involved. Take stock of your life. How resolute are you to complete what has been started? Your model of resolution in the face of difficult circumstances may be the impetus for another believer to "stick it out" and not give up. Are you resolved to be resolute?

Luke 22:39-46

Parenting Point

Every day our children face opportunities to quit what seems hard and to abandon those activities that no longer bring pleasure. We must teach our children to remain resolute in times of difficulty or even simply boredom. Take time today to read the account of our Lord in the Garden of Gethsemane. Discuss with your children how Christ showed a resolute spirit, regardless of the pain and horror He was about to embark upon. Talk as a family about areas in which it is hard to remain resolute. Perhaps now is a good time to talk to your children about why you work so resolutely to teach and train them. As parents, our firm, determined, and unwavering devotion to instilling godly character into our children's lives is a safeguard for them and a matter of obedience to God for us. Resolve today to be a family known for your resolution!

Generosity

G enerous people are characterized by a willingness to give money, help, or time freely. Generosity is also defined as showing nobility of character. Generous people hold on loosely to their "things," realizing that ultimately, everything belongs to the Lord. I believe that part of the reason God has so graciously blessed our family is because of the abundant generosity exhibited by my husband. Read the following verses, remembering that God blesses those who are generous.

Matthew 20:15-16

Parenting Point

How generous is your family? There is a huge difference between being willing to give and eagerly looking for opportunities. Ask your children for suggestions on how your family could practice generosity. Listen for the language of coveting in your home. Children who demand to receive what someone else has been given are not going to become generous children. Teach them to be thankful and willing to share, not covetous and craving more. Here's a practical family project: Spend time together evaluating your children's toys and possessions. If what they have is well cared for and carefully stewarded, good job! However, if you see that your children just have too much stuff, give them a "Generosity Challenge." Remind them just how bountifully the Lord has provided for your family. Then, ask them if they would like to share with another child, or another family, in that same bountiful way. If they say yes, set them to work putting aside toys, puzzles, and games to share with others. Remember, when they want to give away the "good stuff," don't stop them! It is wonderful for our children to learn to share what's best, instead of keeping the best for themselves and passing on their "sloppy seconds." As a family, deliver the toys to their new owners. Perhaps you could make a meal to take along on the delivery run. When we bless others, we always reap a blessing in return. Don't be surprised if your kids get hooked on sharing. What a great problem to have!

The Week in Review

Take some time to gather as a family and discuss the character qualities that you learned this week. Here are some questions to get the conversation started.

- **List the character qualities we studied this week.**

- **Which character quality was the hardest for you to practice this week?**

- **Did you see a family member consistently practicing one of this week's character qualities? Which family member?**

Use your imagination and add questions of your own. After your time of discussion, spend some time praying together, thanking the Lord and sharing one another's burdens. Pray ahead of time for teachable hearts to incorporate and put into practice the character qualities your family will learn in the upcoming week.

Fruitful Self-Control

According to Galatians 5:22, the Fruit of the Spirit is love, joy, peace, patience, kindness, goodness, faithfulness, gentleness, and self-control. Although the Fruit of the Spirit is to be considered collectively, I want us to consider the important role self-control plays in helping us balance out the other fruits like love, joy, peace, etc. Delayed gratification, self-denial, and self-control are all vital disciplines. These disciplines provide strength and health to our character development. When was the last time you exercised self-control? Saying NO to dessert or NO to unhealthy peer pressure is what self-control looks like in daily application. NOT using that credit card next time might just be the important first step you ought to take to begin living a character-healthy life.

Galatians 5:22

Parenting Point

Don't you wish that we could just give our children a "self-control shot?" Unfortunately, it doesn't work that way! For our children to develop the self-control that will be necessary when they grow and leave home, we must continually teach and train into this character quality. In training self-control with your older children, the dialogue question is your greatest ally. Instead of telling your children what they should choose in order to practice self-control, ask them a dialogue question and allow them to make the discovery on their own. A simple question like, "Do you have the freedom to go out with your friends tonight?" puts the responsibility for wise decision-making right in our children's laps, where it belongs. No, they won't always make the right decision, and sometimes, they will suffer the consequences caused by a lack of self-control. However, as you continue to ask the questions and encourage them to consider their answers carefully and prayerfully, they will begin down the road to self-enforced, self-control. They will "own" their own character, and that is a worthwhile goal.

Individual Integrity

Today's scripture, Proverbs 13:6, reminds us that integrity is a character discipline that individuals can possess. Although integrity can rub off on others, it is best thought of as a highly personal trait. Integrity is developed when we consistently elevate virtues above feelings when faced with a moral dilemma. As we choose God's way over our own way, we develop integrity. Integrity further gives us courage and a winsome and compelling testimony that attracts the attention of others. Can you name someone you know who has integrity? What is it about that person that brought them to mind? No doubt they possess individual integrity.

Proverbs 13:6

Parenting Point

Ask your children to name someone they know who has integrity. Next, ask them to explain why they chose that person. Finally, ask them which character qualities they need to work on in order to possess individual integrity for themselves. Around our house, we call this exercise, "Name it, Claim it, and Shame it." Name the character flaw, such as lying or disobedience, etc. Next, in prayer, claim it as your own (no blaming others for your sinful choices), and finally, in prayer, shame it by confessing it to the Lord. Moms and Dads, make sure you lead by example in this exercise. Even though we may hope that our children don't notice our characterless choices, don't be fooled. Children, and especially teens, are quick to recognize hypocrisy. Our actions will scream the truth about our life choices, even when our words are pointing our children toward Christ. Thankfully, unlike many adults, our children have always been quick to forgive and abundantly gracious in their ability to restore with us. Offer the same level of forgiveness to your children, and you will be building a strong family bond of trust, forgiveness, and very importantly, integrity.

The Rewards of Responsibility

As we consider the various responsibilities we are called to fulfill, it would be easy to feel overwhelmed. Let me encourage you that God never calls us to complete any task that He doesn't enable us and strengthen us to fulfill. As you are faithful to diligently uphold your budding, primary, and secondary responsibilities, you will be, at the same time, building a strong testimony of character and Christ-likeness. The unsaved world is watching to see how Christians live out their faith. Careful attention to the responsibility continuum will enhance your ability to share the reason for your actions, actions you take because you are following the example of your Savior, who lived a life of responsibility, service, and ultimately sacrifice for others.

I Thessalonians 1:2-7

Parenting Point

As we teach our children the various aspects of the responsibilities we require of them, it is easy to get bogged down in their failures and forget to notice the positive fruit that our children are producing. I know that every day we can find an area where our children are failing to live up to their budding or primary responsibilities or an area in which they are misusing a secondary responsibility. Let me encourage you to deal with those failures as necessary, but to spend at least as much time looking for their successes and victories and taking the time to celebrate those milestones. As with anything else in parenting, if you want to see more of a particular action or attitude in your children's lives, take the time to encourage and applaud their good effort. Extend verbal praise and positive affirmation. As Proverbs 16:24 reminds us, "Pleasant words are a honeycomb, sweet to the soul and healing to the bones."

Jumping for Joy

What things bring you joy? The dictionary defines joy as that which causes us to experience great pleasure or delight. Unlike happiness, which is dependent upon situations or circumstances, our joy comes from within. The Psalmist found joy in his salvation (Psalm 51:12) and in the name of the Lord (Psalm 89:12). The angels find their joy in the repentance of sinners (Luke 15:17), while the Apostle Paul announced that his joy would be complete when the church at Philippi was like-minded, maintaining the same love, and intent on one purpose. In every case, the things that brought joy in these verses were things that would delight and glorify God. As we become more like Christ through the study of His Word, obedience to His conviction, and growth through change, the things that bring Him joy will be the things that bring us joy. What makes you jump for joy?

Philippians 2:2-3

Parenting Point

As parents, we are called to model what joy looks like, for our children. If our joy is contingent on things going our way or if our level of joyfulness changes daily due to our circumstances, our children will have a hard time grasping what truly brings us joy. Examine your daily attitudes and actions. Are they governed by the steadfast love of the Lord? Or, are you falling prey to fluctuating emotions based on your situation? The greatest antidote to a lack of joy is a time of remembering the Lord's mercies. Gather your family together and begin to list all of the ways that the Lord has protected, provided for, and blessed your family. Spend time thanking Him in prayer; I guarantee you will walk away reminded that "the joy of the Lord is your strength." (Nehemiah 8:10) Make this practice of thankfulness a regular part of your family dynamic, and you will soon see your children and family becoming transformed from joyless to overflowing with joy and thanksgiving.

An Antidote to Anger

D on't you wish that there was some sort of tonic we could take for our anger to disappear forever? Unfortunately, there is no easy fix for the negative character quality of anger; however, today's verse gives us some insight into what is necessary to put-off anger. In order to replace our anger with positive character, we must learn to practice self-control. As we practice self-control in all areas, we will see our anger begin to dissipate as well. Such self-control will be developed in us by the Holy Spirit and through concentrated time in the Word of God. Developing self-control is hard work, but the fruit is sweet!

Proverbs 16:32

Parenting Point

Angry children are often hyperactive and uncontrolled children. A lack of structure for these children will only lead to more issues with anger, hostility, and wrath-filled outbursts. Teach your children, especially the exceptionally high-energy children, to practice self-control. Use a timer and teach them to sit with their hands folded and mouths closed for incrementally increasing periods of time. Make practice time a game and see if they can beat you! Once your children can practice self-control for three minutes, they know what self-control is and can make it their own tool to help them with their reactions and actions. When you see your child heading down the road toward anger, simply stopping and taking time out to practice self-control for a few minutes may waylay the problem. Make sure you take this time before they have succumbed to anger! This is not a "time-out," but rather, a time to exercise their skills of self-control and have victory over their anger. These skills take time to learn, so be patient and give your child lots of verbal encouragement to help them to succeed. Honestly, sometimes when I'm feeling frazzled at the end of a long day, taking just a few minutes to fold my hands, close my mouth, and practice self-control, can keep me from giving in to anger and speaking harshly. Moms and dads need self-control practice, too!

Compassion

The Blessing of Mercy

What does it mean to show mercy? The dictionary defines mercy this way: compassion or forgiveness shown toward someone whom it is within one's power to punish or harm. Showing mercy puts us in the driver's seat because we get to choose when and to whom we will extend mercy. Or do we? Shouldn't the very definition of mercy remind us of the infinite mercy that our Lord showed toward us when it was completely in His power to punish and harm us? Remembering this unmerited mercy should humble us and make us eager to show that same mercy toward others. When we forget the mercy shown toward us, our pride will encourage us to be stingy with extending mercy towards others and will allow us to make them beg for that mercy. May it never be so for the people of God!

Matthew 5:7

Parenting Point

When it comes to parenting, mercy is a thought-provoking concept. Although there are times that it is appropriate to show mercy toward our children's misbehavior and bad attitudes, to always extend mercy will rob them of important lessons of justice and consequences. So, how then can we, as parents, make wise determinations? The key concept in applying mercy is the words "characterized by." A child who is not characterized by willful disobedience or attitude problems in a certain area, should be treated differently than a child who is characterized by such poor choices and attitudes. When a child has a "one-time" problem, it is our privilege to extend mercy toward that behavior; however, if the problem becomes a habit, mercy should no longer be extended. As well, mercy is extended to, not asked for by, our children. You, the parent, should be the initiator of mercy. For strongly compassionate parents, be wise in NOT over-using mercy, but for those of you who are more authoritarian in your parenting, be careful to examine context and characterization. Teach into the extending of mercy and use the opportunity to show your children the great mercy shown to them through the love and sacrifice of Christ.

The Week in Review

Take some time to gather as a family and discuss the character qualities that you learned this week. Here are some questions to get the conversation started.

- **List the character qualities we studied this week.**
- **Which character quality was the hardest for you to practice this week?**
- **Did you see a family member consistently practicing one of this week's character qualities? Which family member?**

Use your imagination and add questions of your own. After your time of discussion, spend some time praying together, thanking the Lord and sharing one another's burdens. Pray ahead of time for teachable hearts to incorporate and put into practice the character qualities your family will learn in the upcoming week.

Patience as Discretion

Patience is defined as the capacity, habit, or fact of bearing pains or trial calmly, without complaint. Manifesting forbearance under provocation or strain, steadfast, not hasty or impetuous. Patience is the vital link in the chain of courageous, Christ-like, character-healthy behavior. Patience is more than a virtue, it is an essential character trait that helps us to diffuse anger, side-step impetuous decision-making, and avoid all manner of frustration. Read the following verse and note the role of patient discretion regarding anger.

Proverbs 19:11

Parenting Point

There are times as a parent that we find ourselves unable to maintain a consistent and even-handed level of patience toward all of our children. In my own life, the children that are most like me in personality are also the children that test my patience the most. Regardless of our children's personalities or annoying behaviors, as the responsible adults in their lives we must be careful to model consistency in our patient responses to ALL of our children. Ask the Lord to help you recognize the times that you are allowing yourself to react impatiently to one child in particular, and when you recognize that attitude, take pro-active steps to replace impatience with patience and irritability with long-suffering. Extra prayer for that child, or children, will arm you with the spiritual muscle necessary to exhibit Christ-like patience, even in the most trying situations. At times, I have shared with the offending child that I was struggling to maintain my patience, and I have asked them to join me in praying that they could obey and that I could be patient. At other times, I have told them that I needed a few minutes alone with the Lord in order to maintain a patient attitude. At those times, I went to my room for a few moments and prayed. First, I thanked the Lord for the life of the child I was struggling to be patient with, and then I prayed for an extra measure of grace, mercy, and patience. Remembering to be thankful for the troublesome child was so helpful in reminding me to press on toward my parenting goals!

Appropriateness • Self-Control

Discipline

The definition of discipline is to make yourself act or work in a controlled or regular way. It also means to teach somebody to obey rules or to behave in an ordered or controlled way. Is it any wonder that our Post-modern culture bristles at the idea of discipline? Most Americans think of discipline as some form of punishment, yet discipline is necessary for virtually every successful venture in life, including successful relationships. I learned many years ago, that if I wanted a successful marriage I had to discipline my actions, thoughts, and words... especially my words. Read and study the following passage on discipline.

Hebrews 12:4-13

Parenting Point

Often, the very lack of discipline that is bothering us in our children's lives is simply an imitation of the lack of discipline apparent in our own lives. Take some time to consider your own discipline or lack thereof. Are there areas that you have allowed to be ruled by laziness or inattention? Just because a certain area of your life is not as interesting or exciting as other areas is no excuse for allowing that area to become undisciplined and out of order. Write down your top five priorities. Are you exhibiting an attitude of self-discipline and diligence? If not, write the steps you must take to bring each of those areas under control. Once you have determined the steps necessary to show more self-discipline in your own life, you are prepared to help your children show more self-discipline in their lives. Follow the same procedure with your children. Help them recognize and record the priority activities in their daily lives. Then, help them to make a practical plan to exhibit self-discipline in carrying out those priority activities. When you see your children practicing self-discipline, take the time to praise their good effort. In fact, exhibiting self-discipline would be a fantastic reason to receive the "You Did Great!" plate in our home. Find a similar way to reward your children's careful and diligent practice of self-discipline. Maybe your spouse deserves some recognition for practicing self-discipline in one of the "adult" areas of life (i.e., spending, eating, Internet time, etc.). When others show self-discipline, discipline yourself to reward them with praise and words of encouragement!

The Thankfulness List

One of the best things I ever did was to make a list of the five things for which I was the most thankful. I then recorded them on a 3x5 card. After I wrote them down, I put the card in my Bible so that I would look at it every time I opened the Scriptures. After 20 years the "thankful" list is still fresh and has been a constant reminder of the goodness of God. Take the time to consider what blessings you can thank God for today.

I Thessalonians 5:18

Parenting Point

Generally speaking, thankful children are happier children. Children who have learned to be thankful and grateful are children who have learned to take their eyes off of themselves. Taking time to consider our blessings and to then show thankfulness for our blessings is an important habit to incorporate in our homes. Children, and adults for that matter, are generally not naturally thankful people. As we spend our days surrounded by all the things we could possess, it takes a heart of discipline to reject coveting and to instead be thankful and content with what the Lord has already provided. Whether it's a new car, a better neighborhood, or a younger wife, coveting threatens to destroy a heart of thankfulness. To build the habit of gratitude in your home, practice habitual times of "Thankfulness Sharing." Good intentions to be thankful will only end in frustration and failure, but being intentional and planning times of thankfulness will bring blessing and new habits of gratitude into your home. The more often you practice the language of thankfulness (i.e., "Wow, isn't the sky beautiful? Thank you God!), the more natural such conversation will become in your home. When you see your children bolting down the road of grumbling and complaining, set up a thankfulness roadblock! Stop what you're doing and have everyone share two things for which they are thankful. Sometimes, it's the parents in the home who need a thankfulness roadblock! I've had times that my children asked me to share what I was thankful for and to do it with a big smile! Just their request reminded me to be thankful and joyful. Thankfulness is contagious, and it's one bug that I don't mind sharing with my kids!

411

Addicted to Choice

Americans are addicted to choice. The next time you go to the store to buy blue jeans you will have to decide between: 501's, 505's, 550's, relaxed fit, easy fit, straight leg, boot leg, pre-washed, stone-washed, hip-huggers, flare bottom, red tag, orange tag, yellow tag, with or without holes, and those are just the offerings from Levi and Co. Commitment means that we make a choice and stick with it, which almost seems un-American these days, but it ought to be what distinguishes us as Christians. Jesus was committed to pleasing His Father. Who are you committed to pleasing?

2 Corinthians 5:9

Parenting Point

Offering our children too many choices is an extremely easy habit to develop. Even before they can voice an opinion, we will hold up two toys and ask our children to choose. Children will quickly become addicted to choices and may consider choices to be a right not a privilege. Then, when they are faced with a situation that allows no choice, they will become angry and resentful. It isn't completely their fault when they respond with these sinful attitudes; they've been trained by their parents. To avoid the choice trap, we should limit the choices to which our children are exposed. Remember, Mom, you are not a short order cook. Offering your children a variety of meal options at breakfast, lunch, and dinnertime will create an addiction to choice. When my children were young and they inquired about what was for dinner, I always answered, "Good food." That was a true reply. I sought to always provide them with healthy and tasty meals. Often, when we tell our children what's for dinner ahead of time, they simply use that information to choose what foods they are going to eat and what foods they will choose to refuse. Once my kids were characterized by eating what they were given and with a thankful heart, then I began to tell them what to expect for the next meal. Too many toys contribute to coveting. Too much time with non-family members can make our children discontent with their family relationships. In fact, too much of anything makes it hard to focus and concentrate on that which is most important: pleasing God! Teach your children to start each day with this simple pledge: Lord, show me today how my thoughts, words, and deeds may be pleasing to You!

The Source of Love

"**B**eloved, let us love on another; for love is of God; and every one that loves is born of God and knows God." (I John 4:7) Whether we show our love through serving, giving, edifying, or preferring, we are only able to extend this love because of the love that God first bestowed on and in us. As I John 4:7 makes clear, the more we know God, the more we will know of His love. How are you doing? Are you born of God? Are you growing to know Him more each day?

I John 4:7

Parenting Point

Take time today to read I John 4:7 together, and then discuss how each family member is doing in their "knowing" of God. Help your children to focus on the ways that God has shown love to your family and to each of them, in particular. Perhaps, you would want to make a giant heart and on it list all of the ways that God has bestowed His love on each of you, individually and corporately. If you have children that are struggling to get to know God better, make a plan to help them in their growth process. At different times, I have met with individual children each morning to share a common devotional time. We each read the scripture, shared our findings, and then spent time praying with and for one another. Sharing this time with me helped them to develop their own consistent time with the Lord each day. During your family discussion, encourage each family member to share the practical and proactive steps they take to ensure that their walk with the Lord is growing and vibrant. Finish your time together by praying prayers of thanksgiving for God's abundant, unconditional, and unchanging love for your family.

Accountability

The dictionary defines accountability this way: an obligation or willingness to accept responsibility or to account for one's actions. Accountability is the reality that we all are responsible to God and others. Do you live your life as one who is accountable to God? To whom, besides God, have you made yourself accountable? Living a life without accountability can lead to an arrogant self-centeredness. Allowing others to challenge, exhort, and when necessary, correct us, will force us to embrace self-examination and growth.

Matthew 8:5-13

Parenting Point

Do your children know that you hold yourself accountable to God and others? Realizing that even their parents must answer to a higher authority will help our children to more easily embrace the concept of their need to submit to our authority. If, however, they see us as unteachable and unable to admit our own wrongs, they will quickly follow our example. Although our children will not often be involved in our decision making processes, those decisions provide us with great teaching opportunities to present to our children. As we share our own need to follow God in submission while we are making decisions, it will easily allow us to speak with our children about their need to submit to the accountability relationships within our home. Share practical examples of how your accountability to God changed the direction of a decision you were making. Ask your children to tell you with whom they have an accountability relationship. Help them to remember examples outside of your family circle, such as: teachers, pastors, babysitters, coaches, etc. For teens, often they will have developed accountability relationships with other teens. Sometimes in those relationships, things will be shared that are too heavy for your child to carry alone (i.e., thoughts of suicide, confessions of abuse, admissions of criminal activity, etc.). Make sure your young adults know that you are available to help them in those close relationships, if they need assistance. Remind them that regardless of their other acco untability relationships, they are first and foremost accountable to God and you. Model accountability and your children will naturally embrace a lifestyle of accountability as well.

The Week in Review

Take some time to gather as a family and discuss the character qualities that you learned this week. Here are some questions to get the conversation started.

- **List the character qualities we studied this week.**

- **Which character quality was the hardest for you to practice this week?**

- **Did you see a family member consistently practicing one of this week's character qualities? Which family member?**

Use your imagination and add questions of your own. After your time of discussion, spend some time praying together, thanking the Lord and sharing one another's burdens. Pray ahead of time for teachable hearts to incorporate and put into practice the character qualities your family will learn in the upcoming week.

Justice

The dictionary defines justice as that which is reasonable or fair, especially in the way people are treated, or in how decisions are made. Yet, we all know that life is not fair; especially in the way people are treated. How just are you when it comes to reasonable fairness? Most of us believe that we treat others fairly, while we, ourselves, don't get a fair shake. The single most important verse regarding justice/ fairness is found in Romans 6:23, "For the wages of sin is death, but the gift of God is eternal life through Christ Jesus our Lord." Justice demands a penalty for sin, and that penalty is death. Aren't you glad God is gracious to us and not fair?

Romans 12:19-21

Parenting Point

Teach your children that life is not fair. Think of the children's birthday party where the mom feels responsible to get a gift for every child in attendance so that nobody feels left out. This week, read the story of the crucifixion of Christ out loud to your family from John 19. Ask them if it was fair for Jesus to go to the cross? Then, take them to 1 Peter 3:18 and read all about justice. When our children tried to fall into the "fairness trap," looking with envy on what other's received, we always asked them a simple question: "Are you happy for your brother/sister?" Because we didn't just instruct them to change their envious attitude, they were forced to look at their own actions. When individuals are compelled to consider their attitudes for themselves, they will be much more likely to take ownership for their behavior, and more importantly, they will become responsible for their own necessary change. Be careful of what they hear from you. Do you rejoice over the good circumstances and blessings that come into the lives of others? Or, do you find yourself comparing and coveting? If you recognize a high degree of grumbling and fairness monitoring in your home, first consider your own life. If necessary, confess your wrong attitude to your children and seek their forgiveness for your poor example. When we are characterized by joy and excitement for others, we will be a winsome testimony for Christ, and we will open the door wide for God to bring blessing into our lives.

The Grace of Being Gracious

Would your friends define you as a gracious person? The dictionary defines gracious this way: courteous, kind, and pleasant, of a compassionate or merciful nature. Being gracious is a choice we must make each day. When we choose to be pleasant to a grumpy spouse, we are choosing to be gracious. When we choose to respond kindly to an impolite cashier, we are choosing to be gracious. Graciousness requires putting aside self and extending care and mercy to others. A gracious Christian brings honor to their God.

Proverbs 11:16

Parenting Point

Gracious women attain honor. Are you teaching your daughters how to act and respond graciously? God, in His wisdom, has provided our daughters with homes and siblings on which to practice the art of graciousness. Take time to gently encourage your daughters to respond to the others in her home in a compassionate and courteous way. Practice at home will prepare our daughters to be gracious outside of their own homes as well.

Are you encouraging your sons to examine the young ladies they show interest in to determine whether they are gracious or not? A girl who cannot be gracious at home will struggle to be gracious once she has moved out. Graciousness may not even be a character quality our sons would think to look for, but we all want them to marry women who attain honor. Of course, our sons need to develop the character quality of graciousness as well. A gracious young man can be an encouragement to his siblings, friends, and peers. Gracious people make others feel accepted and loved. Take time today to discuss the grace of being gracious.

Discernment

O ver the years, friends have often asked me how they could pray for me. My first response has always been to ask them to pray for wisdom and discernment in my life. Without discernment, we cannot differentiate right from wrong. In fact, in Hebrews 5:14 discernment is defined in terms of the distinguishing between good and evil. Are you able to differentiate between good and evil? Read and study the following text and take note of the importance of constant discernment.

Hebrews 5:14

Parenting Point

Ask your children if they believe that there is ever a time when it is okay to let down their guard regarding good and evil. Next, ask them what they think will happen if they do not practice discernment. Since discernment is seeing things as they really are, create an object lesson by comparing an old shoe with a yummy dessert that you have prepared. Ask them which one they would rather eat. Assuming they choose the yummy dessert, reward them for their wise discernment and enjoy the dessert together. While eating the treat, ask them how discernment might impact their decisions about the people they befriend, the activities they participate in, or the places they go on the Internet, etc. You can help your children to share transparently with you by first being transparent with them. Share an instance when a lack of discernment caused unnecessary trouble or heartache and the positive steps that were necessary to mitigate the consequences brought on by that lack of discernment. Often, our children lack discernment because they are young and inexperienced. We frequently told our children that some decisions were just too heavy for them to carry at their age. In those situations, we encouraged them to allow us to carry those heavy burdens for them. As we assisted them in making wise decisions, we shared how to discern God's will in each of those circumstances. The more adept your children are at handling the Word of God, the more able they will be to make discerning decisions. Parents, the same is true for you. Spend time seeking God through prayer and time in the Word. Allow Him to infuse you with godly discernment as you face the myriad decisions necessary to train and equip your family for spiritual battle.

Honesty is the Best Policy

It was William Shakespeare who said,

"Honesty is the best policy. If I lose mine honor, I lose myself."

Do you agree or disagree? If you agree that honesty is the best policy, what are you doing to ensure that your words, deeds, and thoughts are truthful and consistently honest? Since Jesus is our example in all things, and we are to become more like Him, what do you think Jesus meant when He described Himself as the Way, *the Truth*, and the Life in John 14:6? Are you characterized by truth? Truth for God's children is not optional!

John 14:6

Parenting Point

Parents often ask us how to deal with characters like Santa Claus or the Tooth Fairy. In our home, we simply treated those characters the same way we treated Cinderella or Peter Pan. We talked to our children about the difference between pretend and reality. Using their imaginations to pretend about these characters was fine with us, but we never treated the pretend as something that was true. Be careful not to confuse pretend with reality. If your children spend years believing that Santa is real, only to find out that you weren't telling them the truth, you will undermine their trust and confidence in you. You also run the risk of causing them to doubt what you tell them about the Lord. Remember, the wise man sees the danger ahead and avoids it. Remind your children that they do not fill the role of "Personal Holy Spirit" in any other child's life. We simply told our children that although other families might tell their children that Santa or the Tooth Fairy were real, our family chose not to do so. It was never up to us to tell other children what was or wasn't real. If other parents try to talk to your children about the "realness" of those fictional characters, teach your children to respond respectfully but without compromising their own beliefs. Strangely, this is a very touchy subject in Christian circles. Instead of getting involved in controversies over such subjects, find ways to exhibit the love and grace of Christ to those families who might think differently than you.

Proactive or Reactive?

There is no shortage of finger-pointing blame assessors in this world. Highly reactive people rarely take the initiative to problem solve, opting rather to point a finger of blame at anyone or anything that is convenient or available. What are you characterized by? When faced with a moral dilemma, do you deliberately initiate a proactive solution, or do you immediately want to know who or what was to blame for the circumstance? Problem solvers are a rare breed these days, yet the Word of God calls all of God's children to be just that...problem solvers! Are you a problem solver or blame assessor? Are you in the problem solving company of Paul, Timothy, Elijah, and Elisha? Or are you in the finger pointing ranks of Adam, Eve, Cain, Jonah, Haman, and most of Job's friends? Read the following passage and observe the devastating consequences of finger pointing and blame assessing.

Genesis 3:9-13

Parenting Point

While it is easy to make all of the important decisions for our children and to solve all of their problems, we are robbing our children of an important life skill when we do so. Instead, spend time teaching your children to be effective problem-solvers rather than reactive blame assessors. Questions such as: "What do you think would be a good solution?" or "How do you think we can fix this problem?" will start your children down the road to developing solid problem-solving skills. As good coaches and trainers for our children, we must be available to assist them and to be a helpful sounding board but do not take over and solve every problem. Even in the midst of their failures and mistakes, with helpful feedback from us, our children will be growing and learning how to make wise decisions. So, step back and give them the encouragement and freedom they need to solve those problems on their own.

Faithfulness (in Little Things)

Picture yourself on a tour of the Hoover Dam. Suddenly, you notice a small pinhole-sized leak. Would you be concerned? Is it really a big deal? As you ponder the situation, you might begin to rationalize the significance of the leak. After all, it's just a little leak, hardly enough to be concerned about; besides, you wouldn't want to ruin the tour for the rest of the people. You'll just look the other way and pretend it's no big deal. Wow! What a mistake! And, so it is with faithfulness in the little things. Why is it that God is so concerned that we be faithful in the little things of life? Just like the Hoover Dam leak, little things quickly give way to big things! If we look the other way, or rationalize their significance, we risk catastrophic consequences.

Song of Songs 2:15

Parenting Point

Ask your children if a pinhole-sized leak in a dam is a big deal or not. Based on their answer, teach into the principle of faithfulness in little things. If they don't recognize the destructive power of a tiny hole, use a piece of paper, some water, and a cup to illustrate the principle. As they observe how much water can escape from just a tiny hole, they will begin to understand how important the "little" things in life truly are. Ask them to share with you some of the little things that are important to keep your home functioning smoothly. For example, doing laundry is neither glamorous nor exciting; however, if no one in the family takes ownership of the responsibility to complete the family laundry, soon it will be virtually impossible to get dressed. In the same way, sarcastic words may seem like a "little" thing in the daily routine of life; however, a multitude of sarcasm soon builds up walls of bitterness and distrust. Sometimes, the little offenses we perpetrate against one another hardly seem worth mentioning, but the Biblical way to deal with those "little" offenses is still through seeking forgiveness and restoring with the one whom we have wronged. Don't wait; act faithfully now. Quickly repenting and restoring, even in the smallest areas, will build a family dynamic of peace, joy, and unity. Remember, we don't define small; God does, and He wants us to faithfully obey Him even in the smallest of details!

The Week in Review

Take some time to gather as a family and discuss the character qualities that you learned this week. Here are some questions to get the conversation started.

- List the character qualities we studied this week.
- Which character quality was the hardest for you to practice this week?
- Did you see a family member consistently practicing one of this week's character qualities? Which family member?

Use your imagination and add questions of your own. After your time of discussion, spend some time praying together, thanking the Lord and sharing one another's burdens. Pray ahead of time for teachable hearts to incorporate and put into practice the character qualities your family will learn in the upcoming week.

Index of Character Qualities

Contact Us

Steve and Megan travel extensively facilitating parenting, marriage, and men's and women's conferences for churches and other organizations.

Conferences Available Include:

Parenting Matters

Marriage Matters

Character Matters

Second Mile Leadership for Men

When God Writes Your Story

The Wise Wife

The A-Z of a Character Healthy Homeschool

The Discipling Mom and more....

To speak with Steve or Megan please call:
1-877-577-2736

Or send them an email by clicking the Contact Us tab at:
Characterhealth.com

Also, follow them on Twitter:
@SteveScheibner
@Meganscheibner
@CharacterHealth

Other Books by Megan Ann Scheibner:

In My Seat:
A Pilot's Story from Sept. 10th–11th

Grand Slam:
An Athletes Guide to Success in Life

Rise and Shine:
Recipes and Routines For Your Morning
Lunch and Literature

Dinner and Discipleship

Studies in Character

The King of Thing
and the Kingdom of Thingdom

Other Books by Steve Scheibner:

Bible Basics

Books by Steve and Megan Scheibner:

Studies in Character

The King of Thing and the Kingdom of Thingdom

DVD Series Available:

Parenting Matters:
The Nine Practices of the Pro-Active Parent

Character Matters:
The Nine Practices of Character Healthy Youth

Subscribe to Steve and Megan's blogs:

www.SteveScheibner.com
www.MeganScheibner.com

You can find these books and other resources at:

CharacterHealth.com